Val Barra

Bread of Life in Bro

# Bread of Life in Broken Britain

*Food Banks, Faith and Neoliberalism*

Charles Roding Pemberton

scm press

© Charles Roding Pemberton 2020

Published in 2020 by SCM Press
Editorial office
3rd Floor, Invicta House,
108–114 Golden Lane,
London EC1Y 0TG, UK
www.scmpress.co.uk

SCM Press is an imprint of Hymns Ancient & Modern Ltd
(a registered charity)

Hymns Ancient & Modern® is a registered trademark of
Hymns Ancient & Modern Ltd
13A Hellesdon Park Road, Norwich,
Norfolk NR6 5DR, UK

Scripture quotations are from New Revised Standard Version Bible: Anglicized
Edition, copyright © 1989, 1995 National Council of the Churches of Christ in
the United States of America. Used by permission. All rights reserved worldwide.

British Library Cataloguing in Publication data

A catalogue record for this book is available
from the British Library

978-0-334-05896-0

Typeset by Regent Typesetting
Printed and bound by
CPI Group (UK) Ltd

# Contents

# Acknowledgements

My thanks first to Dr Margaret Masson, Principal of St Chad's College, Durham University, who was a sympathetic ear when I was an undergraduate, suggested the William Leech Research Fellowship when I was a postgraduate, and gave my wife and I a roof over our heads when we moved to Durham. Second, my thanks to Professor Robert Song and the members of the William Leech Research committee who are supporting excellent research into theology, church practice and poverty in the north-east of England, year after year, and who funded this project. Professor Song, along with my father Chris Pemberton, read the manuscript in its entirety and made numerous suggestions which extensively improved the final text; 'staged a long-needed intervention' would be more accurate than 'edited the text' if I was pushed to describe their contributions.

My thanks also to David Shervington, Hannah Ward, Christopher Pipe and Mary Matthews at SCM Press who have been prompt, positive and patient in equal measure throughout this process of simultaneously writing a book and for the first time becoming a father. The artist Adam Westerman provided humorous and humane illustrations for the final text as well as genial companionship along the way. My thanks also to my colleagues at the Department of Theology and Religion, Durham University, who have been good natured and supportive to a fault.

To Peter and Tina MacLellan and all the volunteers and clients at County Durham Foodbank my particular gratitude and admiration. This book would not be without your willingness to share honestly from your own lives and your conviction that things can and should be different.

Finally, to Irene, who has done so much to make the writing of this book possible and every day makes again the world worthwhile, my complete love.

# Prologue

It's June 2018, and one of the hottest days of an already hot summer. In Durham United Reformed Church's community hall, three County Durham Foodbank volunteers sit at fold-out tables waiting for anyone who needs a food parcel, and one regular visitor sits at a table in the corner concentrating on a laptop. Her name is Jane and she is in her late forties. After 17½ years working in the care sector, up to January 2016, she was made redundant and she has been visiting the Durham city centre food bank two or three times a month since for a toastie, a tea and free internet access. Along with her job searches, she cares for her elderly mother and volunteers at two Durham charities. We are talking, intermittently, and she tells me that while she has never collected a food parcel from the food bank, she likes coming here, finding it a source of confidence and support. I ask her how she first heard of County Durham Foodbank.

> The food bank was mentioned at the Job Centre, for job search support. I come for the PC access. I like it here, the food bank is good, I can talk with people, home can be lonely. From coming to the food bank I've got more confidence and now I'm doing some volunteering, at the British Heart Foundation and with the Sally Army (Salvation Army).

Jane has a history of working night shifts in residential care with elderly mentally infirm patients. When she was moved from night shifts to day shifts she struggled with the transition and was made redundant.

> The night shifts had an impact on my health. I needed sleeping tablets to help me be able to do the day shifts when I changed over. But I was then struggling in the days, groggy, feeling confused, and that was part of me being made redundant 'cause I couldn't do the job properly.

I ask her about her experience of being unemployed and searching for work in the north-east.

Unemployment has been horrible. I've done hundreds of applications for jobs and had 15 interviews. Nothing yet though. My confidence, it's really brought me down, all the interviews. I do 16 hours a week volunteering and 19 hours a week of job searching for job seekers allowance. Last week, I was at the library writing an email, computers can be difficult for me, but a volunteer here showed me how to attach my CV and when I was at the library I put the CV into the email and it was great. It was so good, 'I did it!'

I congratulate her on her computer literacy breakthrough and say that unemployment sounds like hard work. I ask her what she is hoping for, looking into the future.

I hope for a permanent job, not temporary work, I turned down a job at Sainsbury's, a six-month fixed contract. I want something more secure, permanent.

She goes on to talk about her Methodist father and Church of England mother and reading psalms in church as a child. She's now an intermittent member of a charismatic evangelical church in the Durham area, when time allows.

Evidently, Jane has aspired to live a selfless life for others. And what she has found, over the last two and a half years, is that that kind of life is not perceived to be deserving of trust or worthy of decent financial remuneration. The most basic contention of this book is that food banks sit at the junction of two roads that are orientated in opposite directions. One of these roads is primarily about profits and it sees people and nature as 'resources' or raw materials amenable to the realizing of its own ambitions. The second road, less prominent but always present, is walked by those who believe that the point of life is to love and care for those who populate this shared planet. It is, therefore, primarily concerned with understanding how we participate in each other and the world around us. In this book, the name given to the first road is 'neoliberalism' and to the second 'participation', a route that is explored and defended through the discipline of Christian theology. The problems Britain faces around food, work and ecology are multifaceted and will require the resources of many different traditions to be resolved adequately.[1] My hope is that this book will clarify one small contribution to that general task from one particular reading of the Christian tradition. And that, in doing so, it will add to the realization of a politics, an economics and a society in which people like Jane are perceived to be of infinite value and their discrediting is seen to be, as it really is, a denaturing of our very selves.

# Introduction

There is enough food for everybody but not everybody is getting enough.[1] Since the great recession of 2008, the number of food banks in the United Kingdom and the number of people using them have grown exponentially.[2] The first UK food bank was started in the year 2000 and now there are around 2,000 of them alongside the legacy of soup kitchens, community cafes and breakfast clubs bequeathed to the people of the UK by its complex history of inequality and philanthropic generosity. The Trussell Trust, the largest food bank franchise in the country, has seen an increase in use from 68,486 food parcels in 2010–11 to 1.6 million parcels in 2018–19.[3]

This growth has not gone unnoticed. The dominant political power in the UK over the last ten years, the centre-right Conservative Party, had consistently argued that the cause of increased food bank usage is not the reduction in local and national government welfare spending or a lack of stable work that pays well but bad life choices and the increased availability of free food. Senior Conservatives, like Ian Duncan Smith MP and Lord Freud, have defended the idea that food bank usage is a supply-driven problem.[4] Combined with a moralizing discourse about who deserves benefits, the need to reduce the welfare bill (given the oft repeated claim that 'the centre-left Labour Party was profligate in office'), the increased numbers in employment, and support from large parts of the media and general public, they have been very successful in defending their position over the last seven or eight years.[5]

On the other side, the Trussell Trust have consistently claimed that there is a tight link between welfare benefits and food bank use using data collected from their service users and, along with the All-Party Parliamentary Group on Hunger (APPG), have pointed to increased food prices, real-term benefit cuts and low/stagnant wages aggravated by 'life shocks' as the prime drivers of increased food bank use.[6] In this the Trussell Trust have received support from the UK's academic and religious communities, along with parts of the civil service.[7] From the very extensive *Emergency Use Only* in 2014 which found that for 'between half and two thirds of the people included in the research the immediate income crisis was linked to the operation of the benefits system' to Rachel Loopstra and Doireann Lalor's *Financial Insecurity, Food Insecurity, and Disability*, which says that 70% of all people at the food bank were on a form of state benefits, research commissioned by the food aid sector has consistently argued that real-term benefit cuts and recent welfare reforms have caused hardship for many.[8]

In 2013, the Trussell Trust's Chief Executive Chris Mould said that 'the reality is that there is a clear link between benefit delays or changes and people turning to food banks', as the charity became increasingly desperate for a reversal of the politics of austerity imposed by the coalition government.[9] Following on from Mould's comments, it later emerged that a senior aid to Ian Duncan Smith, then Minister for the Department of Work and Pensions (DWP), had threatened the Trussell Trust with being shut down for politicizing poverty and that the Trussell Trust decided to be less vocal about food poverty in the light of this possibility.[10] In *Breadline Britain*, the academics Joanna Mack and Stewart Lansley give their summary of the current situation by saying that

> the growth of food poverty, while fuelled by the impact of the down-turn and, in particular, the Government's benefit reforms, has not just suddenly emerged. At root, it stems from heightened levels of impoverishment and a steady rise in social and economic risk ... Britain has turned, steadily, into a more brittle and a more fiercely competitive society. A number of trends – from the move from an industrial to a service-based economy and the much greater freedom given to markets, to the impact of globalisation and new technology – have increased levels of insecurity. More chase fewer decent jobs and homes; personal and family incomes have become more volatile; family break-ups are more common; and social support networks are more atomised.[11]

Mack and Lansley's comments have corollaries in the academic communities that study food poverty. After two years volunteering at a food bank in the north-east of England, Kayleigh Garthwaite concludes her book *Hunger Pains* by saying:

> We have seen how food bank use is growing, due to static incomes, rising living costs, low pay, fuel poverty, debt and other complicated problems related to welfare reform. Added to that is the relentless 'shirkers' and 'strivers' dialogue that surrounds people on low incomes, eroding any last scraps of dignity they may have left. As a result of

this, people at the sharp end are mostly existing, not living, and this unsurprisingly leads to stigma, shame and embarrassment for many who are desperately trying to make ends meet.[12]

She says that there would be no need for food banks 'if it weren't for the harsh benefits sanctions, precarious, low-paid jobs, and administrative delays that leave families without money for weeks on end'.[13] Former professor Elizabeth Dowler writes in her essay 'Food Banks and Food Justice in "Austerity Britain"' in *First World Hunger Revisited* that

> while the need grows for UK food policies which take account of environmental, economic and social sustainability, the policy space and opportunities to focus on structural determinants of improving access for all to healthy, low-impact, affordable diets, seem more remote than ever. Individualized 'informed choice' has largely been reinstated, with the state's role merely a light-touch regulation of the food supply and retail sectors, rather than wages or benefits in relation to the cost of food.[14]

The Canadian professor of social work Graham Riches says that food banks in the UK are 'a more recent phenomenon largely driven by the Great Recession of 2008, austerity budgets and punitive welfare sanctions'.[15] Like Dowler, Riches says that his desire for 'poverty reduction and fair income distribution informed by the right to food is inspired more by hope than any beckoning commitment by governments to food and social justice'.[16] With 'risks' growing and 'few friends in the press, in corporate Britain, or in Government, and largely sidelined by the Labour Party in its search for Middle England voters, the poor have – all too often – come to rely on the church, charities and pressure groups to make their case, by offering a collective voice and a corrective, if small, to the gradual erosion of effective countervailing power in Britain. This is hardly new.'[17]

Part of the complexity of food banks and their growth is that food banks sit at the cross-road of religious, political and economic forces. In order to plot a path through this contested terrain, I focus especially on Lansley and Mack's comments about the growth of 'risk' or, as other commentators have called it, 'precariousness'. What does this term mean and why does it deserve to be highlighted? The term precariousness has been used in late-twentieth- and twenty-first-century sociology to talk about labour insecurity and the kind of economy and society that followed Fordism (nineteenth-century industrial, factory-based manufacture which was progressively outsourced to Asia, Africa and

South America over the course of the twentieth century, or automated) and is currently dominant in Europe and North America.[18] Partly, the term is interesting because it is ambiguous, carrying both the common desire for flexibility and control over one's career which was inhibited by Fordist modes of production, while also giving confidence to businesses that they could create jobs in times of growth without the risk of insolvency if the market took a downturn, *and* describing the growth of short-term or zero-hour contracts, unstable or unreliable work and a reduced social safety net.[19] The political theorist Isabell Lorey catches not just the economics but the experience of precariousness when she says in *State of Insecurity: Government of the Precarious*:

> The many precarious are dispersed both in relations of production and through diverse modes of production, which absorb and engender subjectivities, extend their economic exploitation, and multiply identities and work places. It is not only work that is precarious and dispersed, but life itself. In all their differences, the precarious tend to be isolated and individualized, because they do short-term jobs, get by from project to project, and often fall through collective social-security systems. There are no lobbies or forms of representations for the diverse precarious.[20]

As the late social critic Mark Fisher noted in *Capitalist Realism*, a significant part of why neoliberalism successfully followed Fordism was that it managed to incorporate workers' demands for more freedom and choice in how to sell one's labour, but that at the same time what was strengthened in this pact was the logic, ability and importance of selling one's labour in the first place.[21] Fordism was stifling and sexist (the male breadwinner, the female housewife) and neoliberalism built on and partially resolved these frustrations as it came to assume its position at the political and economic apex.[22] Like Lorey, Fisher goes on to link economics and experience. He says that instead of the stable antagonisms of the factory period (workers vs bosses) conflict has been individualized and internalized in neoliberalism.[23] The struggle today is against oneself; to get the next project, secure the necessary funding, entrepreneurialize oneself, build an attractive CV and online presence, disassociate oneself from people, places or actions in one's past that might hold back one's future, always present an appealing public profile.

The experience of precariousness is pronounced in the lives of food bank users, present in the lives of many more, and has tight links to the history, role and remit of government. Lorey goes on from talking about precariousness as 'living with the unforeseeable, with contingency' to discuss the kind of government appropriate to our neoliberal economy.[24] In a labour selling economy, the government has to balance two agendas. On the one hand, 'in the course of dismantling and remodeling of the welfare state and the rights associated with it, a form of government is established that is based on the greatest possible insecurity, promoted by proclaiming the alleged absence of alternatives.'[25] That is, the government must minimize or actively remove anything that inhibits people from selling their labour at the lowest possible price, whether this be social security, environmental protections or traditional cultures which promote or sustain non-commodifiable modes of living (for example, religious traditions which say that work should be 'dignified', forms of education, reproductive labour and even trade union actions can all be seen as problematic in this sense) and it does so by saying that it has to. On the other hand, the government cannot push insecurity and competition so far that the social order is fundamentally destabilized: 'the way that precaritization has become an instrument of government also means that its extent must not pass a certain threshold such that it seriously endangers the existing order: in particular, it must not lead to insurrection.'[26] Lorey concludes quite succinctly that 'managing this threshold is what makes up the art of governing today'.[27]

Even this cursory engagement with the concept of precariousness discloses a series of factors that can illuminate the food bank phenomenon and the conversation I have sketched about individual choice, poverty and governmental responsibility. Food bank users often move in and out of work and face difficult transition periods.[28] They lead precarious lives. This competitive work environment is tiring mentally and physically and these ailments are reported frequently at food banks and to food bank researchers.[29] The degree to which this economy has cognitive downsides can be seen in the rising numbers of GPs (to their own great frustration) prescribing antidepressants to the poor; British society drugs its most vulnerable populations into compliance and conformity.[30]

Wages and taxes are kept low by a government that fears 'capital flight' and that wants to attract international businesses to the UK and the

UK labour force thus faces downward pressure on its wages from a globalized and expanding international labour market, and one of the consequences of this is that many coming to the food bank are in work.[31] The knowledge that work does not pay, despite politicians of both of the largest parties claiming that it is the best way out of poverty, leads to resentment and a sense of disconnect from the political class by food bank users.[32] To cope day to day and week to week, UK citizens have internalized the logic of risk by taking on high levels of debt.[33] But this insecurity adds to a sense of uncertainty and calls for protection from external threats, like migrants, and exposure to trans-national governing bodies, like the European Union.[34] Comparing 2012 and 1983, the numbers who cannot afford basic goods like being able to heat one's home or not living in a damp house have almost doubled to 9%; the 'proportion of households unable to afford two meals a day', which had dropped 'to negligible levels in the intervening' years, was back up to 3% in 2012.[35] Returning to the Conservative Party's association of poverty and individual failings, the narrative they have been telling about poverty's cause, it was the case that individuals that I talked with at County Durham Foodbank told me about links they saw between bad decisions they had made, the flawed kinds of people they were and their poverty.[36] But to claim that bad life choices is the primary driver of poverty is a misrepresentation of the complexity of the current situation and the power of the diverse forces at play.[37]

Aware that food banks eradicating food poverty is unlikely, as probable as a car mechanic sneaking out at night with a sack of gravel to fill in potholes, different denominations of Christians have published their own reflections on the growth of food poverty and food aid in the UK.

A number of common themes mark these documents: the inability of food banks to meet food insecurity, along with the problem of inequalities between volunteers and food bank beneficiaries;[38] the multifarious causes of food insecurity, including unemployment, precariousness and in-work poverty, debt and government policy;[39] the prominence of the church in responses to food insecurity;[40] the need to address questions of justice, politics and economics, along with the tendency for churches to focus on relief rather than solutions;[41] food bank users' experience of stigma or social isolation;[42] Christian attitudes towards food and food in the church's scriptures;[43] and renewed, reconciled or peaceful relationship as the aim of Christian practices and interventions in public life.[44]

These documents contain some useful resources for thinking theologically about food insecurity, some sophisticated analysis of food banks themselves and our current socio-political predicament. Writing in *Mission and Food Banks*, the Anglican theologian Anne Richards notes that

> for Christians, food banks are perplexingly ambiguous: they represent pools of generosity and co-operation, meeting human need and enabling the release of stories we urgently need to hear. Yet at the same time we need to work for a world *where food banks are not needed*. We want food banks to disappear. Consequently, the need for food banks in our society reaches deep into our theology to ask harder and more difficult questions about the nature of our society and its governance.

However, when it comes at the close of the document to talk about the nature of our society and the aims and means of government, Richards largely sidesteps the issue by talking about questions internal to the food bank: how do food banks maximize choice for their users, what is good and bad dependency on charity, what are the limits of the referral system, how will being involved in political campaigning or advocacy affect the food bank's day-to-day services?[45] In this document, important questions – which Richards' analysis has itself implied (for example, how we should affiliate possible policies that would deal with food insecurity and Christian theological commitments) – are not answered. Furthermore, which criteria should guide how Christians vote? Can the church credibly continue its close affiliation with successive governments that bear a mark of culpability in the British food insecurity crisis? Regrettably, and in continuity with a non-partisan tendency in parts of the Church of England's thought to be for social cohesion in general and, therefore, for nothing in particular, these questions are not answered.[46] Towards the end of her essay, Richards does juxtapose a 'trade economy' and a 'gift economy' and this is welcome, but exactly what this means for what Christians buy and consume, how businesses are regulated, for the British farming industry, for taxes and welfare spending are not specified.[47]

A hiatus between the theological and the political marks these church texts. The Church Urban Fund's *Hungry for More: How Churches Can Address the Root Causes of Food Poverty*, for example, observes early on that 'current church-based responses to food poverty are focused on short-term, emergency activities such as food banks, rather than long-term projects that seek to address underlying causes', before culminating in the promotion of a do-more-with-less cookery course.[48] But this is only one side of the problem; it is equally the case that the academic literature on food banks consistently fails to engage the theological imagination that features so prominently in the history of food banking both in the UK and overseas. While the importance of religious communities in founding and sustaining food banks is consistently noted in the academic literature, the same body of books and articles remains mute on the characteristics that these communities exhibit and how their views on the origin, nature and purpose of people and the world relate to what they do.[49] Both the descriptive question, 'Why are Christians inclined to start and support food banks?' and the more complicated, normative question, 'Should Christians be starting and supporting food banks?' are missing.[50] Arguably, the 'right to food' approach that a number of prominent academics in this field take is a tactical decision to articulate a broad enough frame to accommodate a range of non/religious perspectives and stakeholders (an example of the pragmatism the Roman Catholic Jacques Maritain observed in the original UN Human Rights deliberations: 'Yes ... we agree about [human] rights but on condition that no one asks us why') but unfortunately this issue is not explicitly discussed.[51] Nevertheless, failing to engage with the religious narratives that are present in food banking is still potentially problematic. Principally, it divests the sociologist of the ability to address the heart and imagination of a group of citizens who have shown the energy and capacity to act on the issue of food poverty. Conversely, if, as some writers have argued, what we are capable of socially is related to what we can think imaginatively, then the failure of these sociologists to engage in the realm of theology limits the range of possible responses to food insecurity that we might plausibly sustain.[52] The complexity of food banks and durability of poverty calls for more integrated analysis, for interdisciplinary promiscuity.

Food banks will continue to exist while Christians believe they are a cogent expression of their faith. The mass of Christians will not agitate for an alternative political and economic order until politics and the theological have been plausibly articulated so as to resonate with the Christian imagination. It is conventional in a number of theological traditions to stress the need for Christians to show a degree of 'bilingualism' when they talk publicly in secular times, but the criticism runs both ways and there are responsibilities that it would be prudent for the secular to shoulder too.[53]

## The purpose of this book

The American farmer and poet Wendell Berry talks in his book *The Unsettling of America: Culture and Agriculture* about the segmentation of life into distinct parts under the rubric of individual 'specialization' and a 'specialized society'.[54] He says that, looked at from the point of view of a social system, 'the aim of specialization may seem desirable enough … to see that the responsibilities of government, law, medicine, engineering, agriculture, education, etc., are given into the hands of the most skilled, best prepared people.'[55] However, Berry continues, 'the first, and best known, hazard of the specialist system is that it produces specialists – people who are elaborately and expensively trained *to do one thing*.'[56] And so we have, Berry says, 'inventors, manufacturers, and salesmen of devices who have no concern for the possible effects of those devices' and the widespread 'abdication to specialists of various competences and responsibilities that were once personal and universal'.[57] Berry goes on:

> The specialist system fails from a personal point of view because a person who can do only one thing can do virtually nothing for himself. In living in the world by his own will and skill, the stupidest peasant or tribesman is more competent than the most intelligent worker or technician or intellectual in a society of specialists. What happens under the rule of specialization is that, though society becomes more and more intricate, it has less and less structure. It becomes more and more organized, but less and less orderly. The community disintegrates because it loses the necessary understandings, forms, and enactments of the relations among materials and processes, principles and actions, ideals and realities, past and present, present and future, men and women, body and spirit, city and country, civilization and wilderness, growth and decay, life and death – just as the individual character loses the sense of a responsible involvement in these relations.[58]

The purpose of this book is to contribute in a small way to the demise of this kind of specialization by sketching answers to two questions. First, in order to fill a gap in the current academic literature on food banks, this book asks why Christians, in particular, have driven the rise in food banks. Second, to the Christian community, this book asks whether food banks are a satisfactory, contemporary expression of the tradition. In short: this book articulates a Christian narrative for the social scientists, geographers and food rights activists and, vice versa, a political or economic narrative for the Christians.

By focusing on Christian attitudes to food I explore participation, a key theme in the Christian tradition. Food is a recurring aspect of Christian imagery and ritual enactment (paradigmatically in the Eucharist) because it imitates and expresses a core Christian commitment: we are inevitably related to the world, each other and God, as in eating we take in the world, each other and God into our bodies. The Baptist, Methodist and United Reformed Churches' document *Faith in Foodbanks?* illustrates this when it says:

Through foodbanks, Christians are able to express key Gospel values and declare something of the faith that defines us. In real and practical ways we are sharing our bread with one another, welcoming the stranger, loving our neighbour and acting as stewards of God's creation and provision. We might argue that this is a return to an age-old tradition; the tithe-barn was a prominent feature of community life in our nation for centuries – a place where food was stored and shared for the common good, inspired and directed by the teachings of the Old Testament.[59]

Food and charity: both are ways Christians make statements about the character of the world. The American theologian Gary Anderson in his book *Charity* says that for both Christians and Jewish people 'God created the world out of charity' and that consequently 'giving to one's neighbour is not just a Kantian "duty" but a declaration about the metaphysical structure of the world itself. Charity, in short, is not just a good deed but a declaration of belief about the world and the God who created it.'[60] Later in the same book, discussing the books of Proverbs and Ben Sira and what the giver can receive in the act of giving, Anderson says that 'because the Holy One of Israel is a God of mercy, the world he has made is an expression of that mercy. Benefiting from charity isn't so much about advancing one's self-interest (though this cannot be completely factored out of the equation) as it is about giving testimony to the love of God inscribed in the natural order.'[61] The reason why Christians have been so prominent in the history of British charity stems from a belief in who God is, how God sees people (as valuable and worthy of dignity) and consequently about how the world should be.[62] Exploring how Christian theology imagines and enacts a reciprocal circulation of gifts between God, people and world, and how this might inform Christian food banking, is a major part of this text.

Likewise, how Christians produce, distribute and consume food is a classic facet of how Christians aspire to live at peace with each other, the world and God. The field of theology and food studies, which explores these relations from different perspectives, is growing. Ellen Davis' *Scripture, Culture and Agriculture* builds on Christopher Wright's co-ordination of the triumvirate of people, land and God in *God's People in God's Land* and applies this to food and the contemporary food industry.[63] The British theologians David Grumett and Rachel Muers have written an introduction to the history of Christian food practices, *Theology on the Menu*, while the Roman Catholic theologian Angel F. Méndez-Montoya uses the practices and skills of preparing food as a metaphor for doing theology ('theological methodology') in *The Theology of Food: Eating and the Eucharist*.[64] Norman Wirzba and Alexander Schmemann take more systematic routes, focusing their works on the intersections of theology, food and church identity.[65]

Wirzba draws extensively on the texts of Berry and is an important source in this text. He writes that we too often eat quickly, ignorantly, inhospitably, unsustainably and without reverence for the reality that 'to eat is to be implicated in a vast, complex, interweaving set of life and death dramas in which we are only one character among many.'[66] For Wirzba, 'one of the great paradoxes of eating' is that 'to preserve the form of my life, the form of another's life must end'.[67] But this paradox does not inhibit his thought but opens him to a parallel in Christian theology: Christians have often thought that when they eat the body of Christ in the Eucharist they become a part of Jesus and yet also more fully their own selves.[68] Likewise, in making the world 'God wills to be not-God', voluntarily making space for the world without ever ceasing to be all in all.[69] In Wirzba's words, because 'the movement of sacrifice that characterises God's life also characterises created life' it is possible for Christians to see that

> breaking bread together is far more than a fuelling event. It can be a radical, prophetic act of hospitality that is founded upon God's primordial and sustaining hospitality whereby the whole world is created, nurtured, and given the freedom to be itself. It can be the practical site in which existing economies are analysed and challenged. It can even be the foretaste of the messianic age ... 'human beings are

gifts to each other in an endless economy of God's grace whereby we are given in order to give.'[70]

In making space for others by sharing food Christians are imitating God making space for the world, God's hospitality. These relationships, between God and the world, Christians and God, Christians and others, mean that the inevitable overlap of things, their coming and returning to each other preceding their discrete identities, is at the core of Christian belief. For many Christians loving God means loving people, loving people is loving God, caring for creation, humanity and the divine can only be done integrally or not at all; what you do to the least of these you do also to God.[71]

Formed in the ferment of these patterns of thought, and as someone who has described himself as trying to take the Gospels seriously, Berry's works labour to express satisfactorily the interknittedness of things.[72] He says:

> We have given up the understanding – dropped it out of our language and so out of our thought – that we and our country create one another, depend on one another, are literally part of one another; that our land passes in and out of our bodies just as our bodies pass in and out of our land; that we are and our land are part of one another, so all who are living as neighbours here, human and plant and animal, are part of one another, and so cannot possibly flourish alone; that, therefore, our culture must be our response to our place, our culture and our place are images of each other and inseparable from each other, and so neither can be better than the other.[73]

Narrowed by the inculcation of avarice that is endemic to the smooth functioning of our current social order and abetted by the limitations of vision imposed on us by specialization, Berry says that 'the good of the whole of Creation, the world and all its creatures together, is never a consideration because it is never thought of; our culture now simply lacks the means for thinking of it.'[74] Like the Anglican Richards, cited earlier, the contrast that this book builds is, first, between an economic and political order that systematically disassociates us from the natural world, each other and God (and re-embeds us in the social order of the market, more on this below) and a belief system, an imagination, an emotional predilection, a received historical body of practices, which are predicated on and animated by the inverse.[75] Second, I position food banks between these two dynamic orders, being constrained and compromised by the (neoliberal) context of their occurring and yet also animated by a vision at variance with it. Given the importance of participation for Christians, this book argues that the division of society into deserving and undeserving poor (strivers and scroungers) is a theological problem. Feeding the socially marginalized on food produced by degrading the soil, polluting the water, homogenizing plant and animal diversity, driving local communities off the land at home and abroad through industrial farming practices is a theological problem. Sanctifying oneself by addressing the immediate needs in front of one and not contemplating or where necessary contesting one's complicity in the economic and political whole is a theological problem.

## Neoliberalism, precariousness and the structure of this book

In Monty Python's religious and historical satire from 1979, *The Life of Brian*, the protagonist Brian Cohen, played by Graham Chapman, and his mother Mandy Cohen, an aggressive, cross-dressing Terry Jones, are returning into the city of Jerusalem when they are accosted by an 'ex-leper' looking for alms. Played by Michael Palin, this ex-leper, whom we have already seen bemoaning the fancy 'donkey-owning' class who never give him or the other beggars any change, follows Brian and Mandy down the street appealing to them for charity. Brian picks up on this lithe, athletic individual's description of himself as an 'ex-leper' and asks, 'did you say "ex-leper"'? The 'ex-leper', apparently unperturbed, answers back: yes, that is indeed right, I am an ex-leper with 16 years behind the bell and proud of it. Discerning that the essence of the matter has not yet been adequately resolved, Brian tries again, asking exactly what happened to the ex-leper, to which the ex-leper replies that he was cured. Cured? Brian asks. Yes, responds the ex-leper, a miracle by someone called Jesus. Seeing that his pitch for alms is going to require a more comprehensive and involving narrative frame, the ex-leper goes on to tell his tale. So, he was hopping merrily along minding his own business when out of the blue, whoosh, unconsensually cured by a 'bloody do-gooder'. The biggest ramification of this divine intervention: 'One minute I'm a leper with a trade, the next minute my livelihood is gone.'

Showing the kind of forethought and initiative that is going to carry him a long way over the course of the film, Brian sees the nature of the problem and asks the ex-leper why he doesn't just go back to Jesus, say that he wants his trade back and that he would like to be a leper again. But the ex-leper has thought of that already. Yes, he could return to Jesus and ask for the miracle to be reversed but he's been thinking about it and, ideally, he would like to be made a little lame in one leg during the middle of the week. Aware that the exciting process of bar-gaining for a gift is about to begin (the incongruity in the second half of the sketch being the ex-leper's introduction of a market set of norms into the reception of a charitable donation), the ex-leper concludes by agreeing that he does need some impairment but that leprosy is too much: 'a pain in the arse to be blunt, excuse my French, sir'.

While Christians like Norman Wirzba argue that 'the new community called into being by Christ is marked by a new economics and a new politics defined by the work of reconciliation', the actual history of Christian food practices along with the ability of theology to inform human actions and resonate with human's evolving aspirations is far more ambiguous.[76] Monty Python's sketch illustrates a criticism that has been levied at food banks and Christianity: inclusion in the order of salvation engenders new forms of exclusion. A common critique of food banks follows this line of analysis: food banks provide enough food for emergency situations but not enough to either solve the issue of food insecurity long term *or* provide the hungry with socially legitimate ways to feed themselves.[77] A solution at one level causes problems at other levels, and a staple of the academic literature on food insecurity and food banks argues against them as long-term solutions because they do not secure the ability of the hungry to choose what food they want and acquire it in socially conventional ways. Ironically, a tradition that values participation highly inhibits the poor's participation.[78] In this instance it is possible to co-ordinate the triumvirate of food bank, neo-liberal labour market and the hungry with Jesus, the Jerusalem economy in the ancient near east, and an ex-leper.

Even more problematic, the argument has been made historically that charities, including food banks, are not simply compatible with very competitive labour markets and GDP growth-orientated governments but, in reality, are complicit in complex ways in their stability and reproduction. Does Jesus not only do the ex-leper a disservice but also unwittingly reduce the work security of other low-wage workers in the Jerusalem area who now have another unemployed person who wants their job? Jesus: mediocre for lepers, bad for farmers, market vendors and sex workers? Graham Riches suggests that food banks helping those in need enable governments to reduce social security spending and cut taxes for the richest.[79] Do food banks suppress wages by helping maintain a large standing reserve of unemployed people ready to take any job at any price?[80] Or by 'topping up' low wages by helping those who are paid insufficiently reduce their food bills keep the status quo in place? Writing with Tiina Silvasti in *First World Hunger Revisited: Food Charity or the Right to Food*, Riches recognizes 'the strength of human compassion and the moral imperative to feed hungry people' but also asks whether 'this increasingly influential form of global food charity – collecting, sorting and distributing surplus or wasted food to feed the hungry poor in wealthy nations, is part of the solution to or part of the problem of entrenched food poverty'.[81] Do food banks 'de-politicize' hunger, by relieving the government of its basic duty of care for its citizens? Or do they act as a 'moral safety valve' for volunteers who having given in one area believe themselves absolved of acting in others? Or, finally, do food banks provide a means for international food corporations to turn their wasteful production practices and exploitation of the earth for profits into pure and PR-friendly good deeds?[82]

Before outlining the contents of the book's chapters, the book's argument needs to be nuanced and rearticulated in light of what has already been discussed. The initial postulate I've suggested is that Christian theology and neoliberalism are oppositional, with theology on the side of participation and neoliberalism on the side of difference or differentiation. But even in this short survey of Christian thought, the kind of participation that Christianity receives and seeks to reproduce is for the flourishing of the different: Christianity is for relationships that nurture otherness (as God wills creation, and Jesus brings people to find their true selves). Consequently, this book's argument is structured like a chiasm, with the theological initially occupying Side A – relationship and the neoliberal on Side B – separation, with food banks in between. However, because theology is paradoxical, simultaneously for the world disclosed truthfully only in the person of Jesus and yet also for the world as something God loves to the degree that Jesus would give himself for it (the world is its own legitimate, meaningful, distinct thing) the theological also needs to be on Side B, for kinds of separation.

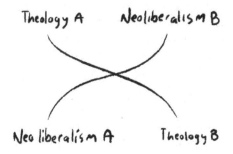

A complicated way of saying something simple: that it is at least plausible that Christianity is for people being able to stand on their own feet *and* a more equal, participatory society; or that embodying our dependency on the earth means taking individual responsibility for one's diet. In short, how do we live out what Wirzba calls 'responsible freedom'?[83]

Likewise, the tendency to simply see neoliberalism on Side B, the side of separation, is untenable. Current writers like George Monbiot, who says that our current neoliberal times are distinguished by 'atomisation: the rupturing of social bonds, the collapse of shared ambitions and civic life, our unbearable isolation from each other', are cultivating a line of investigation formulated by a giant of twentieth-century progressive economics, Karl Polanyi.[84] Polanyi, in his *The Great Transformation*, talked about capitalism (of which neoliberalism is a particular derivative) as a system that 'disembeds', by which Polanyi meant that capitalism extracted money from its life in local markets and economies and inflated it into something bloated and independent that hovers over all markets. The consequence of the freeing of the economy, Polanyi says, was 'an avalanche of social dislocation, surpassing by far that of the enclo-sure period'.[85] Despite the tendency to think of capitalism in economic terms, Polanyi argued that 'what appeared primarily as an economic problem was essentially a social one', for while 'in economic terms the workers were certainly exploited' the more significant issue was that 'a principle quite unfavourable to individual and general happiness was wreaking havoc with [man's] social environment, his neighbourhood, his standing in the community, his craft; in a word, with those relation-ships to nature and man in which his economic existence was formerly embedded.'[86] With implications for the present day, 'the critical stage was reached with the establishment of a labour market in England, in which workers were put under the threat of starvation if they failed to comply with the rules of wage labour.'[87] Martin Konings typifies this view as the tendency to see capitalist money 'as a solvent of social ties, forcing on our interactions the abstract indifference of monetary calcu-lation and the alienating effects of instrumental reason'.[88]

But recent scholarship, like that of Konings, has argued that the story that neoliberalism 'disembeds' is incapable of accounting for the ways neoliberalism reincorporates nature, societies, individuals back into its gambit. Konings writes that 'far from being characterized by a grow-ing externality of economy and sociality, capitalism operates through their imbrication: morality, faith, power, and emotion, the distinctive qualities of human association, are interiorized into the logic of the economy.'[89] The problem with the Polanyi line of analysis is that 'the "disembedding" metaphor encourages us to conceive of the autonomization of money in terms of disarticulation, the rise of possessive individualism and instrumental rationality at the expense of substantive associational logics.'[90] What does this mean? It means that we are inclined to see nature, or poor people, at a distance from the centre and in need of being included, 'accounted for', but not how being at a distance from the centre is useful for the centre itself. Developing this line of enquiry in a recent book on neoliberalism, Konings and his co-author Damien Cahill say that 'capitalism is characterized by a capacity for exploitation through incorporation, for oppression that works not through exclusion but precisely by integrating people into a framework of rights. Or, in the parlance of modern political theory, capital organizes "exclusion through inclusion".'[91] These are the kinds of exclusion that almost 50% of Scottish people feel at being in the United Kingdom, or that some people in the north-east hold against politicians in Westminster, or that the beneficiary of unemployment benefits or personal independence payments feels when they go to the Job Centre, or that nature is subjected to when it is turned into a raw material ready for the market; marginalized through participation. Neoliberalism needs to be thought on Side B *and* on Side A, as a kind of participation. The book's argument is chiastic: theology presumes participation, and separation is the presupposition of neoliberalism; theology is for difference, a monopoly on the same for the sake of the self is the aim of the neoliberal.

## Outline of the chapters

Between the spring of 2016 and the summer of 2018, I volunteered at County Durham Foodbank, conducted interviews with food bank users and volunteers, and collected observations in a research journal. I carried out 20 in-depth interviews during food bank sessions, with volunteers and food bank users. I have anonymized all their names and have drawn on those people's comments in this book. In the interviews, I asked the food bank users about the circumstances that had brought them to the food bank, about their experience of the food bank and finally about their experiences, or lack thereof, of religion or religions. In the first chapter, I present some of these findings in order to describe what food bank users' lives are like. County Durham Foodbank's users, with resolve and good humour, talked about the difficulty of finding good work, their struggles with the benefits system, of isolation and community support, the struggle of ill health and their hopes for stable work and the ability to feed themselves. The chapter proceeds by co-ordinating these stories with trends identified in the larger-scale data analysis on food bank users' lives carried out by Lalor and Loopstra, and the writings of Guy Standing on 'precariousness'.

The second chapter describes the emergence of food banks, first in the USA in the late 1970s and then in the UK in the late 1990s and early 2000s. Food banks are a complex phenomenon and their growth internationally has depended on a number of necessary factors: surplus food in the food industry, food insecurity in the populace, a viable model for transferring food from individuals and companies to those in need, along with a means for that model to spread between different nations (in this instance, predominantly international links between members of the Roman Catholic communion) and, crucially, enough people with the means and motivation to enact their belief that everyone should be fed. Chapter 2 outlines the social and economic conditions necessary for food banks to flourish as they have, introducing research on food waste and food production, austerity in the UK, the history and economy of the north-east of England and the public fallout between various UK religious leaders, the Trussell Trust and the government (first the coalition, then the Conservatives). Predicated on inequality and sustained by generosity, food banks are complex, ambiguous phenomena.

Christian communities internationally and in the UK have been significant actors in the food aid scene and while this is often noted by the academic literature and political commentators, it has not been extensively or critically interrogated. A Christian volunteer at County Durham Foodbank told me a story about the medieval Christian saint Cuthbert when I asked her about her beliefs and her volunteering at the food bank:

Another story for you, do you know the one about Cuthbert and the eagle? A Durham story. St Cuthbert was out preaching in the wild of Northumberland and he had this young monk with him. He's preached about the feeding of the 5,000 and they were going onto the next place and the boy was getting worried, where they were going to get any food for themselves? Cuthbert was saying 'don't worry, God will provide' and just then this eagle flew into the lake and plucked a fish out, probably a sea eagle or an osprey or something, and then it dropped the fish [on the shore]. The boy ran up and took the fish and said 'oh, we got this fish.' Cuthbert said, 'ah, but you've deprived the fisherman of any food.' So, they chopped the fish in half and put one half back down and the eagle came and took it and then they went on to the next peasant's cottage and got them to cook the fish and they all shared it together. In the David Adam version of the story it is all connected to Cuthbert carrying his Gospel of John, a tiny little one which was in the exhibition here [at Durham Cathedral]. The symbol of John is an eagle, and Cuthbert drew the sign of the fish on the floor [of the peasant's hut], the symbol of Christ is the fish, and he connected it all up after they had eaten. So, he was teaching to these people Christianity.

Chapter 3 describes how food has been used in the Christian tradition to teach belief, from God's provision of an abundant land for the Israelites to Jesus' miraculous feeding of a crowd of thousands with five loaves and two fish. The aim of this chapter is, first, to suggest that a significant part of the reason why Christians have been so involved in the food bank movement is because there is a historical proclivity in the Christian tradition to organize and articulate itself around food. Second, along with giving reasons why Christians are inclined by their history to think in terms of food, the second point of this chapter is to begin the process of discerning and articulating norms or principles in the Christian tradition that can be used to adjudicate what is good and bad in current food bank practices, the services they offer and the space they occupy. This chapter outlines a theologically sourced participatory account of food.

Chapter 4 returns to the topic of food banks and asks how well they embody the participatory theology of food outlined in the preceding chapter. Chapters 4 and 5 carry out a form of internal critique and are addressed primarily to Christian communities. These chapters presume, as many do, that the contents of Christian beliefs are plausible and ask what coheres best in present and future practice with these professions. Using the interviews I carried out at County Durham Foodbank with both users and volunteers, Chapter 4 concludes that food banks partially but incompletely satisfy the prerogatives of participation. This chapter draws on two essays, one by the British geographers Andrew Williams, Paul Cloke, Jon May and Mark Goodwin and one by social scientist and theologian Chris Allen, and argues that two areas are particularly problematic.[92] First, the dependence of food banks on an ecologically destructive food industry that shows no recognition of the world's sanctity and, second, the role they play in stabilizing a non-participatory political and economic order which has no place for everybody. The implications of this are numerous: one, the primary problems with food banks lie outside of the food banks themselves and therefore while reforms in food bank practices are arguably necessary (to be in accord with Christian beliefs) they are also insufficient to deal with the problems we face. Second, while we do not know what the solutions to food insecurity, ecological destruction and food waste are, food banks are not it. Food banks are too problematic, too partial, too compatible with neoliberalism. Third, there is the responsibility for those who profess adherence to Christian beliefs to escalate their actions, embody the alternative order they profess and offer publicly their vision of a participatory politics and economics and what this would mean in policy and practice.

The International Panel of Experts on Sustainable Food Systems say in their report on the concentration of power in a decreasing number of international food corporations:

> In almost every sector, new businesses are emerging to meet the 'triple bottom line' of economic, environmental, and social sustainability, building on the principles of social and solidarity economies, food sovereignty, and community empowerment. Some of the most promising initiatives include short food supply chains, direct marketing schemes, cooperative marketing and purchasing structures, and local exchange schemes.[93]

These innovations should be celebrated, and the call for a minimum-wage increase and reform of the benefits system so that it meets minimum income standards by food justice campaigners (including the Trussell Trust) are also welcome. Chapter 5 analyses these demands by UK activists and argues that they are good but outmoded when considered in relation to precarious work and the ecological unsustainability of the (majority of) the current food system. One of the reasons that food banks are popular internationally is that they are perceived to offer solutions to two problems simultaneously: food waste and hunger. While this claim has been found tenuous, Chapter 5 does aim to articulate a framework that retains the concern with the divergent interests of people and nature and disclose that they are compatible. It does this by exploring the idea of a 'Universal Basic Income' – a basic amount of money paid to everybody, unconditionally – as a policy option based on our shared reception of God's gift of the world. The chapter proceeds to ask two further questions: what relationship should there be between the church and the state, and what can individual Christians do today to begin addressing the issues identified in this book? This final chapter suggests that the answers to these questions are reclaiming and restoring (church) land in general and disestablishment for the established Church of England in particular, and changes in one's patterns of consumption (reducing meat eating, vegetarianism or veganism) for the individual. Both of these questions touch on the relationship of the human to the land, explored from a Christian perspective. The frame that the last chapter works to communicate is: what would we need to do to live sustainably and with a fair food system within the territorial boundaries of the land that we have been given, the United Kingdom?[94] How can we divest ourselves of these food banks without either damning the poor abroad or damning the poor at home?

# I

# Food Bank Lives

## Introduction

James tells me that if he had the time and money he would like to start the Durham Liberation People's Front. I tell him that I only believe in the work of the People of Durham's Front of Liberation and we exchange smiles in mutual appreciation of Monty Python's *Life of Brian* and the problematic piety of the politically rebellious. We are in the church hall of the United Reformed Methodist Church on Waddington Street, Durham. We've been talking for about 20 minutes already, about food banks, and work, and James' life and health. He's in his early fifties and hasn't worked since 2009. He's frustrated today that the Job Centre have sent him on another mandatory numeracy and literacy test which cuts into the time he'd like to be spending learning the programming language C#.

> I used to be a PC programmer, my last work was in January 2009, then I was off with illness, a prolapsed disc. Now my skills are out of date, I'm unmarketable.

During his days he works at the Durham Library teaching himself current computer sciences but has limited time and resources. His ability to educate himself is held back by the routine begging trail that has been made his lot. He holds a hand two feet above the table, 'If this is the breadline, what you need to live, then this', holding a second hand halfway between the first hand and the table, 'is what you get on the current benefits.' Because of his government-sponsored poverty, James is forced to conduct a daily tour of Durham's charitable services and institutions. He is 'having to spend a lot of time getting food' and goes through a standard day with me: Sanctuary 21 for breakfast, library at 9.30 for job searches, lunch at County Durham Foodbank or Waddington drop-in, evening meals from Foodcycle when they're open. You have to work hard for your poverty in twenty-first-century Britain.

The food that I get from these charities and groups I wouldn't eat normally. Cake, bread, pasta and pork, you know, lots of ham sandwiches, they're bad for my health because I have diabetes, HbA1c. I'm eating too much sugar and starch. There's fruit on offer, grapes and bananas, it's what they have but it isn't good to me. Eating like this, I know it's costing me the length of my life.

A hot drink off to his right, he rolls a small piece of card between his thumb and forefinger and places it into a coarse-cut tobacco cigarette, the cheap stuff from the marketplace, he says. He continues:

Globalization, offshoring. They have blown my career away. My career was stolen by an undemocratic process. I don't think any government has the remit from its people to offshore employment … There aren't jobs for life now, not any longer. That's changed as well. People are seen as a resource. 'HR', that's what it means, right? Managers see people as a resource, one that can be picked up and discarded. I've got to be available for any kind of job, whatever. I'm filling in forms for being a cleaner or a caretaker.

This chapter is about the lives of those who are using County Durham Foodbank. Like James, many of those I interviewed had histories of precarious and unreliable work in the post-industrial economy of the north-east of England. When out of work, they wrestle with a benefits system that is slow, unsympathetic and experienced as punitive and intrusive. The everyday stresses faced by these individuals whether in or out of work are often related to or exacerbate existing health conditions, or health conditions in loved ones. A proportionate response to the issue of food insecurity in the UK needs to be furnished from an accurate description of the problem, one that this chapter seeks to provide. Included in this description and the chapter's conclusion is a review of recent writings on the idea of 'precariousness': the transition that has been imposed on James and people like him of a new, globalized economy in which country competes with country to drive down corporate tax rates and loosen worker protections in order to attract big business. The experiences of those using our food banks pose questions to us about welfare and its reforms and also of the larger employment and economic context: stagnant wages, decline of manufacturing, rising food prices, employment insecurity and reduced bargaining power for labour.

## Part One: life for food bank users

Like James, a significant number of those I interviewed in County Durham faced overlapping difficulties, often labour marginality combined with demanding caring roles and ill health. The most extensive investigation of the lives of food bank users is Rachel Loopstra and Doireann Lalor's *Financial Insecurity, Food Insecurity, and Disability: The Profile of People Rreceiving Emergency Food Assistance from The Trussell Trust Foodbank Network in Britain.* Working with the Trussell Trust,[1] Loopstra and Lalor used volunteers to collect data from food bank users between October and December 2016 at sites across the UK. They conducted this investigation with the aim of describing the socio-economic situation of food bank users, their degrees of access (or lack of) to social security, the prevalence and severity of 'recent short-term income and expenditure shocks' food bank users may have experienced, the degrees of health and disability challenges food bank users face and the 'chronicity' of household food insecurity experienced by food bank users. Eighteen sites participated in the survey, including my food bank in Durham County, and over 400 food bank users answered an extensive self-complete questionnaire.

What was found in the study? The findings of the study were that 'households using food banks face extreme financial vulnerability'.[2] Second, that 78% of households were 'severely food insecure', which means having skipped meals, gone without food, sometimes for days, in the last 12 months.[3] For the majority, experiencing hunger was the case every month, or almost every month, of the last year. Third, while single male households were the most common household type receiving help from the food bank, it was lone parents with children that constitutes the largest number of people in aggregate.[4] Fourth, one in five food bank users were homeless people and of those who did have a house 50% were unable to heat it.[5]

Food bank users face what Loopstra and Lalor call 'multiple forms of destitution'.[6] Half of those who completed the questionnaires had not only low but unreliable incomes. One in three were awaiting a benefit payment, and Loopstra and Lalor describe the groups of people accessing Trussell Trust food banks as often the 'most affected by recent welfare reforms'.[7]

The question of money was one of the most recurring issues in the interviews I conducted. Talking with a woman in her late thirties in the Durham drop-in centre, the difficulties for those who come to food banks are clear. Jane, who used to be a nurse and is about to start an occupational therapy job in the next few weeks, has been to the food bank twice already. After being forced to sell her flat when the husband of her child left her, she lost her job and now she is caught in debt. She is struggling to pay the bills and provide enough food for her and her child, even with the support she receives.

> I'm overdrawn £800. I've got one child and get JSA and child tax credits, and I have a hardship loan and Durham County Council are paying 70% of my rent but I still struggle. I felt embarrassed, ashamed at coming [to the food bank], but the price of food … so any help I'll take.

The stress caused by these life shocks has had adverse effects on her health. She tells me she has anxiety, has been taking antidepressant medication and has been thinking about suicide. She told this to the Job Centre when she went for her meeting but she tells me that they've refused to give her more extensive help or lighten her burden by transitioning her onto Employment and Support Allowance (ESA, welfare for those who have a health problem or disability which affects how much they can work) and relieving her of the task of constantly searching for new work at a vulnerable time.

> They won't give me ESA, it was rejected and instead they gave me a budgeting loan, the benefits system is crazy.

Other food bank clients I spoke with made similar links between benefits, work, insecurity and health. Miriam, a woman in her fifties, tells me why she's come to the food bank today, showing me the locations of her injuries as she runs through them one by one.

> Hardship, I got sanctioned, they stopped my ESA. I've been on it since 2015. I have COPD (Chronic Obstructive Pulmonary Disease). I'm struggling with liver, and got arthritis in my knee and back. I use my sticks to help walk, compensate for my ankle. But I do struggle to walk a long way, I can't get far. ESA was just enough to cover a fortnight, just. 6 November, 2017 I had a health check, told them about

my medical conditions like I told you. They ask you questions about what you can or can't do, I said that I could walk to the shop, I told them that I'm drink dependent. After the check, the interviewer said, 'after this I think I'll go for a drink', I thought this was because they understood it was difficult and that they understood me. So when I left I felt good, thought I'd still get support. Three or four weeks later I got this letter saying that I am 'fit for work'. I felt sick, really down, I'm smoking more. Now I feel like it's a whole pack of lies, the medical check, like they wanted to cut you off ... I think the government need to treat people like people, not just like points or numbers. It's more like they're trying to get people off the sick to show they are doing good, get brownie points.

Later in the interview I ask her about her future and what she is hoping for.

That's what I'm scared of, the unknown. When will I see a bit of coin again? That uncertainty about the future, being worried about it. You face six weeks of waiting on Universal Credit. How am I supposed to get through that?

Similar frustrations with the assessment for work process brought in by the coalition government were evident in an interview I carried out with a man called Stewart in Brandon Village.

I have a permanent fracture in my left arm. Chronic back pain, osteo-arthritis. My health check in August/September 2016 medical they asked me to do the squats, I told them 'if I do those I'll never get back up'. I was still found fit for work. I appealed and lost the appeal. Now I'm on JSA (Jobseeker's Allowance, welfare for those looking for work) and have to apply for 40 jobs in two weeks. I do online job applications at the Job Centre, 'cause Brandon library is open 2 days per week. It's a struggle to keep up the applications, I might be sanctioned. I struggle with the computers. They want to send me on a PC course, but being around groups of people is difficult cause I don't like groups.
*How does this make you feel, having to put in these applications every week?*
Useless.
*What will you do if you get sanctioned, are you worried?*
Of course. It will affect everything, my rent, everything, you know. I'm worried, worried to death.

Both Stewart and Jane talked to me about the sense of entrapment and futility that marked their lives. For both of them the fatigue had become so severe that they had recurring suicidal thoughts. They are far from alone in this. Malcolm Burge, a retired gardener, killed himself in June 2014 after writing to his council for help with the debts he owed them. The Disability Campaign group Black Triangle keeps a list of welfare-related deaths of sick or disabled people with over 60 names on it back in 2014.[8] Between 2007 and 2014 the NHS Digital's Adult Psychiatric Morbidity Survey said that the number of those out of work on disability benefits who attempted to take their own lives went from 21% to 43% (compared to 6% and 7% of the population generally). The Department for Work and Pensions admits to carrying out 49 'peer reviews' since 2012 (as reported in 2015), reviews 'triggered when suicide or alleged suicide is "associated with a DWP activity"'.[9] Academics working in this area are coming to understand 'austerity suicides as embedded within an affective economy of the anxiety caused by punitive welfare retrenchment, the stigmatization of being a recipient of benefits, and the internalization of market logic that assigns value through "productivity" and conceptualizes welfare entitlement as economic "burden"'.[10]

Those who I talked to at County Durham Foodbank often talked about facing a caustic welfare system and difficult transitions in and out of work, when work was even available and dignified. In relation to work and income, Loopstra and Lalor say that 'part-time work was the most common form of work in the sample, with almost no households having full-time work.'[11] Only 14.8% of households had some work or income from employment. Some 45% of households were economically inactive, due to illness or disability, and 26% contained adults who were unemployed and looking for work.[12] When Loopstra and Lalor asked people about their sources of income, 70% were on a form of state-distributed benefit (70% Employment Support Allowance, 17% on Job Seekers Allowance, 9% on Income Support and 3% on Universal Credit). The research suggests that those transitioning benefits or awaiting a claim are particularly vulnerable, along with those facing benefit conditionality sanctions.[13] On the back of findings from this research, Loopstra and Lalor are worried for those receiving ESA, as further reductions to the income for this group (implemented in April 2017) would leave them even more exposed to food insecurity.[14]

With the difficulty of finding good, reliable work, low levels of benefits payments and frequent hiatuses between payments or suspensions of payments for reviews, appeals, bureaucratic changes or sanctions, food bank users face severe income poverty. In Loopstra and Lalor's questionnaire they asked food bank users to identify the range that best matched their income in the past month. Most households, they say, had incomes between £100 and 500 per month, with average household income at £319 per month. They write that this places food bank users well below the low-income threshold for 2015/2016: 'all households using food banks were experiencing deep income poverty in the past month.'[15] Within the context of inadequate and often unreliable income (44% reported 'somewhat unsteady or extremely unsteady' income), rising and unexpected costs also featured significantly in food bank users' experiences.[16] These included factors from rising food costs (25%), housing expenses (28%), changing health conditions (10%), new children, separation from a partner or debt repayments.[17] On the nature of work done by food bank users, Loopstra and Lalor found very few who had full-time, permanent jobs. This suggests to them that 'certain types of work can give people the security they need to avoid food bank usage'.[18]

The result of a combination of unexpected outgoings and unsteady incomes or reduction in incomes is severe food insecurity. Loopstra and Lalor, following the Food Security Survey used in the United States and Canada, asked food bank users a series of questions: in the last 12 months had they lost weight, been hungry but not eaten, eaten less than they thought they should, cut the size of or skipped meals, or not eaten for a whole day? Those who answered one out of five of the aforementioned questions in the affirmative were classified as marginally food insecure, around 3% in total. Answering two to five in the affirmative makes one moderately to severely food insecure. Of those asked, 78% were classified as severely food insecure, meaning the household had answered two to five questions in the affirmative *and* had 'cut back on food intake, experienced hunger, and/or gone whole days without eating'.[19] Severe food insecurity can be mild or chronic, that is, this degree of food insecurity can be recurrent or intermittent over a 12-month period. Two out of three, Loopstra and Lalor say, over the last year experienced chronic food insecurity – hunger and deprivation 'every month or almost every month'.[20] Putting this in an international context, the level of food insecurity in the UK is 20–40% higher than that reported by food bank users in the Netherlands and Canada.[21] Compared with the poor in other OECD countries, the British poor are particularly badly off.

The survey concluded by asking people about their experiences of illness and/or disability, injury and/or mental or emotional problems, issues already suggested by my interviews. At the food bank three out of four households contained someone with a health condition and/or a

disability.[22] They also found that a third of households included someone with a mental health condition, and stated that these figures make
households using food banks three times more likely to contain someone with a disability than the average low-income UK household.[23] As
Loopstra and Lalor say, 'people with disabilities are at greater risk of
poverty in the UK' and they ask whether 'over-representation of people
with disabilities among food bank users may indicate that current
welfare support for disabled people is insufficient to ensure that such
individuals are not left destitute'.[24] This research reinforces past findings which have confirmed that half of all people in poverty either have
a disability or live with someone who does.[25]

The picture that emerges from Loopstra and Lalor's research is of
food bank users who are worse off according to a range of indices than
even the lowest income groups in the UK, let alone the British public
at large. Those accessing Britain's food banks are the poor among the
poor. Increased food bank usage is related to increased food bank
accessibility, but the problems food banks addressed are not caused
by food banks. To suggest, as recent British politicians have, that food
banks are a supply-driven problem is a case of expedient misrepresentation.[26] Those using the Trussell Trust's services face a series of
adverse circumstances that often overlap and reinforce each other: labour
marginality, ill health, injury, disability, delayed, denied or inadequate
government welfare support; and lonely, isolated or inhospitable living
conditions. These circumstances make food bank users particularly
vulnerable to income and expenditure shocks and, when the household
type is factored into the analysis, those using food banks are the 'most
severely impacted by benefit reforms'.[27] Loopstra and Lalor note that
the government transition of lone parent families from income support
to JSA, their changes to local housing allowance for individuals under
35, conditionality introduced for those disabled but found fit for work,
and the benefits cap will make life for food bank users even harder.
Added to market factors, like the rising cost of food, 'the real value of
benefits has eroded and will continue to do so over the next four years
as the cost of living rises' and the Conservative government's 1% benefits freeze continues to bite.[28] Those out of work are not the only ones
accessing food banks. Those in the 'low pay, no pay' cycles and faced
with job insecurity have also been forced to use food bank services to
maintain themselves.

As we saw with James, it is little surprise that there are deep-seated
anti-politician sentiments expressed by food bank users. A regular visitor
to Durham City Foodbank, where I volunteered, was Antony. He was
born in London and had done two stints in the armed forces. Now in

his late forties with short grey hair and stubble, he regularly walked into Durham in his 'five finger' sandals for a coffee, chat and some food. He'd trained as a nurse and worked for the NHS for ten years before going abroad to teach English, and now, unemployed, he was training to be a long-haul lorry driver. Relocated from the south-east to the north-east with the offer of housing, we regularly talked about his experience of being unemployed and dealing with the Job Centre staff.

*What's it like, going to the Job Centre and signing on?*
The Job Centre? You're like *a priori* a leper ... Who's the guy who did 'Scream', Ed Munch? It makes you feel like that.

He goes on:

It's very demeaning. Abusive staff, not that they mean to be, just they didn't know what they are doing. I've got nothing good to say about it. The people there it's like they have a civil service job mentality. Isn't it my rights to get support, so aren't sanctions illegal, against my rights? But then people have no voice, do they? It's not like if you're unhappy with your benefits you can go on strike can you? You're not going to all get all the people together, they're exhausted.

It's these experiences that led him to tell me that he'd happily 'vote for Guy Fawkes'. He talks to me about politicians seeing politics as a vehicle for themselves or as just a job, and accuses them of lacking the insight or ideals to instigate something like real change. Not that it's just the politicians' fault. Antony also lays part of the blame at the feet of the people who 'have regional voting habits' and are equally myopic. For Antony, while he is currently without stable accommodation and work, he's hoping that his new qualification will allow him to travel to Scandinavia and live and work there long term.

## Part Two: precariat, labour insecurity and neoliberal governance

One of the suggestions made by the 2014 *Feeding Britain* report was for a single office that would have oversight for all food insecurity issues in the UK. The rationale for this was that the lives of people going to the food bank – whether in insecure labour or receiving unemployment benefits – are subject to the practices and policies of eight government departments: from the DWP for benefits to the Department for Business, Innovation and Skills' policies in relation to work, to the Department for Environment, Food and Rural Affairs for food policies.[29] While it is understandable that the Trussell Trust, Feeding Britain and End Hunger UK have prioritized benefits reform because they have been so destructive and are a clear target with achievable 'asks', the social, economic and political processes that have shaped the lives of people like James precede the politics of the post-2008 administrations. Across a range of academic literatures, one of the terms that is being used to describe these processes is 'precariousness' or the rise of the 'precariat'. Precariousness names a process of disembedding or dislocating people from their associations, from stable forms of employment and, for some authors, a separation of people from traditional forms of culture and thus also from past ways of thinking, imagining, relating and hoping.[30] The American theologian Norman Wirzba, for example, writes that 'we cannot live well – as friends, spouses, or citizens – if we do not respect and strengthen the bonds of relationship (human and nonhuman) that make life meaningful'.[31] However, the human need to be a placed animal and participate in the world and people around us is at variance with 'contemporary trends like globalization, corporate downsizing/restructuring, and movable capital' that have 'made all of us much less secure in our economic being'.[32] He continues:

> One of the hallmarks of postmodern life is its precariousness: we can no longer take our socioeconomic position for granted; we feel uncertain about the stability of the things we care most about; and we feel generally unsafe in the face of terrorism, vandalism, rape, and theft.[33]

Given these circumstances, he goes on to suggest with laudable nuance that

> A broad-based discussion on the nature of responsible freedom should be our highest cultural priority. Can we envision and implement lives that encourage creativity, exploration, and self-expression and at the same time promote both the health of the natural habitats we live

from and the vibrancy of communal structures that infuse personal life with meaning and joy? How will we maintain and celebrate the bonds of relationship that nurture life, without coming to regard these bonds as oppressive?[34]

The contribution of this book to that task will be the topic of later chapters. For the moment we turn to Guy Standing's account of the rise of the precariat and its relation to neoliberalism.

In *The Precariat: The Rise of a New Dangerous Class*, Standing outlines who the precariat are, why their numbers have grown and how they have been utilized or cynically exploited by the governments of OECD countries. The political context for their growth, Standing argues, is the global proliferation (often associated with the policies of Margaret Thatcher and Ronald Regan) of 'neoliberalism', a set of economic policies that presumes that 'growth and development [depend] on market competitiveness', that 'everything should be done to maintain competition and competitiveness, and to allow market principles to permeate all aspects of life'.[35] The fundamental link between neoliberalism and precariousness resides in neoliberalism's historical tendency to defend and accelerate processes of disembedding. After the Second World War, the dominant economic model was Keynesian, which 'argued for a more active role for the state', a state that was responsible 'for the welfare of their populations, which included not just maintaining full employment and economic growth but also the provision of a range of social services like housing, healthcare, education, etc.'[36] Part of guaranteeing this arrangement internationally was 'the creation of a system of fixed exchange rates' between currencies that helped shield countries from 'the destabilising dynamics of speculative finance'.[37] However, by the 1960s, with a trade deficit and expensive war in Vietnam, the USA brought an end to this system of fixed exchange rates attached to the value of its own dollar, thereby reducing the power of the state over the economy, a situation that was to become the new norm and see further entrenchment with the stagflation crises of the 1970s and the privatization of the 1980s. Why is this important? Because at the origin of neoliberalism, before it had secured its power over the imaginations of elites and common people alike, is a moment of disconnecting of money not just from gold but from the collective power of people and their particular places. Money floating free, money that no longer refers primarily to the desirability of gold or the power of the dollar and US economy but now refers just to more money in a long chain of deferred value.[38] With fewer state controls, money was free to move across borders to wherever it had most power in a less regulated global economy and take with it jobs, profits and products. Is steel cheaper to produce in China than Sheffield? Then do it there. Is it more profitable to exhume coal in South America than South Shields, or make clothes in Bangladesh rather than Great Britain? Then so be it.

To keep up with these changes, governments across the world had to loosen labour regulations and defeat the unions, as Thatcher famously did in the UK in the 1980s. What these governments offered their people were tax reductions for the rich and increased spending power on cheap (usually imported) goods and services for the poor; Richard Branson on his island and Joe Bloggs on his 18–30 club holiday on Ibiza are, at least in this sense, part of the same process. Standing notes that the domestic consequences of international marketization have been 'labour market flexibility' in industrial policy and the pattern of 'transferring risks and insecurity onto workers and their families'.[39] Standing lists a series of other changes that must be factored into this spread of risk: a shift from manufacturing to services; the 'feminization of labour', or the rising number of women in the workforce; a transfer of capital from OECD countries to emerging market economies; the victory of the Anglo-Saxon shareholder model which sees companies as commodities to be traded or asset-stripped; downward pressure on global wages with the explosion of Chinese industry, coupled with the suppression of OECD wages through the subsidizing of companies.[40] As Srnicek and Williams note in *Inventing the Future*, the numbers of those joining the international economy are astronomical. With the fall of communism and the opening up of China and India, 1.5 billion people have entered the global economy looking for wages in approximately the last 25 years.[41] The rural supply of labour may be slowing in China but continues to rise with more labourers available in South America and Africa. Unemployment rates in the USA and UK have risen from 1% or 2% in the 1940s and 1950s to an 'optimal' rate of 5.5%.

> At a global level, the unemployment rate has continued to rise after the 2008 crisis, both in absolute and relative terms. The global rate of job creation has remained significantly lower, has largely generated part-time jobs, and is forecast to continue its sluggish trend.[42]

The aggregate effect of these changes is a growing group in society, though diverse in age, outlook and background, who 'have lives dominated by insecurity, uncertainty, debt and humiliation', who are underworked or underpaid, or both.[43] Lansley and Mack report that in early 2012 there were 400,000 job vacancies in the UK while 'the official count of unemployed people – those actively looking for work and available to start immediately – stood at 2.69 million.'[44]

Standing identifies the precariat in two ways. First, he says that the precariat are a 'distinct socio-economic group' that can be differentiated from a global elite of plutocrats on the one hand,[45] and below them a 'salariat' who are in full-time employment and are concentrated 'in large corporations, government agencies and public administration'.[46] In the socio-economic sense, the 'precariat' are a contemporary manifestation of the 'proletariat': a classic Marxist term for the members of the working classes. However, Standing does not conflate precariat and proletariat. The precariousness of the precariat 'also implies a lack of secure work-based identity' even if they are able to cobble together bits of piecemeal work.[47] So, Standing's point is not just that there is less solidarity and pride in work among baristas and call centre workers than there was among dockers and miners but that the precarious lack 'labour market security, employment security, job security, work, income, skills and representational security'.[48] He says:

> The precariat can be identified by a distinctive structure of social income, which imparts a vulnerability going well beyond what would be conveyed by the money income received at a particular moment. For instance, in a period of rapid commercialisation of the economy of a developing country, the new groups, many going towards the precariat, find that they lose traditional community benefits and do not gain enterprise or state benefits. They are more vulnerable than many with lower incomes who retain traditional forms of community support and are more vulnerable than salaried employees who have similar money incomes but have access to an array of enterprise and state benefits. A feature of the precariat is not the level of money wages or income earned at any particular moment but the lack of community support in time of need, lack of assured enterprise or state benefits, and lack of private benefits to supplement money earnings.[49]

The question of community support, precariousness and food banks in the north-east is a complicated one. On the one hand, the existence of such a strong food bank network suggests a high degree of 'social capital', an unyielding social spirit in the face of adversity in this area. Food bank users spoke glowingly of food banks as social and friendly spaces, an issue in individualistic and lonely times that is very important and will be discussed later. However, in my interviews, a number of those I talked with shared a concern with me that they'd be seen at the food bank. In my conversation with Miriam, for example, we were talking about her desire to continue to contribute socially, and what she liked to do with her money when she had it:

> When I've got some I like to give to the food bank or to the animal charities, for the dogs. It feels good to donate, help the animals and people that are going short.
> *What does it feel like to receive, come to the food bank for a parcel?*
> A bit like a tramp, a leech, you're taking. It's worse in the food bank when it's full. Less people showing up or no people, then less people see you or talk about it. That's much better, how I'd like it to be.

A similar sentiment was shared with me by Jane.

> *Is there anything you think the food bank could do to improve?*
> Yes, it would be good if there was home delivery, help to avoid the shame of coming out. Better, it would be more discreet, more comfortable. I know that lady there, I'm worried about being seen, the confidentiality isn't great with coming to a food bank is it?

Looking around the food bank, Jane then spotted a man at another table and strongly differentiated herself from him. For her, this man who smoked and was losing his teeth shared little or nothing in common with her. She wasn't poor or homeless, she just needed a little help. In the first instance, these feelings of shame at being at the food bank suggest that food bank clients have internalized a social narrative (about independence, worth and wages, self-sufficiency) in which they have come to understand themselves as failures. It suggests, furthermore, that a correlate of these food bank users' idea of success was not depending on others, or being seen to depend on others. By arranging links between how people think and the material circumstances of their existence, the economy they are caught in, Standing's work unpacks this complicated area in greater detail.

Along with socio-economic changes comes the spread of correlate modes of thought, Standing says. It is not 'just being in jobs of limited duration and with minimal labour protection', it's also 'being in a status that offers no sense of career, no sense of secure occupational identity and few, if any, entitlements to the state and enterprise benefits that several generations of those who saw themselves as belonging to the industrial proletariat or the salaried had come to expect'.[50] This new form of vulnerability breeds 'anger, anomie, anxiety, and alienation'.[51] Unlike the British working class, which became in time a 'class for itself' with robust pride that helped forge it into a political force with a clear agenda, the precariat is still a 'class in itself'.[52] This means that a temporary low-wage worker may be induced to see the 'welfare scrounger' as obtaining more, unfairly and at his or her expense. A long-term resident of a low-income urban area will easily be led to see incoming migrants as taking better jobs and leaping to head the queue for benefits. Tensions within the precariat are setting people against each other, preventing them from recognising that the social and economic structure is producing their common set of vulnerabilities.[53]

Standing calls the precariat 'the new dangerous class' because of the possibility that the root of the problem of precariousness will not be fixed, while the anger and anxiety it produces will be diverted by academics, politicians, commentators and religious leaders towards other social, economic and political ends. Precariousness precedes political populism; the question of job security and global competition were significant factors both in Donald Trump's election in the USA and in the vote to leave the EU in the UK.

Standing identifies those most vulnerable to being pulled into the classes of the precariat as those who come from poorer communities or are identified as different (the precariat is a gendered and raced phenomenon), especially the disabled and episodically disabled. Despite the range of measures governments have taken to react to the growing recognition of disability through specialized workplaces, anti-discrimination laws and equal opportunity workplaces, the drive to reduce welfare budgets and 'make more of the disabled employable' by pushing them into work has fostered a strong link between disability, precariousness and poverty, as a range of research around disability and benefits has already suggested.[54] The relationship between precariousness, poverty, and race is an established part of the American account of neoliberalism, with Reagan's 'welfare queen' a particularly salient image of the 1980s which tied together race, poverty and gender with the political purpose of rolling back the responsibilities of the state.[55] Globally, 'women are more likely than men to be in precarious forms of work', while in Europe 'migrants are more likely than native-born workers to be in temporary rather than permanent employment'.[56] Whether neoliberalism is inherently racist or misogynistic is open to contention. What is beyond doubt is that precariousness is more problematic for people of ethnic minorities and women in the UK *and* that defenders of neoliberal social and economic policies are comfortable speaking in normative terms about the family, the defence of traditional cultures and the failings of significant proportions of those coming to the UK from other countries.

The political discourses around 'troubled families' and, prior to that, 'single mothers' contain these links between state dependency, gender and poverty.[57] In a poorly attended debate in the House of Commons on holiday hunger among school children in the summer of 2019, the Conservative MP and evangelical Christian Fiona Bruce, while recognizing the complicated causes of child hunger, laid a significant portion of the blame on poor mothering and the denigration of mothering more broadly. For Bruce, one reason for child hunger is that

> family life isn't as strong as it was a generation ago ... what can we do to strengthen family life ... I think we've undermined it in recent years, and this Government also [is responsible for that], the role of mothering, the value of a mother, the vocation that many women have to be a mother in the home ...

While she does recognize that poor mothers often have to work the longest hours and during the most anti-social times of day, she maintains throughout her speech the contention that children are going hungry because their mothers have failed them and that this was not the case when she grew up, despite the fact that they were not well off. No more food banks, because 'home cooking is nutritious at a lower cost'?[58]

Moving in and out of low-paid and short-term work along with 'dealing with the unfriendly complexities of the welfare system' can lead many people to 'drift into chronic debt', a problem so severe that County Durham Foodbank has placed debt advice workers ('Durham Money Advice Centre' or DMAC) into a number of its food banks.[59] Being born into poverty makes one more vulnerable to other forms of poverty, insecurities accentuate each other, a lack of 'social capital' or 'community resources' can increase your chances to enter the precariat. And once there the poverty premium (the increased costs of goods and services for those who are poor) makes it harder to get out.[60] Standing says that whereas once, 'before the welfare state', 'individuals relied heavily on informal mechanisms of community help these are no longer there. They were weakened by the growth of state and enterprise benefits. For several generations, people came to think there was no need for them, so they faded' and now, with state benefits and enterprise benefits also in withdrawal, the social, political and economic levers needed to resist the pull of the precariat are no longer available for many.[61]

## Conclusion

I'm coming to the end of a conversation with a man called David in his mid-forties. He's talked extensively and movingly about his experience of becoming a Christian, the new life it brought him, and his history of mental health difficulties, employment and benefits. He's got a face-to-face assessment coming up to review his Disability Living Allowance (which was a great relief to him after moving off JSA) which gives him a lot of anxiety, but someone at the food bank is helping him prepare for it and write a letter to the Job Centre, for which he is very appreciative. I ask him in closing what he is hoping for in the future and he says:

> A secure future? Not having to worry about money and things like that. I guess I hope for contentment mostly. Age has changed my perceptions, I'm sure that I look at things differently now with how I've grown. Like how technology and jobs change, they're always evolving aren't they? The Terminator in *Terminator 3*, it's not like Arnie in the first movies is it? ... The government with the benefits system, it is difficult to keep up. It was that if I didn't apply for ten jobs a week I'd get sanctions, all that. I got pushed into this job that I wasn't happy with at all by the government. It was a dead-end job that wasn't going anywhere. If I could go back, do some of it again, I think I would try to be more ambitious in this unambitious world.

The Terminator movies tell the story of a human rebellion against a dystopic Artifical Intelligence (AI) called Skynet in the near future. In an attempt to stop the human rebellion, Skynet sends increasingly sophisticated 'hunter killer' robots back into the past to assassinate the leader of the rebellion, John Conor (while he is still a child) and his mother Sarah Conor.

In David's analogy, the old industrial economy and its associated technologies (the factory, the mine, the printing press) are like the original Terminator, the Cyberdyne Systems Model 101.[62] A traditional, metallic robot under a human veneer; solid, inflexible, unstoppable but predictable, reliable but not amendable, strong but not sophisticated. In the later films in the franchise, all that was once solid melts into 'mimetic polyalloy' – mercury – when a T1000 and a T-X are sent back into the past by an increasingly desperate AI. These new technologies (computers, GM crops, financialization tools), like the new precarious economy that has followed on from industrialism and Fordism, are adaptable, flexible, responsive. The new Terminators are equally misanthropic but harder to grasp as they innovate quickly, shift form and move seamlessly into all spheres.

With his history of health difficulties, David told me, 'I always assumed that I couldn't work, but my experience of Handcrafted has definitely changed my view.' Handcrafted is a charity based in the north-east of England that helps people struggling with health issues, debt or addiction to retrain, refurbish their homes, build themselves their own goods and find paid employment. They currently use 18 houses to accommodate 31 people, building whatever is needed for the homes in their workshops and including those who will live in the homes in the processes of production.[63] For the last year, David has been visiting one of Handcrafted's wood workshops; the freedom, the creativity, the company, the purpose that making give him were all positive parts of his experience of being there and have, in his own words, moved him from 'a can't do to a can do attitude'. While his last job left him feeling depressed at the pointlessness of it, the kinds of labour that he can carry out at Handcrafted, within his own capacities and at his own speed, have been life affirming for him.

In his book *Bullshit Jobs: A Theory*, the American anthropologist David Graeber writes about an early twentieth-century psychologist, Karl Gross, who 'discovered that infants express extraordinary happiness when they first figure out that they can cause predictable effects in the world'.[64] Graeber continues:

Let's say that they discover that they can move a pencil by randomly moving their arms. Then they realize they can achieve the same effect by moving in the same pattern again. Expressions of utter joy ensue.

Gross called this 'the pleasure at being the cause' and Graeber says that 'confirmed by a century of experimental evidence' the baby's experience of making something happen and, then, making it happen again, is 'a species of delight that remains the fundamental background of all subsequent human experience'.[65] Writing on the preceding page, Graeber notes that 'even in those prisons where inmates are provided free food and shelter and are not actually required to work, denying them the right to press shirts in the prison laundry, clean latrines in the prison gym, or package computers for Microsoft in the prison workshop is used as a form of punishment'.[66]

Academics like Loopstra and Lalor, along with others in the field, are right to question recent benefit reforms, the future trajectories of welfare and to point out that those using British food banks face 'severe financial insecurity' coupled with physical and mental health trials and high rates of social isolation. But food banks, as the next chapter will show, precede these recent benefit changes and the issue of denying many 'the ability to cause' either through unemployment or pointless work is to the detriment of people's sense of wanting to be around in the world at all. Following James' comments, the link that needs to be followed is not only food banking and the dereliction of duty being undertaken in the dismantling of the welfare safety net, but the proliferation of insecure, short-term and poorly paid labour. Our current employment situation is so confused and there is such little consensus on the cumulative point of our habits of work that Graeber rightly notes that 'in our society, there seems to be a general rule that, the more obviously one's work benefits other people, the less one is likely to be paid for it'.[67]

James' story has been contextualized in this chapter in a narrative, provided by Standing, about changes in work practice and habits of mind that follow on from deregularized globalization and the capture of the state by neoliberal norms of thought. It is not the case that neoliberalism simply disembeds people from the labour market, citizens from their country's governments, people from their local communities and ecologies, nor even people from their own bodies (malnutrition is Janus-faced, with food insecurity looking one way and obesity the other). Neoliberalism also works the other way, it re-embeds people back into intrusive welfare regimes, it forces them to be amenable to the demands of the labour market or starve, it ropes countries into a global economy in which their people, habitats, natural resources, technical innovations, and historical inheritances of mores and institutions are sold off to the highest bidder. But what about food banks and the people who run them? Are they enacting another form of 'exclusion through inclusion', practically and conceptually compatible with the circumstances that caused the problem they now seek to address? Or are they illustrative of a more fundamental inclusivity, a participation in each other, the creation and in its Creator which is also freedom?

# 2

# International Growth of Food Banks

## Introduction

Loopstra and Lalor end the report I cited in the last chapter by saying that the drivers of food bank use are, primarily, 'insecure and insufficient incomes'.[1] Consequently, they say that food charity or food aid in the form of food banks 'cannot address the widespread and severe problem of food insecurity'.[2] In an article from 2019, Loopstra and her co-authors Hannah Lambie-Mumford and Jasmine Fledderjohann elaborate on this point:

> To be able to reduce food insecurity: [food banks] must provide a quantity and quality of food to meet the nutritional and food security needs of their clients, and they must be accessible to people who experience food insecurity. On the former, previous studies have found high risk of dietary inadequacies and high levels of severe food insecurity among food bank users, and food banks have been found to provide an inadequate supply of dairy foods, and insufficient amounts of calcium and vitamins A and C in the parcels provided.[3]

Along with studies that have highlighted the high (but understandable) reliance on non-perishable goods, Loopstra says that the current consensus is that 'food banks are limited in their ability to provide the quantity and quality of food needed to address the food insecurity and nutritional vulnerability of their clients'.[4] In terms of food bank accessibility there are also problems: how often are food banks open? How flexible can they be given their dependence on volunteers? Are they located in regions that need them, those with higher numbers of welfare caseloads, unemployment and percentages of child deprivation? How reliable are the referrers who act as gatekeepers for the vouchers? Does the 'three times in six months' cap (while subject to the discretion of the food bank manager) inhibit access when it's needed?[5] Loopstra is normally very sympathetic in her accounts of the work done by food banks, but when it comes to meeting the needs of the hungry she says quite bluntly that 'inherent features of charitable responses to hunger often restrict their effectiveness. Public policy interventions are needed to address hunger.'[6]

If the inability to deal with food insecurity long term are food banks' weakness, what are their strengths? What rationales have been provided for their growth and legitimacy? What, conversely, has been neglected from academic reviews of the rise of food banks in the USA and UK? This chapter surveys the international rise of food banks and identifies some of their key features, before telling the story of the rise of County Durham Foodbank. Beginning in the USA in the 1960s, food banks moved through international Roman Catholic channels into the rest of America, Europe and Asia. Arriving in the UK at the end of the millennium, they grew exponentially after the 2008 financial crash. From their inception, food banks have creatively negotiated a range of complicated forces: the Christian desire to serve God and their fellow people, waste in the food system and the mixed motives of international food corporations, rising levels of unemployment and changes in labour markets (as the last chapter identified), volunteering and the increased size and prestige of the charity industry, and the government's changing understanding of their role and responsibility in relation to the citizenry. It is this confluence of elements, compounded by post-industrialism in the north-east and austerity everywhere, which together led to the emergence of County Durham Foodbank, the site from which the stories of the last chapter were told.

## Part One: the international growth of food banks

The American sociologist Janet Poppendieck has given a history of US food aid in the twentieth century and its origins. She says that the US government's response to the mass unemployment and hunger of the 1930s was addressed, at least in part, by the transfer of the food bounty of surplus farm products to the poor.[7] Both Hoover and Roosevelt administrations contributed to the national school lunch programmes, provided free distribution of food through state and local agencies, and innovated through the introduction of the food stamp programme.[8] In time, the Federal Surplus Relief Corporation was created within the United States Department of Agriculture in order to systematize the transfer of agricultural surpluses to charities in order that they might feed the unemployed and poor. With the renewed visibility and attention given to poverty in the 1960s, Poppendieck notes that 'anti-poverty activists in the US made a strategic decision to pursue the reform and expansion of food programs rather than the more adequate cash assistance that might have made them unnecessary'.[9] The idea of hunger in a land of plenty resonated with the American public and food programmes seemed like a common sense solution to two problems: food waste and food insecurity. On top of their practicality, part of the force of these policies was their moral appeal, as 'increasing concerns about the environment and economic costs of food waste are now driving the food bank movement'.[10]

The historical decision to deal with hunger through the redistribution of waste food in the 1930s helped foster a set of conceptual boundaries and institutional practices for later food aid in America and abroad. The first food bank was set up in Phoenix, Arizona, USA, in 1967, with 'Feeding America' launched 12 years later in 1979. John van Hengel launched the first food bank following an encounter with a woman who had ten children and a husband on death row but had, according to him, no problem feeding her children because she 'shopped' in the refuse bins at the rear of a nearby grocery store.[11] According to van Hengel, it was she who came up with the term 'food bank'. Having been moved by a documentary about hunger in Africa and with the help of a grocer, a church donation of $3,000 and an abandoned bakery, van Hengel began collecting and distributing any surplus food he could find under the motto 'the poor we shall always have with us. But why the hungry?'

Riches speaks in passing of the importance of Christian believers in the spread of food banks internationally. The international communion of Roman Catholicism was central in the transition of food banks out of the United States and into Canada, Mexico and Europe in the early 1980s. Van Hengel and his early colleague Robert McCarty 'were both volunteering at the local St Vincent de Paul Society mission. McCarty was a Catholic deacon and van Hengel a business man, social activist and also a devout Catholic.'[12] McCarty travelled to Canada to help found a food bank in Calgary, Edmonton and Regna in Canada.[13] A Catholic nun, Sister Cécile Bigot, from Paris, heard about the Edmonton food bank and helped establish the food bank of Paris Ile de France in 1984, and John van Hengel visited France and Belgium in this period. French and Belgian food banks later launched the European Federation of Food Banks (FEBA) in 1986. Within six years, as Riches reports, Spain, Italy, Ireland and Portugal, all historically Roman Catholic countries, had established food banks with FEBA support. FEBA are now active in 27 EU countries and have close ties with Die Tafel – Germany's food bank network – and the Global Food banking Network (GFN) which was established in 2006.[14] The GFN is working in 32 countries, including high- and middle-income countries: Australia, Chile, Israel, China, South Korea and the UK.[15] Van Hengel also visited Mexico at the request of Richardo Bon Echeverria and a Mexican food bank was first launched in 1987.[16] Riches notes that the international spread of food banking in the 1980s owed much to 'American practices and the warehouse model of food banking and to international Catholic outreach including the work of Caritas', an influential, international Catholic faith-based organization.[17]

Through the 1990s food banks spread across the EU, being launched in Germany (1993), Poland (1994), Greece and Finland (1995) and Austria (1999), reaching the UK for the first time in 1994 with Fareshare and 2000 with the Trussell Trust. Protestant groups like the Salvation Army, Lutherans and Anglicans increasingly came to the fore in founding and running food banks in the 1990s, though it would again be the international Roman Catholic Church which (through Jeanna Rockey and Charles Scarf in association with the St Vincent de Paul Society) would open Sydney food bank in Australia in 1992.[18] A second significant factor in the growth of the international food bank network are the strong links it has developed with big international food corporations. GFN's current corporate partners include Cargill Inc and Kelloggs, General Mills and Unilever with Coca-Cola, Pepsico, Mondolez and Walmart as significant sponsors. Feeding America's supporters include celebrities like Ben Affleck and Sheryl Crow, and it has the financial muscle to pay its CEO the competitive salary of $651,083 a year.[19] Despite the support Feeding America receives and its ability to attract the best in corporate leadership through high pay and high publicity, Riches reports that 42.2 million (13.4%) of the population in the United States are 'food insecure', a term which means a 'limited or uncertain availability of safe and nutritious foods and limited or uncertain availability to acquire it in socially acceptable ways'.[20]

Long before the great recession of 2008, food banks were already well established in the majority of OECD countries, 'warning signs of the impact of neo-liberalism and shrinking government support for the poor long before the financial crash'.[21] Riches goes on to conclude that 'while food drivers and [food bank] fundraising are built around themes of "ending" or "alleviating" hunger, the strategies of corporate food banking are a long way removed from the goals of food and social justice and from advocating for a living wage, let alone adequate welfare benefits'.[22]

## Part Two: Fareshare and Trussell Trust

Food bank use in the UK has increased exponentially in the last ten years and British food banks have notable differences to their American counterparts. Riches, for example, praises British food banks for retaining the political nature of food insecurity in their advocacy work.[23] Along with the rise in food bank use, food banks have become much more broadly discussed phenomena in the national press. In a review of the media coverage of food banks, Rebecca Wells and Martin Caraher note that there were four mentions of food banking in 2010, 42 by 2012 and 131 in 2013.[24] The two largest of Britain's variegated food bank network are Fareshare and the Trussell Trust, each operating a different model. Fareshare aim to reduce food waste and food poverty simultaneously. They do this by taking surplus food goods from across the supply chain (producers, manufacturers and retailers) and distributing it to a range of frontline services, like homeless shelters, women's refuge centres and children's breakfast clubs.

Fareshare was formed in 1994 by Crisis, the homeless people charity. In 2004, Fareshare became an independent organization with regional bases in London, South Yorkshire, Dundee and Edinburgh. By 2013 it was supplying food to 1,000 charities, rising to 9,653 charities by 2017/18. In 2017/18 the number of people accessing food from Fareshare was 772,390 each week (up 59% from 484,376 in 2016/17); the charity provided 36.7 million meals (up 28% from the previous year) and received 16,992 tonnes of food (up 25% from 13,552 in 2016/17), providing an estimated £28.7 million worth of food to its charities (up 28% from £22.4 million in 2016/17).[25] According to research commissioned by Fareshare, the charity saves the UK economy approximately £51 million a year, of which £7 million is saved for the beneficiaries of the food, and £44 million is saved for the state (i.e. to the National Health Service, the criminal justice system, to schools and for social care).[26] In February 2018, the Walmart-owned supermarket Asda pledged £20 million to Fareshare and the Trussell Trust to help them extend their operation, while also committing to having all its shops ready to donate surplus food to food banks by 2020.[27]

A common reason for food banking is that it makes waste food useful. According to Fareshare, drawing on data from WRAP's (the UK Government's Waste and Resources Action Programme) 'Quantification of Food Surplus', 1.9 million tonnes of food is wasted annually, an amount they find galling given that 8.4 million people are struggling to eat in the UK, and 4.7 million are severely food insecure.[28]

The total tonnage of food redistributed by the charitable and commercial sectors stood at around 43,000 in 2017, up from 38,000 in 2016 – that is, 102 million meals valued at around £130 million, according to a report produced by WRAP on Surplus Food Redistribution.[29] It's still only a fraction of the 1.9 million tonnes of food that is wasted annually, of which, according to the UK government, the vast majority is used for animal feed or for anaerobic digestion or sent to landfill.[30] Moving more of this food to the hungry is a major aim for Feeding Britain. It is seen as desirable by those in the food production, distribution and retail sectors too, for a number of reasons, including the tax breaks companies receive for these donations and the good publicity it generates.[31] Where is all this waste coming from in the system?

Only a minority of it happens at the retail stage.[32] The majority of food waste happens at the farm stage: between 100,000 and 500,000 tonnes.[33] Overproduction is endemic to industrial farming, Berry writes, because 'farmers individually and collectively do not know, and cannot learn ahead of time, the extent either of public need or of market demand ... Either because the market is good and they are encouraged, or because the market is bad and they are desperate, farmers tend to produce as much as they can.'[34] The 2013 *Food Wastage Footprint: Impacts on Natural Resources* makes for sobering reading when we consider UK food wastage in its ecological and international contexts. This report, published by the Food and Agriculture Organization of the United Nations, notes that approximately a third of all food produced for human consumption in the world is lost or wasted (between 1.6 and 1.3 Gtonnes).[35] Focusing on 'impacts on climate, water, land and biodiversity', the report says that, without accounting for greenhouse gas emissions from land change (deforesting the Amazon rainforest in order to produce beef, for example), 'the carbon footprint of food produced and not eaten is estimated to 3.3 Gtonnes of $CO_2$ equivalent: as such, food wastage ranks as the third top emitter after USA and China'.[36] To produce the food wasted in the UK takes 1.4 billion hectares of land (approximately an area the size of Wales), around 30% of the world's agricultural land area, and consumes 250 km³ of blue water (surface and groundwater), equivalent to the annual water discharge of the Volga, the EU's longest river with the largest discharge and drainage basin.[37]

In the UK there have been improvements in dealing with food waste, with a 9% reduction in 'post-farm-gate' waste between 2007 and 2015, a 13% reduction in household waste and a year-on-year increase in the amounts of food waste being redistributed to people.[38] However, despite the appeal of joining up food waste and food poverty, there is widespread scepticism in parts of the academic, food justice campaigning and food charity leadership about its coherence as a strategy. In a webinar promoted by FIAN (Food First Information and Action Network) called 'Right to Food and Emerging Strategies of Resistance', Pete Ritchie, executive director of Nourish Scotland, said that redistribution of surplus food is not the solution to waste *or* poverty, a sentiment echoed by Paul Taylor, Executive Director at Foodshare Toronto.[39] Riches shares these concerns, saying:

> Food waste and domestic hunger are two critical but separate structural issues, the former a symptom of a dysfunctional global food system and the latter a consequence of income poverty and inequality, broken social safety nets, pro-rich income distribution and neglected human rights. Neither are solutions to the other. Distinct public policies are required to address these systemic problems. The neoliberal reliance on surplus or 'left-over' food can never be more than a palliative for 'left-behind' people.[40]

Paul McMahon writes in *Feeding Frenzy: The New Politics of Food* that 'in high-income countries, education campaigns and a shift away from "best before" dates to more sophisticated food management tools' are needed as these 'have been shown to change consumer behaviour'.[41] Ironically, he continues, higher food prices would better reflect the 'external costs' of the current food system, bring investment into the agricultural sector, sharpen in the consumer's mind the value of food and (if governed well) give a better price to global food producers, many of whom live on poverty-level incomes.[42] As McMahon says, 'people go hungry not because of high food prices but because they cannot afford to pay these prices. And inability to pay has as much to do with income levels and purchasing power as the price of food.'[43]

The Trussell Trust was founded in 1997 by Carol and Paddy Henderson. They began the trust with a legacy gift from Carol's mother and were initially supporting children in Bulgaria, having already worked for Tearfund in the former Soviet Union.[44] In 2000, Paddy started Salisbury food bank after having received a call from a local mother who challenged him to help deal with British destitution. In an interview with *Reform* magazine, Carol and Paddy talked about their experiences of becoming Christians and how this had informed their involvement with food banks. Going overseas because they believed that poverty 'had been removed by the welfare state' in Britain, they were shocked to find how much residual poverty there was in the UK and how much need there has been for food banks since the financial crash.[45] Taking referrals from social services, children's organizations, doctors and nurses who gave out vouchers to make 'sure that food went to the right people, as opposed to those who were just scamming the system', they collected 46,000 tins from a town of 40,000 people in the first year.[46]

For the Hendersons, the food bank gave a way for the churches of Salisbury to work together, a way for Christians to serve outside the church in the world, and a way for them to do 'the work that God gave us to do – feeding the hungry and empowering them'.[47] Later in the interview, Paddy said that 'the number of people abusing the system was really, really small, and, taken against the number we were feeding, in many ways really irrelevant' and Carol asked whether 'in some cases God may have sent those people to us for his purposes and [that] they may therefore be a gift'.[48] The Christian narrative featured heavily in the Hendersons' interview at a number of levels: as a principle to be applied in caring for one's neighbours at home and abroad, as a specific calling on their lives, as an expression of their own dependence on God following major life changes, as a practice for the church, as a normative way for the church to be in the world, and as a way to receive others. Both of them, now living with their daughters in New Zealand, expressed complex feelings about the growth of the Trust. Carol, more politically direct, talked about 'benefits and wages both [falling] short' and claimed that 'the welfare state is not fulfilling its role to provide for those who are most in need', which 'seems like a failure of government' to her.[49] For Paddy, stressing the role of government may detract from the recognition that food insecurity is a problem for all of us, one that will require changing our education system, facing our social breakdown.[50] On the growth of the Trussell Trust over the last ten years, they said:

It's a hugely mixed emotion. You see a project that's been really successful during this huge economic downturn, juxtaposed with a huge sadness. It's a total travesty – we've seen poverty in Britain equal to poverty we saw overseas. For a country that's supposed to be one of the leading countries in the world, I find that really difficult to get my head around. I think we've lost our way.[51]

By 2018–19, the Trussell Trust (which operates a franchise model, providing resources and institutional structures to local food banks in exchange for a yearly fee) gave out 1.6 million parcels to those coming to their 1,200 food banks.[52] But 1.6 million parcels does not mean 1.6 million individual users; if a family of three were referred on two occasions, that would be six parcels. The Trust reports that on average people need around two parcels a year.[53] Recognizing that 'ending hunger is about more than food', the Trussell Trust also runs a 'More than Food' programme which, through holiday clubs and budgeting courses, aims to 'prevent people from reaching further crisis and help them break free from poverty'.[54] However, they stress in their advocacy work that the three primary causes of food bank referrals relate to benefits and spending power: 'income not covering essential costs', 'benefits delays' and 'benefits changes'.[55] Emma Revie, Trussell Trust Chief Executive, talks about the campaigning work that goes along with the other operations carried out by the Trust:

> What we are seeing year-upon-year is more and more people struggling to eat because they simply cannot afford food … Our benefits system is supposed to protect us all from being swept into poverty. Universal Credit should be part of the solution but currently the five week wait is leaving many without enough money to cover the basics. … it's unacceptable that anyone should have to use a food bank in the first place. No charity can replace the dignity of having financial security …. we're urging the Government to ensure benefit payments reflect the true cost of living and work is secure, paying the real Living Wage, to help ensure we are all anchored from poverty.[56]

Between 2010 and 2019, the Trussell Trust has gone through periods of being very politically critical. The UK Department for Work and Pensions Secretary Amber Rudd's recent admission that there are links between food bank use and governmental policy – in particular the rolling out of a welfare reform and simplification programme, Universal Credit – marks a significant victory for the Trussell Trust, the campaigners 'End Hunger UK' and academics and journalists who have addressed these issues. The Trussell Trust was once a darling of former Prime Minister David Cameron's 'Big Society' (a programme of devolution of services from the state to civil society, in line with Tony Blair's 'Third Way'). The influential Conservative blog, Conservative Home, for example, commended the Trussell Trust as 'a fantastic Christian Charity' in 2012 and the 'epitome of Big Society', and in front of the UK parliament in December 2012 Cameron praised the work of food bank volunteers as 'part of what I call the big society'.[57]

However, in 2013 a major rift developed between the then Work and Pensions Secretary Ian Duncan Smith and the Trussell Trust. While Duncan Smith, a devout Roman Catholic, was blaming the rising numbers of people accessing food banks on 'an increasing number [of food banks] and/or [their] marketing activities', Chris Mould, the Trussell Trust's Chief Executive, was trying to broker a meeting with the Work and Pensions Secretary to discuss the fact that 'many of the problems people were facing could be traced back to changes in their benefits, and to delays in the payment of them'.[58] Ian Duncan Smith strongly denied this claim, as he did the criticisms levelled at him by former Archbishop of Canterbury Rowan Williams and the Roman Catholic Cardinal Vincent Nichols in early 2014, by stating that the Trussell Trust was running a business that requires 'you to continuously achieve publicity' and that they were achieving this by 'making [their] political opposition to welfare reform overtly clear'.[59] In Duncan Smith's mind, this was a supply- not a demand-side problem. Despite his long-standing criticism of foreign aid and the foreign aid budget, a second Conservative Catholic MP, Jacob Rees-Mogg, praised the rise of food banks as a good thing. He said that the state does provide

> a basic level of welfare ... but on some occasions that will not work and to have charitable support given by people voluntarily to support their fellow citizens I think is rather uplifting and shows what a good compassionate country we are.

The Labour Party, according to Rees-Mogg, was responsible for the government's fiscal exposure because of its excessive welfare spending while in government, the subsequent austerity and the rise in food bank use under coalition and Conservative governments:

> The real reason for the rise in numbers is because people know they are there and Labour refused to tell them.[60]

For the academic Kayleigh Garthwaite there are links between Labour and welfare given the conditionality brought into the benefits regime by that party but there is also a strong correlation between the Conservative government's policies following the 2008 crash and the rise of food banks. She recognizes that 'historically, there have always been soup kitchens for people who are homeless, but the extent to which provision has grown and expanded in recent years is staggering'.[61] The combination of rising food and fuel costs, stagnant wage growth, and a harsh sanctions regime with the Coalition's continuation of (New) Labour welfare policy trajectory in the Welfare Reform Act 2012 has 'led to more and more people being pushed into poverty'.[62] The Welfare Reform Act, which includes 'caps on levels of entitlement', introduction of the 'under occupancy charge' (or 'bedroom tax' as it is more commonly known) on housing benefit, longer waiting periods between becoming unemployed and benefit eligibility, and the establishment of local welfare assistance to replace the discretionary social fund' were all aspects of the 2010–15 coalition government's attempt to 'cut the deficit' through a politics of austerity.[63] The later Welfare Reform and Work Bill outlined £45 billion in savings from the welfare budget, with a further £12 billion to be cut by 2019/20.[64] The most controversial measure included 'reducing the welfare cap; abolishing child-poverty targets; cuts to child tax credits; disability benefit changes; and cutting housing assistance for young people'.[65] For Garthwaite, it is quite clear that 'frontline experience of foodbank use and academic research have both consistently contradicted the idea' that benefits reform and food bank use are not related.[66]

## Part Three: austerity and the north-east

The north-east of England has one of the strongest regional identities in the country, a positive trade balance that sets it apart from the trade deficits present in most parts of the country and a proud heritage of socialism and collectivism, and female involvement in twentieth-century manufacturing.[67]

Despite this, industrialism, post-industrialism and austerity have all left deep marks on the landscape and identity of the north-east, the area in which I carried out my food bank interviews. Peter MacLellan, Director of Durham Christian Partnership and County Durham Foodbank, believes that the disjunction between the north-east's proud past and its current difficulties is a major factor in the culture and mentality of the area:

> [The] first thing that really struck me when we moved up here, I remember after a little while I thought 'I must look up and see when the last mine closed in some of these mining villages' and in many cases it was over 40 years, even then. 'And the DLI, when did the DLI stop being the DLI and just become the light infantry and part of it?' And that was 40 years. And I thought, 'My goodness, if you didn't look it up and you didn't know you'd think it was yesterday.'

MacLellan went on suggest that a sense of frustration and stifled hope was passed from generation to generation in the north-east and related to the decline of the security that came from the employment of the pit. He continued by saying that some

> see it as its been taken away from them. Whereas I wouldn't see it as something as malign as that, it's a global economy or whatever that's taken it away from them, it's not a person saying 'we don't want people in Durham to work any more'.

A pining for the past is in many senses a very valid inclination – in the late eighteenth century, as the economist Adam Smith observed, the pitmen of the Great Northern Coalfield were 'the highest paid manual workers in the UK'.[68] A historian of the north-east, David Byrne, quotes from a meeting for the British Association for the Advancement of Science held in Durham in 1970 in which W. M. Hughes said that 'it is perhaps hard for us to realise after the years of the inter-war depression that for sixty years before 1914 the Durham (and Northumberland) pitmen and the shipyard workers of the Tyne and Wear were among the most highly paid workers in the world outside the USA ... the decline into the poverty of the inter-war years was from the heights to the depths.'[69] These working-class wages, made possible by the connection of inland coal to the sea and workers' solidarity, led to mass migration into the north-east and an explosion in the population from 600,000 in 1801 to 3 million in 1921. By the second half of the nineteenth century, 30% of the adult males in County Durham were immigrants, from

Ireland, Scotland, Germany, Scandinavia and the Baltic.[70] This is ironic, arguably, given the support for Brexit and reduced migration in parts of the region.

Byrne talks of a 'culture of industrialism' developing through this period which 'is not now, nor was it ever, solely or even primarily a culture of the poor. In industrial regions industrial culture was something which was in important respects shared by all of the aristocracy of manual labour, the very important employed industrial middle-class, and industrial capitalist.'[71] With a landscape speckled with pit villages which exported people and products across the world, the 'carboniferous capitalism' of the north-east incubated a range of social and political institutions: from a strong radical tradition manifest in the trade union movement, to a strong Conservative tradition of local nobility and landed gentry.[72] Steel from the city of Middlesbrough (with motto emblazoned on one of its gates: Born of iron, made of steel) can be found in the Sydney harbour bridge and the Golden Gate bridge across San Francisco Bay; it also laid the basis for much of India's railway network.[73] In the book *Geordies*, Byrne writes that 'the north east was an industrial hellhole, but it was a prospering industrial hellhole with a particularly self-confident and well organised industrial working class.'[74]

The shift from an industrial to post-industrial economy has not destroyed this culture, Byrne says and the yearly Durham Miner's Gala makes this clear. However, it has put immense strains on the north-east. 'The industrial to post-industrial transformation happened essentially between the late 1930s and the mid-1980s' and led to the 'massive loss of industrial jobs and the development of service employment'.[75] With a new international availability of oil, the National Coal Board, which had until then 'pursued a policy of maximising production more or less regardless of cost', had to change to a profit-led system.[76] Under the direction of Lord Robens, a huge programme of pit closures was carried out, between 1957 and 1974. The north-east lost 100,000 of 150,000 mining jobs.[77] Consequences of this lost industry were largely mitigated in the region by a significant Conservative and Labour funded programme of social and economic investment, and with it the rise in manufacturing employment.[78] The appointment of Margaret Thatcher marked a significant watershed in the history of the region:

> the pursuit of a monetarist, macroeconomic strategy, favouring finance capital at the expense of industrial capital, took the particular form of a grossly overvalued pound in the early 1980s, and contributed to the general decline of UK manufacturing industry across a range of sectors and to massive industrial job losses in the North-East as in all industrial regions.[79]

Between 1973 and 2009, manufacturing employment as a share of total employment shrank from 32% to 11%.[80] The north-east saw both absolute and relative deindustrialization over the last 40 years.

> What industry that remains is more productive and employs fewer people to make more, but there has also been an absolute loss of industrial capacity. Between 1973 and 1988, the region lost 250,000 industrial jobs from an original total of 625,000. Between 1976 and 1987, industrial production declined by more than 10 percent in real terms.[81]

Early in his premiership Tony Blair claimed that the north–south divide was a thing of the past.[82] With prominent New Labour politicians holding safe seats in the north-east, the region saw falls in unemployment, diversification in the economy and extensive public sector funding.[83] New Labour's commitment to regionalism bore dividends in the north-east in the context of sustained national economic growth from the mid-1990s up to 2008. However, the public investment in the region, with an estimate of 79% of new jobs created by the state, and the still unequal history of disparity between the north-east and other parts of the country left the area vulnerable after the 2008 crash.[84]

In written evidence submitted in 2018 to the UN Special Rapporteur on Extreme Poverty and Human Rights, Tracey Shildrick and Claire Bambra (health geographers at Newcastle University) among others, wrote:

Welfare reforms have hit hardest where reliance on benefits has been greatest and the most affected places are older industrial areas, many of which are located in the North East of England. These places have also been among the most affected in terms of cuts to local government, reducing statutory funding to voluntary and community sector bodies. The high unemployment rate in the North East is set against a severe skills shortage and a population that is on average older and getting older faster than the rest of the UK.[85]

Pointing towards the regional disparity in the UK, they noted that net wealth in the south-east of England is 233% higher on average than in the north-east and that during the period between 2012 and 2016 median wealth in the south-east rose 14%, in the north-east it fell by 7%.[86] In 2012 in Hartlepool, a coastal town 30 miles south of Newcastle, every job was attracting 16 applications and 1 out of 10 men were claiming benefits. House prices in the north-east fell from £174,053 in 2007 to £155,925, while in the south-east they rose from £285,137 to £311,037 in the same period.[87] At this stage, in the early 2010s, job losses were four times higher than in the rest of the nation.[88]

These changes in wealth had significant impacts on the people these academics worked with and knew, with reductions like the bedroom tax affecting 'purchasing power for essentials, particularly food and utilities. Participants recounted negative impacts on mental health, family relationships and community networks.'[89] The conditionality and sanctions of what they bitingly refer to as the 'welfare' system

> negatively affect wellbeing. The inadequacy of benefit levels, with or without the 'bedroom tax', left people feeling excluded from normal social participation, but significantly, this included cutting back on food, surviving primarily on cheap, filling foods such as bread, pasta and noodles, and unable to afford fruit and vegetables, even when required for medical conditions. People reported continued stress, shame and embarrassment.[90]

With a 49% cut to government funding for local authorities, adult social care, transport, residential rehab and detox treatment centres have all been cut or asked to do 'more with less', with disproportionate effects on poorer communities, disproportionate effects on black and minority ethnic (BME) groups and women.[91] Ninety-seven per cent of the reductions in local spending on social care, children and homelessness since 2011 have taken place in the fifth most deprived councils, they report.[92] Some local authorities in northern cities and boroughs lost £150–200 per head while in the south-east, the west country and parts of the midlands cuts ranged between £0 and £50. The government was spending £2,731 per person on transport in London at this time, and £5 per person in the north-east.[93] It must have been hard to keep a straight face as a member of the coalition government while blaming the people of this and other regions like it for being 'benefits scroungers', 'skivers', 'workshy' or 'welfare dependent' when the public purse was being liberally poured into sustaining the service sector of London and the south-east. Despite the fall in unemployment from 10.4% in 2011 to 4.9% in 2018, working-age poverty has got worse in the north-east, going from 22% to 23% in the same period.[94]

Combined with the trend for there to be less voluntary, civil society services in deprived areas, the last ten years have seen improvements in the area undermined and historically rooted weaknesses exacerbated.[95] Based in Newcastle, the first city to have Universal Credit full service in all its Job Centres, Bambra et al. reflected that during the system's roll-out 'there has been an increase in requests for short-term financial support, such as Discretionary Housing Payment (DHP), the Crisis Support Scheme and food packages from food banks'.[96] They note the significant increase in fuel poverty in their city during the same period, with an increase from three residents being supported by the Council's Energy Service rising to 136 in 2017/18. 'Of all of them, 122 had energy debts that they were unable to pay, 27 had either disconnected their energy supply themselves, or were being threatened with disconnection by their energy supplier, and 48 households had children present.'[97]

## Part Four: County Durham Foodbank

CDF was established in 2011 and is run by Durham Christian Partnership (DCP), an institution started almost 20 years ago. The current director of County Durham Foodbank, Peter MacLellan, explains its origins:

> [DCP] got set up as a direct result of a sermon given at St Nicks [St Nicholas' Church, in Durham city centre]. It was coming up to the millennium, in Durham the Prince Bishop Shopping Centre was just being built and obviously St Nick's is the church on the market and marketplace was a theme of this sermon. They were basically saying 'look we've got a brand new marketplace being built out here, we've got the old marketplace out there, what are we doing as a church out there in the marketplace beyond these four walls?' Encouraging the

church to be outward-looking ... A group of them said 'well what should we be doing? What's out there?' So they did various surveys and questionnaires to try and find out what the needs were in Durham city. Out of that they identified that there was a gap to provide people to listen, simply to listen to other people and they developed what became the Cathedral Listening Service.

The Cathedral Listening Service continues and is one of a number of activities lodged in DCP, including a fuel bank, debt advice service (Durham Money Advice Centre), and Street Pastors. Tina and Peter MacLellan started the food bank in 2011 and already had some experience of food banks from their time living in the United States. MacLellan again:

> There had been a food bank in the States, or food pantry as they call it, which I had never really engaged with much. But the church had got frustrated with the system there, where the Government provides the food through large manufacturers and things and big warehouses, which food banks go and collect from and give out. There are tight restrictions on how [the food pantry] can operate, you know you mustn't mix church and state in the United States, so they weren't allowed to say anything about church or Christian things and they were just seeing the same people over and over and over again twice a week queuing up for food. And the church there had basically come to the conclusion that they weren't doing people any good, didn't like the system, wanted to make more impact on people's lives. So, they stopped doing it and instead went with a different arrangement called 'Loaves and fishes', which was basically to provide a hot meal five days a week through volunteers. So, come in, sit down, have a nice hot meal and have a chat, so much more of an engagement, much more relational, far less transactional. So that's what I'd seen, from afar in the US.

Peter and Tina, who had felt called by God to plant a church in Durham and be with the marginal people of the north-east in 2005/2006, were invited by the Trussell Trust to a meeting on food banks in the winter of 2010/2011, before food banks had made the news in a significant way. Peter was ambiguous about being involved but thought they should go along and learn more.

> So, talking about food banks here I didn't necessarily have a warm fuzzy feeling about it. Went to the presentation which [the Trussell

Trust] did and in the course of it they talked about their experiences in Salisbury. We didn't particularly know Salisbury but we did know the south-west having moved up from there. And they talked about the kind of numbers that they saw down there and all the rest of it, and we thought 'oh for goodness sake, if it's like that there then what is it like around here?' So, I felt very clearly that this was something that we needed to take forward. I talked to the presenter afterwards and he linked me up with other people from the area who had enquired ... and we said, 'what are we going to do about this?' So I said, 'let's call a public meeting.' We set a date, managed to pick Pentecost, not being very into the church calendar I didn't realize that this might not be the best evening to have it. As soon as the letter went out to all and sundry and every connection I'd managed to find on email I started getting emails back: 'You do realize ...' Well it's too late now we'd booked the space at St Oswald's, it's going to happen. And it did. We had about 45 people turn up, which was pretty amazing, at this place ... I said, 'I think there's a need for this, I think we should explore it' ... A couple of stumbling blocks, there is a £1,500 franchise pay to get started. Big intake of breath from the room. 'That's a lot of money' ... I saw a couple of people have a little confab and then they stuck up their hands and said, 'we'll fund that', which they did, very gracious of them, both still involved in the food bank. So, then we needed to start.

The first food parcels went out in September and in the following 12 months CDF fed 3,209 people. New centres quickly followed at Newton Aycliffe, Chester-le-Street, The Well at West Auckland. By December 2015, the number of distribution points had grown from one to 28 and they fed over 1,000 in a month for the first time, a rapid scaling up of the procedures in a short period of time. The model for expansion and launching new centres was already in place: hold a public meeting in a central, accessible location, involve as many community leaders as possible, offer no-strings-attached information and training, and then launch a new distribution point. The Trussell Trust resources, database, training guide, manual, collections advice provided a transferable infrastructure that, according to Peter, allowed them to begin quickly.

Another part of this expansion in coverage of the Durham County area was a grant of £400,000 from the National Lottery, though Peter informed me that money has been a recurring challenge.[98] In 2018, CDF's own data says they fed 18,550 people of which 6,468 were children. In 2019 they've seen another rise in demand (13%) due to the implementation of Universal Credit along with 'no signs that [demand] is slowing', according to MacLellan. In terms of tonnage of food, CDF moved 138 tonnes in 2017, up from 123 in 2016. Durham Christian Partnership's unrestricted income is £302,705, but this doesn't account for the value of food that is donated to the charity (approximately £265,000) or the volunteer hours offered (around 40,000 or a value of £338,000). In the words of the charity's trustees, 'although neither donated time nor food is recorded in the accounts, it is important to note that the charity is providing a level of service greatly above that which the financial accounts ... would indicate'.[99] In 2015, CDF, along with Npower and National Energy Action, pioneered a programme called 'Fuel Vouchers', which has now gone national. Fuel Vouchers, which can be applied for at the food bank, give the food bank client a set amount of money to put onto their pre-payment meter at home, as long as they are referred by the right agency. A popular scheme, Fuel Vouchers went up from 3,670 in 2016 to 3,947 in 2017. The National Lottery money has now finished, but with stable donations and support from Durham County Council Welfare Assistance funding they have financial stability.

## Conclusion

Riches' account of the origins and globalization of food banking is important for a number of reasons. First, the United States case shows that food banking alone cannot deal adequately with the issue of food insecurity. Second, Riches' book draws the reader's attention to the fact that food banks existed and were growing before the 2008 global crash and, in the UK, the Conservative Party's austerity programme. For Riches, food banks and neoliberalism chronologically and, in some ways, conceptually overlap because food banks address a need and fill a space abdicated by a worldview whose 'guiding mandate is economic growth, deregulation, lower taxes and freedom from state control'.[100] He continues a couple of pages later by saying that when 'outsourcing domestic hunger ... to corporately dependent charitable food banking is accepted as an effective no cost solution' the state is enabled 'to claim its austerity driven prescriptions are responsible public policy while repeating *ad nauseam* that work is the only way out of poverty and even lower personal and corporate taxes will raise all boats'.[101]

While food banks and neoliberalism have longer histories, the particulars of the 2008 great recession were catastrophic in two ways. First, financial investors after the 2008 crash were looking for stable markets to invest their money and turned to commodities speculation, pushing up the price of food globally. The 2008 food price spike led to a doubling in corn export prices, the cost of rice tripled in three months, and civil disobedience followed in Egypt, Cameroon, Ivory, Senegal, Ethiopia and Haiti.[102] Vandana Shiva, one of the world's leading environmentalists, noted: 'After the US subprime crisis and the Wall Street crash, investors rushed to commodity markets, especially oil and agricultural commodities. While real production did not increase between 2005 and 2007, commodity speculation in food increased 160 per cent. Speculation pushed up prices and pushed an additional 100 million people to hunger.'[103] Combined with the UK government deficit reduction policy (austerity) and bank bailout, the spending power of many in the UK was cut at the same moment that prices were rising everywhere.

It is in this context that the Department for Work and Pensions produced a leaflet about benefits sanctions that included stories from benefits claimants and their photos. The leaflet suggested that benefits claimants appreciated the sanctions regime, with one claimant called Sarah 'quoted as being "really pleased" that a cut to her benefits supposedly encouraged her to re-draft her CV'.[104] Following a freedom of information request by the *Welfare Weekly* website, the DWP were forced to retract the leaflet in the following weeks and confessed that 'the quotes were not actually real cases and that the photos were not of actual claimants'.[105] The economic prudence of the deficit repayment imperative and consequently austerity is a contested topic, but when George Osborne repeated the call for austerity cuts in 2015 while also proposing tax cuts some, like the Oxford-based economist Simon Wren-Lewis, saw not just 'ignorance' but another example of a political party 'deliberately deceiving the electorate'.[106] Wren-Lewis says that austerity 'if it started as ignorance rather than deceit, it turned into the latter as Osborne prepared to repeat the policy all over again before the 2015 election, while at the same time cutting taxes'.[107]

But to argue that food banks are fully compatible with these kinds of neoliberal machinations is untenable. Neoliberalism is not in any clear or straightforward way beholden to the welfare of the poor.[108] In contrast, van Hengel, the Hendersons, the MacLellans all share a concern for and interest in the lives of the most deprived, and they showed a willingness to make changes in their own lives to see the poor empowered. They all share the belief that their concern for the poor is a facet of God's concern for the vulnerable; they have all consciously participated in a story that precedes and transcends them and to which they have added a small part. The conditions necessary to predicate food banks' necessity are stark: changing labour markets, falling purchasing power, government neglect, seismic shifts in international food markets and the corporations that run them. But the existence of the food banks themselves cannot be reduced to these political and economic forces; they also testify to another set of drives and a vision of an alternative order in which abundance trumps scarcity and gift means as much as ownership, an order in which compassion is more fundamental than deserts. It is to that vision of another order that we now turn.

# 3

# Food, Faith, Food Banks

## Introduction

In *Feeding the Other: Whiteness, Privilege and Neoliberal Stigma*, Rebecca de Souza notes that the United States food banks she volunteered at had strong Christian links. She reports that 'religious beliefs [were] often described as the key motivation for volunteers' and that 'volunteers talked about the role of Jesus in the lives of the poor and saw themselves as fulfilling a God-given mandate.'[1] However, despite this observation, de Souza's engagement with Christian stories, symbols, beliefs and histories is tentative and prescribed. De Souza rejects the American 'food pantry' model and two questions consequently follow on from her social observations: if Christianity is being misappropriated by food bank volunteers, isn't a robust articulation of the Christian tradition and a sympathetic but firm refutation of these volunteers' 'Christian' identity needed? Inversely, if food banks are plausibly and coherently embodying Christian teaching and yet also disempowering the poor, does Christian teaching itself not need to be called into extended examination? These questions are not addressed. Instead, her concern with the intersection of racism, neoliberalism and charity repeatedly orientates her engagement with Christian thought towards the overlap of Calvinism and capitalism put forward in the early twentieth century by Max Weber.[2]

In the introduction to *Religion and Sustainable Agriculture*, Todd LeVasseur notes an analogous problem in a related set of fields. Beginning his work in 2009 on religious agrarianism, he found that when it came to the social scientific literature,

> many studies exist about agriculture, and sustainable agriculture, but only a minority attempt to tackle the tougher 'values' element by researching why farmers, consumers, or legislators advocate for sustainable farming. When the values element is incorporated into social science studies, it tends to focus on ethics or political values – very rarely on religious values and identities.[3]

Similarly, in *Food, Farming and Religion*, Gretel Van Wieren writes that one of her book's key contentions is that

> the neglect of religious and spiritual perspectives and narratives in scholarly and societal discussions of agriculture and food ethics has been detrimental to developing a more fully representative dialogue around some of today's most pressing environmental problems.[4]

This chapter is concerned with Christian perspectives on food and with beginning the process of discerning what might be usefully retrieved from Christian theology and practice and brought into dialogue with the present. It begins by looking at some historical examples of Christian food practices drawn from *Theology on the Menu* by Grumett and Muers, a book that asks: 'Can alternative Christian food practices be identified which express and inculcate hope for the renewal and trans-formation of embodied life and for just and sustainable relationships?'[5] Second, this chapter discusses how food (and humans' relationship to the land) features in the Hebrew Bible or Old Testament and in the New Testament, before outlining some aspects of the Eastern Ortho-dox theologian Alexander Schmemann's influential discussion of the Eucharist. As this book's introduction noted, the theological perspec-tive developed here is chiastic. That is to say, this chapter begins by noting how the recognition of our embeddedness and entanglement in God, nature and each other is endemic to the Christian imagination and processed through Christian food practices. But, second, that the sense of dependency and emphasis on relationship inherent in Christian thought and practice does not preclude a Christian sense of generosity towards and benefice for the other. Christian understandings of rela-tionship (and of creation more broadly, as this chapter suggests) are Christologically shaped: love for the other to the point even of detri-ment to the self (participation, properly understood, is 'kenotic').[6] To interrupt or pre-emptively foreclose this circulation of gift-giving from self to other and back again, to prioritize the extraction of value in service of the self or non-reciprocal ownership is, as Schmemann writes, what Christians call sin.

## Part One: sacred food

I'm in Newcastle, home of the largest food bank in the UK. On the first floor above a pawnbroker's, just off the West Road and a mile from the city centre, is the Islamic Diversity Centre (IDC). The IDC was set up in 2002 as a charity with three aims – to educate, engage and empower – and they organize a range of social and educational activities in Sunderland and Newcastle. Abu-Tayeb Khairdeen, one of IDC's founders, is telling me about their engagement with the local food bank and how that is related to his identity as a Muslim. He's in his mid-forties, with glasses, broad shoulders and is dressed in a yellow t-shirt and tracksuit bottoms. The room is hot with summer and the windows are open to the noise of the road as he talks about their work.

> In 2013 we started our first food campaign. Now, we've done a num-ber over the years. Ramadan in 2013, while we were fasting we would collect all the leftover food from the Mosques and then distribute it to the poor people in the evenings, or those who would need it basic-ally. That's where it all started ... That's when we realized that this is a serious problem, this is something we need to do ... We did our weekly street kitchen, we got a couple of local restaurants ... they cook it fresh, and we distribute it Tuesday evenings ... We did origin-ally get in touch with Trussell Trust [but] we thought 'ok, no point setting up a new one' ... So, what we ended up doing was, the [food bank] down in Whickham View, a couple of years ago they had a real shortage of food, so we did a massive campaign within the Muslim community. We collected the food here and then we dropped it off with them over there. And I don't know, there was tonnes of food, literally the whole place was full of food items and we raised about £1,000 of cash as well and we just supported them in that way ... We believe that those who are going hungry, those who are in most need, those who are at the edges of society, it's our Islamic duty and respon-sibility to ensure that they have the right support that they need.

Abu-Tayeb talks about the importance of collaboration with other groups in the area addressing hunger and his discomfort with waste food. He goes on to mention the diverse needs of some of the people in the area and the work of local opticians and pharmacists who have been offering their services through their Tuesday night soup kitchen and their befriending scheme for those who have various and complex needs. *Zakat* (charity) features as a part of a single, coherent Muslim identity, Abu-Tayeb tells me, and has a prominent place in the story of the Prophet Muhammad who was reassured by his wife Khadija, after he first received his calling from God, on the basis that his life has been marked by acts of justice and generosity. Abu-Tayeb went on:

Let me establish a principle. Whatever we do, we're doing it not for fame, not for PR, not to just get a pat on the back, we don't do it for these types of reason ... Allah always links two kinds of things: prayer and charity. He links the two things together and He mentions in the Qur'an 'establish prayer and give charity, and bow with those who bow, those who submit and are obedient to God'. So, everything we do has an element of worship to it. Every righteous deed, we look at it as worship.

Eating, Abu-Tayeb says, is an act of worship, as much as bowing one's head in the mosque. Food, how it is eaten, when it is eaten, in what quantities, how it is reared and killed, cannot be separated off from questions of theology. The bounty of the world and even our bodies too are a gift from God, which we should not abuse:

> The Qur'an talks, first of all, it talks about Allah as the one who provides and gives sustenance. And He has given us from the blessing of this land, so that we can enjoy it and eat it. So, we grow it, enjoy it and eat it, as long as it is *halal tayyab*, meaning it is permissible and it is good and nourishing, and He said He has made those things which are *haram*, impermissible, those things which are bad for you and harmful for you. So, the Prophet has said, we need food, we need food to live and survive but at the same time if we don't take care of it, we can end up destroying ourselves with it.

Abu-Tayeb is concerned with articulating a sophisticated account of food practices, one that seeks to sustain how we receive the abundance of the world as a gift and return that gift back to God in worship. Islam, he tells me, 'can't be secularized. We can't just leave our religion at home and do what everyone else does. For us, Islam is an integral part of our identity. So when we go and pray, praying isn't just bowing and putting your head to the ground, it's obedience to God as well.' Eating, charity, justice, economics, they can't be separated off from their rightful place in relation to the divine; to do so would be to denature them and disfigure the self.

Across many different religious traditions there are shared commitments to the reception of food as a gift from the divine (or divines), to its utility in defining the boundaries of the community, to its significance as a means for our participation in each other and the natural world. Food, contemporary scholars of religion say, is wrapped up in three forms of participation: the self in relationship to God (or gods), to others, and to the world. Corrie E. Norman writes in *The Oxford Handbook of Food*

*History* that 'religious people have related to their gods, each other, and the world through food'.[7] Likewise, Todd LeVasseur says that 'how we eat matters because eating is an intimate act for human beings, establishing our connections to natural, social and ultimate reality'.[8] Vandana Shiva writes about food in the context of the Indian notion of *dharma*, the 'right way of living', and *rta* 'the right order that makes life and the universe possible'.[9] She says 'the seed, the soil, the water, and our food are sacred gifts of the earth' and that 'all faiths are in unity when it comes to sacred seed, sacred soil, and sacred, sacred food. No faith says to destroy the earth and starve your neighbours.'[10] Those who recognize this, who see that *dharma* 'arises from the interconnectedness of all life and from our duty to care for all humans and all species', are beholden 'to give back to the earth in gratitude', to participate in 'The Law of Return'.[11]

## Part Two: food in the Christian tradition

The history of the Christian tradition bears witness to the same investment in food practices; Christians have used food to clarify and enact the human role in the drama of God and the world, particularly through the Eucharist. David Grumett and Rachel Muers' helpful overview of the history of Christian food in *Theology on the Menu: Asceticism, Meat and the Christian Diet* makes this clear. The first example they give is the early Christian anchorites, who withdrew into the deserts of Egypt, Palestine and Syria in the second and third centuries AD 'in the search [for] a simple, solitary existence devoted to prayer and meditation' and away from the constant distractions of the world and threat of military conscription.[12] Through what they ate, the anchorites 'became part of a structural dimension of Christian identity in which the countercultural dimension of Christianity was witnessed anew in a harsh and alien environment that imposed tight natural constraints on diet'.[13] Grumett and Muers recount a number of the practices of eating found in the *Lives of the Desert Fathers* (stories from the lives of some of the earliest Christians) to make this point. Macarius of Alexandria 'ate for seven years nothing but raw vegetables and rehydrated pulses'.[14] Some ascetics like John the Hermit, they say, were 'reported to have subsisted exclusively on the Eucharist host'.[15] Presumably John the Hermit looked down on the wanton Hero of Diospolis, who complemented the host with 'one meal every three months as well as any wild herbs he found'.[16] Even more radical:

in Palestine and Syria, where especially rigorous practices existed, there was a tradition of 'shepherds' or 'grazers' who ate only grass, often alongside wild animals – a practice analogous to that of the *turytta* class of Indian ascetics, who perform *govrata* or 'cow-vow'.[17]

There are viable alternatives for interpreting these practices today: as a facet of the view that animals were unclean, or, more plausible for Grumett and Muers, that the anchorites' abstinence from animal flesh came from 'a sense of kinship with animals resulting from a life spent close to nature'.[18] They conclude this section by writing: 'In the desert, meat abstinence needs to be understood as part of a wider discipline of which the central principle was the spiritual government and transformation of the ascetic's body.'[19] Against the contemporary tendency to see these forms of practice as denigrations of the material or religiously inspired self-loathing, Grumett and Muers see an inverse positive inflection to them: these practices of self-discipline are expressions of self-control, invitations to and examples of power.[20]

As asceticism moved from the desert into the lives of the Christians in the cities of the ancient near east, the social function of food shifted. Grumett and Muers say that 'the rules of the new communities promoted not the extreme abstinence witnessed among many solitary anchorites, but a moderated asceticism that enabled members to participate in the common life and manual labour necessary to sustain the community'.[21] In part, this was due to the doctrinal diversity of these early protomonastic communities, which ate rather than articulated their common identity: 'In this context of an absence of agreed detailed doctrinal formulations around which community identity could be constructed, the role of common dietary rules in fostering such identity was vital.'[22] In their review of the history of the early church they conclude that what constitutes a 'good diet' is not prescribed once and for all on 'biological arguments or a scripturally-derived authoritative model of the ascetic – but is discerned in each location in a way that acknowledges the reciprocal relationships between the ascetic community and its wider social, economic and geographical context'.[23]

Along with the place of asceticism in the control of the self and the distinction of the Christian from the self-involved gluttonies of the world, Grumett and Muers frame asceticism as a means for the encroachment of the redeemed order into the structures of the world. Food practices are a part of salvation history. They write: 'The physical body of the individual ascetic and the social body of the monastery become sites of blessing for a wider community.'[24] In some instances, this redeemed community includes animals. Grumett and Muers tell the stories of Abba Macarius and Abba Gerasimos who receive a hyena and a lion respectively into their monastic communities on the condition that these predators give up their practices of eating meat. The lion who needed a thorn removed from his paw is eventually given the name Jordanes and is entrusted with overseeing the community donkey that is used to collect water.[25]

Animals that eschewed meat in a specifically Christian context were therefore regarded not as pursuing supererogatory asceticism but as reverting to the diet which God had always intended for them through a combination of their own spiritual obedience and guidance by a holy person, who adopts the animal as a disciple.[26]

A second example that Grumett and Muers give of the redemption of the Christian coinciding with the redemption of the world through attention to food is fasting and the rise of dietary moderation. As late as 1662, the Book of Common Prayer listed an extensive calendar of fasts (principally Lent and Advent) which cumulatively counted for 'well over half the days of the year ... meat could not be eaten on any of those days'.[27] Grumett and Muers point to research that sees fasting as flourishing in 'regions with obvious seasonal cycles of abundance and scarcity when hunger stalked rich and poor alike'.[28] The major Christian fasts coincide with the natural scarcity of winter and early spring, 'fasting can thus be regarded as the sanctified acceptance by humans of the natural rhythms of the earth and of the wisdom of nature.'[29] Fasting, sanctified scarcity, was deployed as a way to re-enact Jesus' time in the wilderness and the Jewish community's tithing of one-tenth of its possessions, as a means by which the church could live out its scriptural narratives.[30] Can fasting be seen as indicative of a tendency to show disdain for the world? For Grumett and Muers this would be too reductive, but there are clear ambiguities in their account of the Christian diet, especially for women. Grumett and Muers contend that the extreme asceticism shown by some medieval Christian women should not be seen 'as the simple "subjugation" of dangerous bodies by external force, or as the claiming by women of political and social power which they would otherwise have been denied'.[31] Re-narrating these women's lives, these authors argue, as simply oppression or empowerment is insufficiently attentive to the multiplicity and complexity of their lives.

Food is endemic to the Christian imagination. It features in attempts to define the boundaries and identity of the Christian community and as a means for and result of the transformation of the world beyond the boundaries of the ascetic community. Food practices truck theological meanings and commitments and this can be seen in the Hebrew Bible and the New Testament.

## Part Three: food and Christian scriptures

In the Hebrew Bible, questions of land and food feature recurrently in the context of God's creation of the world and the call of the people of Israel to covenant. Ellen Davis writes in *Scripture, Culture and Agriculture* that,

> beginning with the first chapter of Genesis, there is no extensive exploration of the relationship between God and humanity that does not factor the land and its fertility into that relationship. Overall, from a biblical perspective, the sustained fertility and habitability of the earth, or more particularly of the land of Israel, is the best index of the health of the covenant relationship.[32]

The people of Israel, unlike ourselves, 'belonged to a culture that recognized land care as the life-and-death matter it unquestionably is'.[33] The responsibility to care for the land came, furthermore, from the belief that the land belonged to God. Deuteronomy 11 says:

For the land that you are about to enter to occupy is not like the land of Egypt, from which you have come, where you sow your seed and irrigate by foot like a vegetable garden. But the land that you are crossing over to occupy is a land of hills and valleys, watered by rain from the sky, a land that the LORD your God looks after. The eyes of the LORD your God are always on it, from the beginning of the year to the end of the year.[34]

In Leviticus 25, YHWH says to the people that 'the land shall not be sold in perpetuity, for the land is mine; with me you are but aliens and tenants'.[35] For Davis, the land was made by God and because the land is God's it has a relationship to God independent of the Israel community, or of any human. She says that the writers of the Hebrew Bible hold that the

land is a semi-autonomous moral agent. Though it can be victimized by its inhabitants, it remains accountable to God even for the defilement it suffers at human hands. Ultimately for the land, divine presence trumps human presence. The land, which retains its healthful instinct for God, must finally expel the unhealthful presence and make up the Sabbath years that Israel failed to observe. So the land retains a capacity to act for God, even when humans have forfeited their high yet humble calling to work with God.[36]

Less pronounced in the Christian New Testament, the agency of creation and its relationship to God, unmediated by the person, is still suggested in Romans 8. Paul writes here that 'creation waits with eager longing for the revealing of the children of God' for it was subject to the 'bondage of decay' brought to bear by human failing and is 'groaning in labour pains' waiting for redemption to be completed.[37] The world has its own agency according to these texts and exists independently to the imposition of human needs and values.

Four conclusions are drawn from this theological framing of the world, points at which Davis sees overlap between the Hebrew writers of the ancient near east and contemporary agrarian writers. First, the land is not an inert object but 'a fellow creature that can justly expect something from us whose lives depend on it'.[38] The world predates the human and humans have a place in it as a part of a communion of subjects, not a collection of objects.[39] Norman Wirzba summarizes this nicely when he says that 'there is an integrity to creation that depends on humans seeing themselves as properly placed within a network of creation and God'.[40]

Second, if the world precedes the human and continues to exist independently of them then humans will never, can never and should never pretend to know it fully. The appropriate human posture to take towards the earth is humility, wonder and awe. For Davis, this cuts against the 'modern conceit that human behaviour is invariably ameliorated by more knowledge: 'If we knew for certain that some of our behaviours were wrong, we would stop them. [Contemporary agrarians] share the biblical writers' view that what underlies moral failure is not simple ignorance but rather sin ... a culpable pride, a destructive lack of humility.'[41] A due reverence for the world leads logically into point three: that materiality is endemic to this spirituality. The question we should be asking in the present, according to Davis is: 'How can we meet our material needs, in the present and for the indefinite future, without inflicting damage? The biblical writers are likewise concerned with ordering material existence in ways that are consonant with God's will and the design of the world.'[42] The materialism Davis advocates includes a respect for the finiteness of things and a due reverence for their limits. In a similar vein, Grumett and Muers point out that the idea of the world is a 'gift' is 'prominent in current theology' but that its 'implications ... for a theology of eating are ... ambiguous' because 'notions of excess can unwittingly buttress a view of the world as little more than the legitimate object of progressive annihilation driven by advanced consumer capitalism'.[43] They go on to say that 'the world's food resources are not only structured but finite and exhaustible, as classical liberal economics, with distant origins in scholastic natural law theory, correctly recognized in its founding concept of "scarcity"'.[44]

Our failure to recognize these boundaries, or, more often, to outsource the responsibility for recognizing and maintaining these boundaries to the market (with its price mechanism), is a widespread and deep-set collective blind spot.[45] Davis quotes from Barbara Kingsolver:

> Most of our populace and all our leaders are participating in a mass hallucinatory fantasy in which the megatons of waste we dump in our rivers and bays are not poisoning the water, the hydrocarbons we pump into the air are not changing the climate, overfishing is not depleting the oceans, fossil fuels will never run out, wars that kill masses of civilians are an appropriate way to keep our hands on what's left, we are not desperately overdrawn at the environmental bank, and really, the kids are all right.[46]

This leads into the fourth point of continuity between agrarianism and the Hebrew Bible, the Hebrews gave a very high value to the land.

Unlike their neighbours in Egypt and Mesopotamia, the 'Israelites seem to have had no concept of arable land as a commodity to be bought and sold freely'.[47] Instead a piece of land was 'the possession of a family to be held as a trust and transmitted from generation to generation ... there is to be no permanently landless underclass in Israel'.[48] Davis summarizes: 'the covenant is properly conceived as a triangulated relationship among Israel, the land, and YHWH'.[49] When God is betrayed the land is degraded, to the detriment of person and creature alike. Conversely, when God is feared nature flourishes, to the benefit of the human and animal alike.

Within their imaginative space, the Israelites engaged in a task of 'making whole' the ruptures of earth and heaven. Davis, drawing on the work of Berry, talks of maintaining the imagination of Israel, defining imagination as

> the means whereby writers with diverse gifts may enable their communities literally to 're-member,' to work toward their own wholeness, a goal that can be achieved only by claiming a 'membership' ... in 'the wholeness and the Holiness of the creation.'[50]

Food, the product of healthy, whole and holy (all etymologically linked terms) earth, attended to by caring humans, is an aspect of God's generosity towards the people of Israel. The story of manna from heaven, sent to give respite to the Jewish people in their exodus from slavery in Egypt (Exodus 16), is atypical of what would mark the attitudes, commitments and experiences that Davis endorses. The gift of manna from heaven 'shows that food is more than anything else, an expression of God's sovereignty over creation and generosity toward humankind'.[51] The books of the law – Leviticus, Deuteronomy – seek to codify these experiences in the desert with strict rules for what can be eaten: presenting the Israelites with ways to communicate who they are. Food is 'a symbolic system that says something about holiness, and at the same time, about the nature of creation'.[52] It says God made the world, that it is good and that it is a gift, and that like all gifts it holds open the invitation for something to be given back in return.

The theme of land is less pronounced in the New Testament. There are different possible reasons for this: Jesus' claim that no particular place would be the locus of true worship; for Davis it may be because a number of the New Testament writers believed that the imminent second coming of Christ would lead to a radical recreation of everything, heaven and earth.[53] Nevertheless, food is still a prominent topic in the Gospels and is used regularly to demonstrate various forms of participation and non-participation: primarily Jesus' participation in God and the world (the 'I am the bread of life' in John's Gospel and saying 'unless a grain of wheat falls to the ground'), the natural and created world's participation in Jesus (the feeding of the 5,000), the disciples' participation in Jesus and each other (Eucharist), and the early Christian communities' non-participation in the food rules of Israel (nothing is unclean, Acts 10).

In his book *Miracles*, the writer of the Narnia stories C. S. Lewis explores the presuppositions we hold and how they influence our reading of history. Miracles, Lewis argues, do not interrupt gratuitously the patterns of nature. It is wrong to think they are ungainly because they are brash. Instead, Lewis says,

> I contend that in all these miracles alike the incarnate God does suddenly and locally something that God has done or will do in general. Each miracle writes for us in small letters something that God has already written, or will write, in letters almost too large to be noticed, across the whole canvas of Nature.[54]

There is nothing anti-natural about Jesus' changing of water into wine at the wedding of Cana, Lewis continues:

> Every year, as part of the Natural order, God makes wine. He does so by creating a vegetable organism that can turn water, soil and sunlight into a juice which will, under proper conditions, become wine. Thus, in a certain sense, He constantly turns water into wine, for wine, like all drinks, is but water modified. Once, and in one year only, God, now incarnate, short circuits the process: makes wine in a moment: uses earthenware jars instead of vegetable fibres to hold the water. But uses them to do what He is always doing. The Miracle consists in the short cut; but the event to which it leads is the usual one.[55]

Jesus, who 'does nothing except what he sees the Father do', likewise multiplies the bread and the fish to feed the multitudes who come to him.[56] The story goes that a crowd is following Jesus. Jesus turns to the disciples and asks them where food can be found for these followers as they traipse through the hills and fields around the Sea of Galilee. In doing this, Jesus takes on the responsibility of Moses who fed the Israelites in their exodus. Philip, a follower of Jesus, comments that feeding the crowd would be too expensive for them. A second follower, Andrew, brings a boy to Jesus who has five loaves and two fishes, Jesus gives thanks for the food, it is distributed to the crowd and is miraculously sufficient for all. Along with the Hebrew Bible passages that associate the provision of food with God's saving actions in history (David and his men receive food in 1 Samuel 21.3–7, Elijah is fed bread by the ravens in 1 Kings 17.6), the New Testament scholar Jane Webster says that 'the miraculous provision of bread is also associated with the messianic age of the last days'.[57]

Jesus moves away from the business of the crowd again but the people follow him and Jesus takes the opportunity to talk to them about 'food that endures', rather than perishing as the food of the world does. He says, in a passage that Webster sees as the most eucharistic foreshadowing passage in John's Gospel, 'I am the bread of life. Whoever comes to me will never be hungry, and whoever believes in me will never be thirsty.'[58] A theme already present in the text (Jesus is the 'Lamb of God'[59]) is stated explicitly here: Jesus is 'both the provider and the substance of the food that God gives'.[60] The 'I am' phrase, repeated numerous times in John's Gospel (John 8.12; 10.9, 11; 11.25; 14.6; 15.5), harks back to YHWH's revelation to Moses in the desert, affirming Jesus' identity as the Word who is God.[61] Lewis says that 'every year God makes a little corn into much corn: the seed is sown and there is an increase'.[62] Likewise, the same day, 'He also multiplied fish. Look down into every bay and almost every river. This swarming, undulating fecundity shows He is still at work "thronging the seas with spawn innumerable" ... that day, at the feeding of the thousands, incarnate God does the same: does close and small, under His human hands, a workman's hands, what He has always been doing in the seas, the lakes and the little brooks.'[63]

The Gospel of John, which contains a range of important food passages, gives one of the New Testament's most theologically developed frames in which to see the complicity of the miracles in the normal actions of God. The first chapter of the Gospel says that Jesus – the Word – 'was God' and 'was with God' from the beginning and that 'all things came into being through him' and that without the Word 'not one thing came into being'.[64] The miracles only disclose in accelerated form the world's creation by and dependence on God. The miracles are microcosms or synecdoche, as the manna from heaven for the Hebrews was indicative of a wider order. The Gospel proceeds – as Jane Webster's *Ingesting Jesus: Eating and Drinking in the Gospel of John* explores – to elaborate on how Jesus shares in God and what this means for humans' sharing in Jesus.

Webster's text examines a number of 'ingestion motifs' in the Gospel and the matrix of theological ideas which they iterate. Along with the obvious references to bread, wine, grain, fish and water, Webster picks up on the eating scenes (weddings, suppers) and the passing reference to words drawn from the domain of ingesting language: 'tasting death' and 'being consumed', for example.[65] She summarizes her findings by saying that 'ingesting language provides a way to describe both the role of Jesus and the role of believers'.[66] First, Jesus provides food for others; in the feeding of the multitude, the wedding at Cana, and in the post-resurrection narrative in which Jesus has fish on the fire for the disciples' breakfast. Second, Jesus offers himself as food, giving life to others through his death.[67] Along with the already mentioned identification of Jesus with the Passover lamb (an animal sacrificed for the safety of the Israelites when in slavery in Egypt, Exodus 12, John 1.29), Jesus talks about himself as the grain of wheat that, unless it 'falls into the earth and dies, it remains just a single grain; but if it dies, it bears much fruit' (John 12.24). Participating in Jesus means sharing in this love for the world, love so excessive it makes one vulnerable, even to the point of death. As God gives up being everything, wills something that is not-God in order for creation to be, so Jesus' life climaxes in a self-curtailing:

> By evoking the ingesting motif, however, and coupling it with actions that anticipate Jesus' death, the Gospel again sets before the reader, albeit in allusive form, the fact that Jesus must die in order that others might 'eat him' and live. Jesus' death is to be celebrated rather than mourned, for his death brings life to others.[68]

Jesus shows how, and lives out how, God loves and in doing so re-affirms John's contention that this *is* God. The God who makes space for others for the sake of relationship. In John 13, when Jesus offers to wash the disciples' feet and Peter refuses, Jesus responds by saying 'unless I wash you, you have no share with me'.[69] On this idea of what 'sharing' with Jesus means, Webster says that to eat with Jesus in the narrative present would mean to share the only food which Jesus partakes – the cup of his death: he says, 'Am I not to drink the cup that the Father has given me?' (19.11; cf. 15.20). In other words, to eat and drink with Jesus suggests that the disciples must be prepared to die for the sake of Jesus, a theme that pervades the Gospel (see, for example, 13.37, 15.13, 21.18–19).[70]

The disciples are called to share in Jesus, to share in his death, a death that makes life possible for others: 'finally, the ingesting motif is used to describe the way in which believers are to respond [to Jesus]: they are to feed others.'[71] Webster notes that in John's Gospel the disciples are called to gather an 'imminent harvest', they are told that their dependence on Jesus will produce 'much fruit', Peter is told to feed Jesus' sheep, and that after the resurrection the disciples pull up a great catch of fish at Jesus' request.[72] Feeding others is simultaneously the most natural and supernatural thing a Christian can do because it is not only what Jesus asks for explicitly from the disciples but also what Jesus does constantly through creation.

## Part Four: sacrament and Eucharist

From these observations on the place and function of food in Christian scriptures and its histories of practice, it is possible to begin tentatively outlining recurring values or norms in Christian engagements with food. These, once elucidated, will help us to judge whether a practice (like food banking) is consistent with the commitments of the tradition: in short, are they 'eucharistic'? Do they fulfil 'the eucharist, the sacrament of the coming of the risen Lord, of our meeting and communion with him "at his table in his kingdom?"'[73] The twentieth-century Orthodox theologian and priest Alexander Schmemann has been very influential in the field of theology and food, and I'll draw on his work here to summarize some of what we have already seen.

First, the world, matter and food are not secular. Their natures are participatory. Schmemann says that Christians have thought about the world separate from God, 'as an end in itself and not as transparent to God', so often that it is now 'in the air'; 'it seems natural for man to experience the world as opaque, and not shot through with the presence of God. It seems natural not to live a life of thanksgiving for God's gift of a world. It seems natural not to be eucharistic.'[74] The church surreptitiously appropriates this logic when it accepts 'the reduction of God to an area called "sacred" ("spiritual," "supernatural") – as opposed to the world as "profane"', thereby denying that 'God is all in all'.[75] For Schmemann, one of the results of this is the paradox that when things are treated as ends in themselves (separate from participation and end in God) they lose rather than gain value.

> When we see the world as an end in itself, everything becomes itself a value and consequently loses all value, because only in God is found the meaning (value) of everything, and the world is meaningful only when it is the 'sacrament' of God's presence. Things treated merely as things in themselves destroy themselves because only in God have they any life.[76]

Second, then, the world is sacramental, it is completed or remade in the person of Jesus. Jesus 'ate and drank, and this means that the world of which he partook, the very food of our world became His body, His life. But his life was totally, absolutely *eucharistic* – all of it was transformed into communion with God and all of it ascended into heaven.'[77] Thus, in the act of communion 'when we receive this bread from His hands, we know that He has taken up all life, filled it with Himself, made it what it was meant to be: communion with God, sacrament of His presence and love'.[78]

Third, the whole world is the site of God's blessing and humans can by their practices participate in God through their lives in the world. Schmemann says that 'Man must eat in order to live; he must take the world into his body and transform it into himself, into flesh and blood.'[79] Rightly practised and understood, the human act of making, eating and sharing of food shares in God's blessing of the world. Schmemann writes:

> All that exists is God's gift to man, and it all exists to make God known to man, to make man's life communion with God. It is divine love made food, made life for man. God *blesses* everything He creates, and, in biblical language, this means He makes all creation the sign and means of His presence and wisdom, love and revelation: 'O taste and see that the Lord is good'. Man is a hungry being. But he is hungry for God. Behind all the hunger of our life is God.[80]

Fourth, humans are involved in a story of descent and return, as is the grain of wheat which falls, dies and becomes life for others. Through eating, humans participate in the divine, and the particularity of the human resides in their role to say thanks for the food he or she eats, Schmemann says. To '*bless* God for the food and the life he receives from Him' is endemic to the human vocation.[81] To sin is to illegiti-mately interrupt this reciprocal circulation of gifts. It is to deny the human vocation to be a priest (to return the world to God in thanks), sin stems from when we 'made the world *material*'.[82] Food is part of a complex Christian stance towards the world, similar in ways to that outlined earlier in the chapter by Abu-Tayeb. The Orthodox Christian tradition has held open 'both the goodness of the world for whose life God has given his only-begotten Son, and the *wickedness* in which the world lies'; moments of return and moments of refusal.[83]

Berry makes a similar point when he writes that farming should be 'the proper use and care of an immeasurable gift'.[84] Our failing, Berry goes on, is in transitioning the world from its lodging in God to the acquisitive economy, in refusing to return the world to God, which also means refusing to share it with each other.

> Among the commonplaces of the Bible, for example, are the admoni-tions that the world was made and approved by God, that it belongs to Him, and that its good things come to us from Him as gifts. Beyond those ideas is the idea that the whole Creation exists only by partici-pating in the life of God, sharing in His being, breathing His breath ... Such thoughts seem strange to us now, and what has estranged us from them is our economy. The industrial economy could not have been derived from such thoughts any more than it could have been derived from the Golden Rule.[85]

The Christian imagination is foreign to the cultural mainstream for 'if we believed that the existence of the world is rooted in mystery and in sanctity, then we would have a different economy'.[86] The land is a gift, and if this is right 'then it is a gift to all the living in all time. To withhold it from some is finally to destroy it for all.'[87] Like Schmemann and Shiva, Berry says that 'what is most conspicuously absent from the industrial economy and industrial culture is this idea of return'.[88]

## Conclusion

The picture of Christian theology and food that emerges in this chapter is deeply at variance with the otherworldly orientations, stigmatizing of the different, and individualizing tendencies that de Souza observed in the American food banks she participated in. In the history of the church, in the Christian scriptures, and in some of the most influential twentieth-century Christian voices, eating embodies and exemplifies the intractable links that suspend the human in the natural and spiritual world. Theology is the practice of 're-membering' in which 'industry is for mending the bent bones and the minds fractured by life', as the Welsh priest-poet R. S. Thomas writes in 'The Kingdom'.[89] Because the kind of participation theology advocates is 'reciprocal', a circulation of gifts, it includes an affirmation of existence of the other and a desire that they persist. Like the rationale for food banks which sees them as solutions to the issues of food waste *and* hunger, the theological vision elucidated here affirms that the restoration of the world and the human occur simultaneously in the wider horizon of reconciliation with the divine.

Furthermore, it is possible, from this provisional investigation of the Christian tradition, to posit that a significant part of the reason why Christians are involved in food banking is that food is so prominent in its writings and history. In continuity with how food practices have featured in the history of the church, as discussed by Grumett and Muers, food banks give contemporary Christians a way to contribute to a common world outside the boundaries of the church *and* a means to show the distinctiveness of the Christian identity. However, the question still remains as to how participatory, or reciprocal, food banks are and whether they syphon the Christian community's attention away from non-reciprocal extraction in either the food or welfare systems (in short, do they surreptitiously deny the sacramentality of the whole world, gathered up in Christ)? The next chapter takes up this issue, assuming a broadly agrarian, theological perspective, and asks what theology has to offer to contemporary neoliberal arrangements and the place of food banks within them. Do food banks realize the participatory character of the world, real at many levels, or do they exhibit the estrangement that is endemic to our economy?

Davis develops a number of analogies in her work between the writers of the Hebrew Bible and contemporary agrarians. Before bringing this agrarian perspective into further conversation with contemporary food banking, it is worth pausing to define the term more specifically. Berry, in a recent set of essays, lists a number of characteristics that mark agrarianism. Berry says that agrarianism is 'an elated, loving interest in the use and care of the land'; it is informed by 'submission to nature' and 'her laws of conservation, frugality, fullness or completeness, and diversity'.[90] As such, it is diametrically opposed to 'an almost-general approval of the so far unrestrained industrial prerogative to treat living creatures as comprising a sort of ore, and the food industry as a sort of foundry'.[91] It includes 'the wish, the felt need, to have and to belong to a place of one's own' along with the suggestion, articulated by the freed slaves who asked for 'forty acres and a mule', that a place of one's own is the 'only secure source of sustenance and independence'.[92] Agrarianism acknowledges the importance of neighbours, the continuity of local cultures, good work or 'vocation', and a 'lively suspicion of anything new'.[93] It is not a movement with a distinct hierarchy or theological edifice but 'a sort of summary existence as a *feeling* – an instinct, an excitement, a passion, a tenderness – for the living earth and its creatures'.[94] Putting this feeling in touch with the British food aid scene is the task of the next chapter.

# 4

# Coincidences of the Neoliberal
# and the Food Banks

## Introduction

In his book *The Unsettling of America*, Berry writes that 'for some time now ecologists have been documenting the principle that "you can't do one thing" – which means that in a natural system whatever affects one thing ultimately affects everything. Everything in the Creation is related to everything else and dependent on everything else. The Creation is one; it is a uni-verse, a whole, the parts of which are all "turned into one".'[1] The problem that Berry identifies is the disregard for this truth enshrined in the practices of our economy. In an essay called 'In Distrust of Movements', 20 years later in 1998, he writes:

> Study of the history of land use (and any local history will do) informs us that we have had for a long time an economy that thrives by undermining its own foundations. Industrialism, which is the name of our economy, and which is now virtually the only economy of the world, has been from its beginnings in a state of riot. It is based squarely upon the principle of violence towards everything on which it depends and it has not mattered whether the form of industrialism was communist or capitalist; the violence toward nature, human communities, traditional agricultures, and local economies has been constant.[2]

One of the results of this entrenched disorder, our variance with the most basic constituents of our being, and there are many,[3] is that 'the split between what we think and what we do is profound.'[4] Berry observes:

> the tendency of modern organizations to perform in opposition to their stated purposes ... governments that exploit and oppress the people they are sworn to serve and protect, medical procedures that produce ill health, schools that preserve ignorance, methods of trans-

portation that, as Ivan Illich says, have 'created more distances than they bridge.'[5]

It's no use pretending that we are exempt from this confusion. Berry 'cannot think of any American' whom he knows or has heard of 'who is not contributing in some way to [this] destruction.'[6] And

> the reason is simple: to live undestructively in an economy that is overwhelmingly destructive would require of any one of us, or of any small group of us, a great deal more work than we have yet been able to do. How could we divorce ourselves completely and yet responsibly from the technologies and powers that are destroying our planet? The answer is not yet thinkable, and it will not be thinkable for some time – even though there are now groups and families and persons everywhere in the country who have begun the labour of thinking it.[7]

What about food banks? Are they another example of an organization that performs in opposition to its stated purpose? What, second, of the (Anglican) churches that preach peace on earth while renting their buildings to arms traders;[8] advocate for freedom from debt while holding shares in payday lenders;[9] call for the common good while holding extensive private lands;[10] declare that love and justice are the true nature of things while remaining integral to the decision-making processes of successive governments which lie to their people in order to push through policies that are detrimental to those same people's health?[11] How well do the church and food banks meet the standards of participation already elucidated? Are the food banks (at least for the Christians working or volunteering within them) and church actions internally consistent with their beliefs? This chapter focuses on food banks and neoliberalism, the next on the church and its relationship to the economy and state more broadly.

While we are in no way 'readily divisible, into environmental saints and sinners', there '*are* legitimate distinctions that need to be made ... distinctions of degree and consciousness'.[12] In the case of food banks, not only are there distinctions that need to be drawn between food banks and the industrial (neoliberal) economy in which they operate, there are also distinctions between different types of food banks that are important to bear in mind. Andrew Williams (along with his co-authors) addresses four possible points of overlap between neoliberalism and food banks: they operate in and depend on a food system that is highly non-participatory and unsustainable; they compensate for the reduced remit and role of the state; they nurture neoliberal ways of thinking in volunteers (differences between 'deserving' and 'unde-serving' poor, a distinction shared with Victorian thinkers); and they distract volunteers from more potentially effective forms of (political) action. For the Liverpool-based theologian and social scientist Chris Allen these critiques are correct, but for Williams each of these critiques is only partially true and it is best to think of food banks as 'contested space' with 'contradictory dynamics'.[13]

Beginning with the reflections of volunteers and food bank users I interviewed in County Durham, this chapter concludes by agreeing with the position put forward by Williams. Food banks are deeply contra-dictory spaces in which food bank users can feel great shame or express real agency; in which volunteers can be hardened by their exposure to suffering or softened by the stories they hear; in which an economy that is built on scarcity and competition is both reaffirmed and juxtaposed with generosity and the gift of the creation's abundance. Alongside the question of how neoliberalism and food banks do and do not overlap, this chapter provides a series of theological means for thinking through some of the problems food banks raise: how should Christians think about hunger? What links are there between food banks, choice, guilt and responsibility? Is the agency of the poor a means by which God moves?

## Part One: food and company in County Durham Foodbank

In the interviews I carried out, both clients and volunteers expressed mixed feelings about the food bank but were consistently inclined to see them as a net positive. Volunteers praised the food bank as an example of human generosity, whether religiously motivated or not. Emma, a retired schoolteacher who had a long history of involvement with the Labour Party and the trade unions, told me about her experience volunteering at the Durham City drop-in, on Framwellgate.

> I'm enjoying it, I think I am giving something back to society, it's my Catholic upbringing. One of the commandments: love your neigh-bour as much as yourself. I've been Catholic all my life and done charity work before, at the Crown court as a witness support, was on the rates there, but now my grandchildren are the priority and I can't be sure I'll be there so I've given it up.

She went on:

[Food banks are] a marvellous thing, what they do. Only thing that bothers me, and it bothers me a lot: the government are copping out of their responsibility to help the poor people, homeless people. I give to different charities through the post and the TV. When I see those kids who are hungry on TV it upsets me massively. If I saw those kids in the UK I'd take them in, though I wouldn't be allowed to. I think the majority in the UK would do the same. How can you justify just sitting there with what you have? You must give something ... It's evil what the government is doing. Food banks are a dichotomy, is that what you call it? These people should be fed and housed, it would be better if the food bank didn't exist. But I do think it's going to get worse, until Labour comes in. Then they'll disappear. It's a scandal, a scandal.

While Emma told me that she was more concerned with attacks on trade union rights and zero-hour contracts than Brexit and the then prospects of the Prime Minister Theresa May and 'those southern papers', volunteers like Susan who held very different political outlooks shared many of her views.

Susan, who is in her sixties, gave up her career working as a tax officer early in order to care for a loved one. She now volunteers at the food bank in order to give something back, to help people. She's been coming to the food bank for six weeks now, first at Chester-le-Street and now Durham, and told me that:

I think its brilliant, absolutely amazing. I am here to stay, not just for a couple of years but for as long as I can. I'm very impressed with the food bank. There are a great number of donations coming in from people ... It's brilliant these [volunteers] came out 'cause they don't have to be here, it's great that they are helping people.

Historically, she's supported the Conservative Party and tells me that she voted for Brexit as she thought it was 'the traditional British thing to do' and that we'd 'be better off by ourselves'. But this didn't stop her being critical of the government, especially now she was having to find some part-time work to top up her income.

It's not going to change, [food banks] are here for the foreseeable future, unfortunately. They can't be got rid of. Sanctions, politics, there are lots of different variables. Universal Credit ... the problems are too complex, there is a lack of staff in the Job Centre, it isn't the workers' fault, it's what is up the heights. I do think the mandatory job applications is a problem, why force people to do this, just to box tick? People get put into impossible jobs, it's not good. I've been looking for some work, you forget about ageism and sexism in applications. It's bureaucratic crap, I don't think I'll be able to find work. I've got a friend, they're a cleaner, 54, and have no experience of PCs, what are they supposed to do? I'm a political Conservative, but now feel sick of the whole lot. Its groundhog day, round and round and round.

Despite her criticism of the bureaucracy in work and the current benefits regime she was also highly critical of people manipulating the benefits system or trying to live off it, commenting to me that some of those on welfare benefits should be given university degrees for the level of ingenuity they've shown in manipulating the system.

A third female volunteer, Rachel, a retired town planner, gave her reflections on the development of the food banks and the changes they went through over the course of her time with them. She said that they are meeting a local need, especially for people who are socially isolated.

It's definitely fulfilling a need. I like the expansion into the drop-in centre system, because it's meaning that people could come for some company or to use the laptops and things. Particularly when we were being used more as a place where you could access information, like on the fuel poverty side, housing issues and debt advice and things like that, 'beyond food' as it were, that was very positive.

The 'drop-in model' refers to a diversification of services in the food bank commensurate with the variety of needs of food banks' clientele. Peter explained the thinking behind them:

There are two things about the Brandon model, the drop-in model, of food available to anybody [served in the food bank cafe] whether they need the food bank or not. Part of it is obviously trying to get away from a stigma of being in that place and potentially accessing the food bank. If you've got people going there just because it is happening and it is a social event how do people know whether that's why people are going or whether it's because they are desperate for some food? It's less obvious, that is a plus. Second, we know social isolation is an issue, so it helps break down that. And it builds up that normalcy of being there, makes it less likely that people rush in and rush out of having done something very transactional and not relational, without their story being heard. And being listened to, I think that's a really important part of the food bank. Because people who use the food bank will often have been dealt with by people who haven't got time to listen to them, the Job Centre or advisors who are pushed against time, or whatever it is. People may have been really struggling to give them any time and if volunteers give time to listen to somebody that is an immensely healing process for that person who gets listened to. It goes back to the origins of DCP ...

In a report by the Durham County Director of Public Health, the extent of loneliness and some strategies to deal with it are laid out.[14] Following national estimates that 'suggest that 20 percent of the older population are mildly lonely and a further 11 percent are intensely lonely', the report estimates that 19,000 over-65s are experiencing loneliness and 10,000 experience intense loneliness in the county.[15] With 7% of the 18–64 population socially isolated, there are another 22,000 people in County Durham experiencing some form of loneliness.[16] The effects of extended loneliness are 'depression, decreased immunity and longer recovery from illness, poor nutrition, increased anxiety, fatigue, social stigma and ultimately increased morbidity and (premature) mortality'.[17] The report cites statistics from the Office for National Statistics which says that the UK is the 'loneliness capital of Europe', and it was clear in my interviews that a number of food bank users appreciated the time and companionship of the space.[18]

Stewart, who talked earlier about his experience of the Job Centre, told me in the interview about how he came to Brandon food bank and what he thought of it. He moved to Brandon a couple of years before we talked and just after his marriage had broken down. He had come to appreciate being recognized and welcomed in the food bank and told me that he couldn't fault the food bank for anything:

They are good people to talk to. This other volunteer ... is good. I heard about the food bank from a friend, I came along to explore and felt very welcome. [The food bank co-ordinator] is great. I give her a hug every time I come in. I've explained food banks to my friends: 'If you're feeling down and out, if you need help they will help you.' I couldn't think of any improvements.
*What were you looking for at the food bank?*
Support. I was in a hell of a mess. I'd be in the house for too long my own. I was in the house too long to sleep, I was only getting two hours' sleep a night.

For David, the hospitality of the food bank was a part of the hospitality that Christians have experienced from God. What Christians had experienced spiritually was reflected in how they acted socially. He told me:

> Every Christian affects people. Everyone is touched by Jesus, you can see that at the food bank, the feeling here, the atmosphere. People get helped here, all people, people on the streets, people who got nothing. I like how the food bank works. But there is a non-positive side. Three days' food? I don't think that really does anything for people. It's a difficult balance because if you give people more or let them come all the time that could build dependency.

Despite the inability of food banks to ameliorate food insecurity long term, they do provide short-term, immediate respite for some people experiencing hunger. Garthwaite includes in her book a statement making this point from the Trussell Trust, which says that 'food banks represent a community response to the problem of hunger that people have identified in their local areas. Food banks provide a mechanism for local people to provide effective support to people at the point of crisis and, as long as a need exists, it is good that communities can be part of the solution.'[19] In his book *Hunger: A Modern History*, James Vernon writes that hunger is 'never simply a condition grounded in the material reality of the human body'.[20] By this, he does not mean that 'there is no such thing as reality' or that 'bodies are merely cultural' but that 'hunger has a cultural history that belies its apparently consistent material form. This history matters not just because hunger hurts, but because how it has hurt has always been culturally and historically specific.'[21]

Méndez-Montoya makes a similar point when he says that 'the body is not a mere pre-social or absolutely determined biological entity'.[22] The body is both personal and public, it is always 'socialized' by 'a series of social constructions such as gender, race, class, age and so forth'.[23] We experience our body through these categories and therefore never directly; we always experience ourselves in a mediated way. Seen in this light, food insecurity and hunger are both individual and social cleavages, an antagonism inside the self and between the self and others. Méndez-Montoya goes on to say that 'bread, and the lack thereof, has to do with the power of sharing and the potential refusal to do just that. It is therefore a profoundly theological issue, for it has to do ultimately with God's gift and the sharing (or refusal to share) of this gift with one another.'[24] He goes on to quote a document produced by

the inter-religious group Zero Hunger, which says that 'hunger results
from injustice and represents an offense against the Creator, since life
is the greatest gift of God'.[25] Building simultaneously on the bodiliness
of the person and a theology of creation, Méndez-Montoya argues
that there is an 'ethical-political' dimension to hunger because 'hunger
reflects society's practice of the disempowerment of certain groups, and
[its] lack of common vision, virtue, and caritas'.[26]

One of the complexities in judging food banks is balancing the social
participation volunteers and food bank users value and the immediate
needs they meet and make publicly visible with the possibility that food
banks surreptitiously facilitate the dismantling of other ways we share
in each other: our relationships to each other as citizens through the
vehicle of the state and as creatures living sustainably from the land.
There is the widely noted possibility, seen in previous chapters in the
work of those like Riches, that the generosity that sustains food banks
enables atavistic politics and inhibits more proportionate, remedial
political opportunities.[27] Peter expressed a version of this to me when
talking about food banks and Universal Credit.

> And I think it's interesting: if you had tried to bring in Universal
> Credit, with that waiting time, without a food bank infrastructure
> in place, would it have been accepted as readily? I think that's a real
> question because food banks have provided a safety net of sorts. And
> if that safety net had not been there at all, could you have seriously
> said to people 'you're going to have to wait six weeks before you get
> any money'? I don't think you could ... The poll tax caused riots, and
> telling people that they are not going to get any money for six weeks
> and there is nothing out there that they can go to, I think it would
> have radicalized rather more rapidly.

Peter articulates an oft historically noted relationship between charities
and neoliberalism. Are the principles of community, care, hospitality
and relationality embodied by food banks at variance with the dis-
aggregation of people vertically (through inequalities of wealth and
health) and horizontally (through the destruction of local communities
of support, workplace solidarity, furthering competition, auditing and
individualized pay grades, the distinction of deserving and undeserving
poor) from each other that characterize neoliberal precariousness?
Andrew Williams, along with his co-authors, usefully outlines four
possible points at which neoliberalism and food banking overlap, but
also ways in which this overlap is not a complete coincidence.

## Part Two: four food bank criticisms

Williams and his co-authors turn to the criticism that food banks '[undermine] collectivist welfare, and [deflect] attention from fundamental injustices in the food system' by drawing on their own ethnographic work in a UK food bank.[28] They say that food banks may contribute to the atrophying of other forms of welfare; in particular they point to the Trussell Trust's voucher system, its concern with 'welfare dependency', the ways it may reinforce differences between deserving and undeserving poor, and the lack of attention paid to larger questions of the politics around food systems.[29] But they also argue that these problems do not fully stymie food banks as a place of transformative 'encounter where predominantly middle-class volunteers come into contact with "poor others"'.[30] Food banks are still places of care, and places in which food bank clients retain and express agency. It is important to retain the question of distinction and degree noted by Berry. In practice, in the complex processes at work on the ground, Williams finds that the neoliberal context in which food banks occur is being contested *and* reaffirmed. I broadly agree with this assessment; there are 'contradictory dynamics' to food banks and the one I participated in in the north-east of England.[31]

So, Williams et al. identify four narratives in which food banking has typically been discussed, each of which 'points to the limited utility if not also damaging politics of food banking'.[32] The first of these is that food banks are dependent on exactly the kinds of agribusiness and exploitation of the earth (including the many people who work it) criticized by Wendell Berry, among others, in the last chapter. Food banks '[depoliticize] problems of food insecurity, by apparently meeting the need for emergency food without confronting the systemic injustices that lead to problems of hunger in developed countries'.[33] Dowler makes this point when reflecting on the pressures of competition in the retail sector, food production and labour markets:

> The only way retailers and others can try to keep food prices down (and most big supermarkets compete on low price) is by causing more problems to those who work in the food sector, here and elsewhere – and this compounds the problems of low wages and unstable jobs. Low wages and job instabilities are contributing to rising numbers having to use food banks.[34]

Add to this the pressure food megacorporations feel to produce food on industrial scales at low prices *and* the need to maintain corporate prestige by supporting a good cause like reducing hunger through donating your surplus (waste) produce to a food bank and the PR, political, ethical, ecological and economic quagmire in which food banks are currently located becomes a little clearer. When a Tesco employee, as Williams' essay reports, is forced to go to the food bank and receives there Tesco value beans that they stocked on the shelves we see a little of the inconsistencies of the current system.[35]

In terms of 'participation', we have two problems here: food banks are downstream of a type of farming (often forced by the increasingly concentrated power of food corporations) that is closer to strip mining than gardening: the non-reciprocal and unsustainable prioritization of the extraction of value.[36] Second, these forms of farming and the retail sector that sustains them have large human costs: displaced peoples, low-waged farm labour, low-waged retail labour, destruction of cultures, and pollution.[37]

The most lucid proponent of this ecological-political point is the Liverpool-based theologian and social scientist Chris Allen. Allen has argued that 'the Christian churches and their leadership have historically occupied privileged social and economic spaces' and consequently 'their message has historically borne the imprint of its privileged origins'.[38] Allen says that it should not be a surprise to us that food banking 'constitutes the predominant Christian response to food poverty in Britain' as

> it is entirely consistent with the historically dominant Christian social tradition that has oriented largely middle-class church organisations and their leadership towards charitable giving activities rather than radical social change. Foodbank theology is merely the product of a church whose privileged being has shaped its theological episteme such that it understands charitable giving, rather than radical social change, to lie at the heart of God's message.[39]

'Radical social change' is necessary, Allen continues, because our current levels of consumption set us at odds with the sustainability of the earth. Does our focus on poverty in the UK '[render] the earth and its inhabitants in the food producing regions of the Global South politically and analytically invisible'?[40] Allen is very critical of food banks and 'food justice campaigners' because they have had 'nothing to say about the "death machines" of agribusiness, which are destroying the earth and its inhabitants in food producing regions in order to serve food consumers in countries such as Britain'.[41] The same issue marks food justice, or social justice campaigners, who promote the human right to food. He goes on: because food rights campaigners identify that 'a key cause of food poverty is low income and an unduly punitive welfare system',

> they have called for a 'campaign for social justice' so the 'underlying structural causes of inadequate food access' can be addressed. The core objective of this campaign is to secure minimum income standards so that people routinely 'acquire the food they need through socially acceptable means of market income or state support.' This involves appealing to the state to meet its obligations under the 1948 Declaration of Human Rights and Article 11 of the 1966 International Covenant on Economic, Social and Cultural Rights to 'recognise the right of everyone to an adequate standard of living for himself and his family including adequate food,'

to which the UK state is a signatory.[42] However, for Allen, by placing the issue of food insecurity into the context of human rights we render it anthropocentric, and by damning hunger as a failure of our extension of the franchise of consumption to the poor we indict ourselves as ecologically destructive capitalists. 'Food consumerism appeals to a privileged and individualised life of buying, possessing, and gratification, and is incompatible with a Jesus that used food to emphasise our "communism of being."'[43] To bring more people into the current British order by extending them credit would only further bury the earth and many of its inhabitants, it would be another example of neoliberalism excluding by including.

What Allen is arguing is that Christian charities and social justice campaigners have been insufficiently critical of the categories that they inherit and the ways in which these categories inform the boundaries they draw and the conclusions they reach. The first of these is an occlusion endemic to nationalism that informs both the local orientation of food banks (the poor here at the expense of the poor there) and the prioritization of the agency of the state by food justice campaigners (policy as the primary culprit and cure). While it is appealing to hold the UK government to account for years of hypocrisy in relation to its human rights record on food security,[44] it is prudent to remember that neoliberalism limits the power of nation states. Before the election of Margaret Thatcher in the UK, the 1976 Labour government's appeal for a loan to the IMF following an acute crisis brought about by speculation against sterling was a seminal moment in the history of UK neoliberalism. The Labour government, which had been elected two years earlier on the back of promises to maintain (and in some cases extend) aspects of the post-World War Two social-democratic, welfare arrangement, was now manoeuvred into a loan which was 'conditional on the Government willingness to implement a domestic austerity programme that involved large cutbacks on public spending'.[45] It was in this period that the World Bank and IMF, 'instead of assisting countries with the management of their external position in ways that promoted their domestic policy autonomy', was now 'dominated by US interests – became key enforcers of the "discipline" of global finance'.[46] The strings attached to the IMF loan 'subverted the policy autonomy that was required for the continuation of such social-democratic policies' which the Labour Party promised the country.[47] During this period, the UK experienced the same kinds of 'structural adjustment' that the IMF would impose on countries in South America and Africa as they sought to escape their financial debts.[48]

Like the Stockholm syndrome exhibited by the Labour Shadow Chancellor Ed Balls in 2013, when he promised to match Conservative spending cuts if a Labour government got into office,[49] the 1967 British bailout marked a new watershed in the national capture of the British state by the institutions of global finance. The promise of renewed national sovereignty following the British exit from the European Union has always seemed facile to those familiar with the reality that in recent history those 'countries whose financial health and economic competitiveness were considered to be in doubt became subject to currency speculation, forcing them to seek funds from the IMF in exchange for promises to cut state budgets and neoliberalise economic regulations more generally'.[50] The way the Eurozone dealt with the Greek debt crisis in 2011, following on from the 2008 great recession, was the most vivid recent example of national impotence and had significant effects on the British political landscape: both legitimized austerity to the deputy Prime Minister Nick Clegg at a key moment in 2011 and undermined the confidence of the British political left in the Eurozone project in the years leading up to the Brexit vote in 2016.[51]

For Allen, a further assumption that diminishes Christian thought and practice in these areas is the allocation of divine activity to some spheres and His or Her exclusion from others. From the chief proponent of 'Radical Orthodoxy', John Milbank, Allen learns that in 'acquiescing to capitalism and treating it as an autonomous secular realm legitimately governed by the state, the Christian Church has surrendered its claim to produce its own metadiscourse about social and economic problems in capitalist societies'.[52] According to Allen, those like Milbank, Wirzba, Méndenz-Montoya (and we could add Berry) 'are helpful here because they achieve this epistemic break with [neoliberal] political economy' and its secular state 'by starting instead with the world as "God's universal gift of creation and our relation to it as consumers"'.[53] The task for Christians is to embody 'the living unity that Jesus restored between human beings and the gift of creation – exemplified in his sharing of food' and to work out how to show that this 'means that there is no autonomous space outside of God in which Christians can operate'.[54] The segmentation of life into discrete spheres can produce pronounced inconsistencies, as Williams notes:

> In terms of challenging corporate agribusiness and retail, very little is currently done by Levington Foodbank around the wider politics of the food system ... Some volunteers even acknowledged the contradiction that the food bank operates within the conventional (capitalist) food chain system, distributing 'surplus' or donated commercial products to those who cannot afford the (escalating) market price.[55]

The first problem, or narrative, around food banks is that they depend on the exploitation of the earth. The second narrative, which again sees overlap between food banks and neoliberalism, suggests that food banks inhibit another kind of participation: our participation in each through the mechanism of the state. In Williams' words: do food banks inadvertently serve 'as a smoke-screen for Government to shirk responsibility to its citizens and institutionalises charitable forms of support in place of universal state welfare?'[56] Since a low point following the Second World War there has been a marked increase in the level of support for charitable forms of poverty alleviation. A historian of charity and volunteerism, Frank Prochaska, notes that an opinion poll conducted in 1948 'found that 90% of people no longer thought that there was a role for charity in Britain'.[57] Interestingly, Prochaska suggests that when we are collectively inclined 'to attribute the source of social problems to individual failings' then we are logically forced into the conclusion that 'the remedy must be found in personal reformation, assisted by discretionary charity'.[58] As the landscape has changed from a Fordist, welfare state with Keynesian economics regnant to a neoliberal state and market, the size, role and legitimacy of faith-based organizations has also undergone a transformation.[59] For those opposed to neoliberalism, 'third sector involvement in emergency food provision has typically been viewed as caught up in the wider incorporation of voluntary sector organisations and resources in the vacuum left by retreating central and local state welfare provision ... and represents a privatisation of political responsibility – one that enables policy makers to "look the other way" ... and construct food poverty as a matter of charity rather than a political obligation and human right.'[60] As previous chapters have shown, some of the most prominent writers on the topic of food banks have taken this line, including Graham Riches, Kayleigh Garthwaite and Elizabeth Dowler.

The rationale for these reductions in the remit and responsibility of the state is multiple. At the most superficial level, reducing the size and spending power of the state can mean lower taxes and increased spending power for the rich.[61] But a project so basic would not have been so successful, and there is evidence from the British Attitudes Survey that there has been no general change in people's desire for rolling back the state in the last 30 years.[62] It is necessary, therefore, to take up Martijn Konings' questions about why austerity caught the public's imagination and explore neoliberalism's conceptual and moral history.[63]

To do this, I'll begin with the basic view that rolling back the state increases freedom, that freedom is the prerequisite of choice, and that it is important that we are responsible for the consequences of our choices. These big terms are important parts of how neoliberalism legitimizes itself and is experienced as legitimate. Adam Kotsko writes that 'the key concept in neoliberalism's attempt at self-legitimisation is freedom, which neoliberalism defines in deeply individualistic terms that renders market competition the highest actualization of human liberty'.[64] Institutions that inhibit the actualization of our freedom in the market, that create kinds of dependency, must consequently be dissolved.[65] The argument continues that people who fail to exercise their freedom responsibly are the architects of their own ill-fortune; in Kotsko's terms, neoliberalism gives us 'forced choices that serve to redirect the blame for social problems onto the ostensible poor decision making of individuals'.[66] Consequently, neoliberalism is not simply the expansion of financial metrics into more spheres of life or the rolling back of state services. No programme this simple could have caught the voting public's imagination so successfully. Instead, neoliberalism is 'a remarkably cohesive moral order' which appeals to the inclination towards the moral in the person.[67] It is the widespread acceptance of this moral economy that allowed David Cameron while in office to speak in highly emotive terms about 'fairness' as getting nothing, or social justice as hunger, and for neoliberalism in general to see freedom as labour, independence as conformity, debt as self-sufficiency, and responsibility as indifference to suffering.

Liberty or libertarianism, Kotsko goes on, 'does not describe the actual workings of the neoliberal economy, but it does perfectly capture its moral dynamic of using freedom as a mechanism to generate blameworthiness. If you fail, it is your fault, and yours alone.'[68] For one volunteer called Victoria that I spoke to over coffee in her sitting room:

> There [are] such a range of views on food banks, but one of them is definitely that people want to be reassured that the people in the food banks really deserve the food, which I find problematic.

Not only are there people around food banks checking deservingness, she also recounted stories to me of food bank users offering up, unsolicited, stories justifying their needs:

> I've had multiple people try to justify to me what kind of person they are and why therefore they deserve their food parcel, which is always something I've felt really uncomfortable with. Because my take on it is that they don't have to come in and justify themselves to me, but I've had people completely unprompted say 'I'm not on drugs, I've not done this, I've not done that, I'm just struggling with whatever thing' and not want themselves put into a certain category.

It is indicative of the success of neoliberalism that even those who have lost most by it reproduce its legitimizations.[69] Kotsko's primary claim is that neoliberalism 'demonizes' us. He defines demonizing as

> to set someone up to fall, providing them with just the barest sliver of agency necessary to render them blameworthy ... And to add insult to injury, the [neoliberal] social order alternates between declaring [disadvantaged groups'] plight a deserved result of morally culpable decisions and congratulating itself for generously providing opportunities for individuals to succeed despite their background.[70]

In summary, the historical overlap of faith-based organizations and the shrinking of the neoliberal state is not simply historical coincidence or cost-cutting convenience. Rather, it is emblematic of the popularity of a kind of morality shared broadly in society that builds around choice, freedom and responsibility the remits of the relative spheres of state and civil society and the responsibilities of the citizen within them.[71]

How should we respond to this theologically? On 25 March 1963, the 29-year-old boxer Davey Moore died following injuries sustained during a fight with Sugar Ramos.

The next year, Bob Dylan performed a song interrogating the event, called 'Who Killed Davey Moore?', in a concert at the Philharmonic Hall. In each verse of the song, a new character in the story of the fight is introduced: crowd, gambler, referee, manager, sports writer and, ultimately, the opposition boxer, all of whom deny responsibility for the death. 'Not us,' says the crowd, though they found their spectacle there. 'Not I,' says the referee, constrained by the rules. 'Not me,' says the boxing manager puffing on his cigar. The sportswriter pleads innocence too, and Ramos concludes the song: 'I hit him, yes, it's true, but that's what I'm paid to do.' Each time Dylan sings with increasing desperation in response to these protestations the refrain: 'who killed Davey Moore, why an' what's the reason for?'

The association of choice, freedom and poverty elucidated by Kotsko highlights two issues. First, that food banks are caught up in a secular society's search for righteousness; the existence of food banks is indicative of an excess, rather than deficit, of morality. Second, that this morality is reciprocally constructed; in this instance, the poor have failed to express their autonomy and agency in a way that contributes back to the commons. The poor have broken the law of return and it is not simply legitimate but necessary to jettison them to their fate, how else will they learn? However, unlike neoliberalism which presumes distinct debtors and creditors, the implicit assumption of Dylan's song is that at its most basic, and tragic, guilt is the denial of culpability. Who is responsible for the rise of British food banks? Not the government, we are told, not the food industry, not the food banks themselves, not the churches who support them or the people who go to them, not the financiers, and yet still somehow they exist, causelessly. The theological contribution to this conversation, developed from the giftedness of creation, is that everyone stands in debt to God for the gift of life. And, second, that everyone who has benefited through welfare payments, wages or rents from this economy has profited from the pollution and erosion of the earth, from deforestation and the displacement of indigenous people *and* from the hard work and imagination of past generations. The real fallacy here is sustained in the widespread assumption, cherished by many and manipulated by a small minority, that the world did not exist in a meaningful way before they were born. Working through the giftedness of creation in economic and political terms is a major part of the next chapter.

The third narrative Williams identifies (which should probably be called '2b') elaborates on the overlap of food bank and neoliberalism by reflecting further on the question of worldview and the things food banks do day to day: 'the ways in which the discourses of charity constructed in the organisational practices of food banks might serve to uphold and further embed neoliberal ideologies of welfare by elevating a modus operandi in keeping with dominant discourses of dependency, deservingness and self-responsibility.'[72] This is a complex way of saying that food banks reinforce the dominant culture. One example of this for Williams is the voucher system which institutionalizes 'a calculation of "genuine need" – thus implicitly betraying a moral judgement of who is considered "deserving" and "undeserving" of food assistance'.[73] While there are a number of possible rationales for using vouchers: managing the food bank's stock, keeping track of referrers, checking the possible dependency of clients, being accountable to food bank supporters and keeping records of food bank referral causes, Williams thinks that this system is the most vivid example of the incorporation of neoliberal ways of thinking into the practices of the food bank. The voucher system introduces a degree of bureaucracy and the demonstration of compliance into the process of accessing the service (even if you self-refer). The voucher, which the food bank volunteer checks on the Trussell Trust user database, is a part of a decision-making process of whether this person needs and deserves the food.

A number of social scientists, including Williams and his co-authors, have written about charities as 'places of care'.[74] But Williams also points to a body of literature that highlights 'the "darker side" to food bank environments, and in particular the emotional nexus of shame, stigma, and gratitude [that some] argue is experienced by many food aid recipients'.[75] What is it like to exhibit publicly your lack of ability to feed yourself and your loved ones? What is it like to receive surplus food that might be close to out of date? Or ask for food that can be eaten straightaway because you don't have a home or the electricity and gas has been turned off? In an article for *Anthropology Today*, Pat Caplan wrote that 'many clients of food banks consider themselves and are considered by others, to be stigmatized ... they see themselves as failures, excluded from normal society ... they have internalized the stigma, because worth and self-worth are measured in terms of the ability to stand on one's own two feet, be independent of others, and exercise choice.'[76] Do people experience interactions with volunteers 'in which clear hierarchies of provider and recipient are upheld'?[77] For Caplan, the tendency for those receiving food parcels to promise that they will give back to the food bank when they can, or become volunteers themselves, shows that an imbalance is intuited by some users, who seek a mode of redress.[78]

The fourth narrative criticizes food banks for distracting their volunteers and organizers from more emancipatory forms of actions, a question Williams addresses by asking what impact volunteering at the food bank has on the volunteers themselves. While I am not aware of any extensive datasets which compare attitudes held by volunteers before they start at the food bank and their views after volunteering for a period, Williams puts forward anecdotal evidence that suggests that volunteers can change in diverse ways. The cumulative effect of the volunteer–client power imbalance and the technologies of rationing is that it is possible that there are kinds of encounter between client and volunteer in which the volunteer's receptiveness to the client is closed down, not opened up, by the engagement. Williams says: 'food banks can "politicise" volunteers in another direction; whereby individuals learn to accept as necessary and just a set of exclusionary technologies predicated on calculations of "deservingness", rationing and "dependency".'[79] Williams notes that 'scholars have also critiqued the ethos of charity claimed and performed by volunteers and supporters of food banks' by asking whether food banks 'diminish activism by "assuaging liberal guilt"', helping the volunteer to feel better about themselves while potentially placating 'political action that might otherwise be put towards more just alternatives'.[80] Can volunteering contribute to a sense of finality that leads to political lethargy (Popppendieck) or a sense of ethical satisfaction in having acted on the good (the 'moral selving' that Allahyari identifies as a part of what volunteers act out and achieve through their good works)?[81]

The Christian theological overlay of these social interactions can heighten the problem, rather than diminish it. De Souza's account of two different food banks, one of which, Ruby's Pantry, is run by a conservative evangelical church, demonstrates how volunteering may be problematic not because it gives too little but because it takes too much. De Souza records sayings and teachings given through the church's website by the church's pastor and food bank founder Lyn Sahr in her book. These letters 'articulate, interpret, and unify the values and mission of Ruby's Pantry' and in de Souza's estimation, 'seamlessly [narrate] Christian doctrine in relation to neoliberal values of individualism, entrepreneurialism, freedom of choice, and minimal Government'.[82] In a letter dated from February 2016, Sahr 'invokes Christian imagery of the death and resurrection of Christ' when talking about the significance of the work done by Ruby's Pantry's 15,000 volunteers.[83] Sahr says: '[The volunteers] lay down their life for four or five hours for our guests at each distribution. Thank you for all you do! Volunteers are the lifeblood of our organisation.'[84] What Sahr identifies is, as we saw in John's Gospel, a confluence of the sacrifice made by the Christian with the sacrifice made by Christ. Read in the light of Berry's claim that our problem is taking without returning, we have here the hunger of the poor facilitating the holiness of the Christian. Is giving food, money or the time to distribute food sufficient to legitimize identifying with the crucified God?

For Williams et al. there are significant truths to aspects of these claims and they cannot be simply sidelined or off-handedly dismissed. The shrinking of the welfare state and growth of civil society as a (perceived) legitimate site for the reduction or mitigation of poverty is an issue Williams is significantly concerned by, as is the environmental catastrophe we are already living through. UK government job centres signpost to local food banks (though in County Durham they do not have access to the food bank vouchers and do not make referrals), and many food bank clients need food banks because of delays over accessing or retaining benefits. Williams sees a complicated relationship between state and civil society in the current mixed economy of welfare. Food banks may be inadvertently contributing to a shifting political landscape by taking local authority funding following the abolition of community care grants and crisis loans in 2013 and expectations from central government that these withdrawn services would be covered by local welfare schemes, including food banks.[85] Williams seems to tend towards scrapping the voucher system because it reinforces neoliberal differentiation of deserving and undeserving, despite the 'widespread public as well as political support for such systems – praised for ensuring assistance is only provided to those who are most "deserving" of help'.[86]

Four narratives: (1) food banks depend on an unsustainable food economy; (2) they legitimize the diminishing of the responsibility of the state; (3) they inculcate punitive modes of thought; (4) they shortcut people's sense of justice by giving them an unwarranted sense of satisfaction. What these narratives miss, Williams says, is the complexity, diversity and contradictions of the British food aid environment. Along with the growing antagonism between food banks and the UK government that has already been noted in Chapter 2, there are also the stories of care and community noted at the beginning of this chapter, which Williams also values.

## Part Three: differentiating food banks from the neoliberal

Williams says that

> longitudinal analysis of client experience, for instance, suggests food banks often come *after* difficult and stigmatising interviews with other kinds of welfare official, and may sometimes be performatively easier than these previous encounters. Equally while the first visit may be difficult subsequent visits may be a lot easier when the unknown turns into a hospitable 'known'.[87]

To this, Williams and his co-writers add common underestimations of the diversity of food banks in the current food bank literature, which includes 'a number of independent food banks [which] have taken a deliberate decision not to operate a rationing/voucher system, preferring instead to operate according to an ethos of direct access and/or unconditionality'.[88] There can even be diversity within different food banks in the same franchise, with the range of religious, social and political outlooks held by food bank staff and volunteers affecting how food banks are experienced by their clients. Williams concludes the article by making a number of points that are salient for our study. First, food banks can be places where volunteers are transformed. Volunteers can be sensitized to food bank users' stories and the article quotes from a volunteer called Lydia who reiterated this:

> I think my approach was quite patronizing when I started. I had an idea that it's a good thing to do, to help people in need. Which is fine. But ... I don't think I'd really thought about it in terms of poverty particularly ... I didn't have any strong political views; I wasn't very politically aware. And I think gradually it made me look at the bigger picture, and start to look at some of the causes. Whereas initially I was motivated a lot by a sense of just grace, I suddenly became more integrated with a sense of injustice and feeling that more needed to be done to address the causes of that. And actually, just the experience of sitting down and talking to people had an effect on what I did with the rest of my life.

Some volunteers moved from apolitical stances to active political engagement, joining anti-austerity groups, writing to local and national political representatives on issues of food justice. Victoria, a former student of Durham University whom I have already quoted, told me a similar story of how volunteering at the food bank had changed her outlook, her plans for the future and brought her home to truths she already believed about herself but until then hadn't been able to realize. Volunteering

> challenged me a lot, and I learnt a lot. I enjoyed my degree so much but I started to feel towards the end of it that actually like studying and writing and reading books was starting to get in the way of the things I wanted to be doing. And that actually I wanted to be out there supporting people and if I went down an academic role or particular jobs that English grads normally went for I could end up very closed off from ordinary people, locked in an office or in a library, disconnected from a lot of what was going on in the world ... I think it was a feeling that I'd had for ages, actually, feeling that there was stuff I was supposed to be doing, to be helpful, that I wasn't doing. So being at the food bank, partly it showed me ways of being helpful and things that I could be doing, but also, more, the problems that people were facing.

Later on she told me, in the same vein,

> I would say I had no idea what hope was until I started volunteering at the food bank because I didn't need it. Because my life was

fine and I had enough to eat and I knew that I was saved or knew Jesus or however you want to phrase that. And so I had no need for hope or need for an understanding of it. But actually seeing people who do need hope was a completely different and new experience for me and they were very much linked. On the one hand there is the whole big redemption-future-what happens when I die thing but also there's that immediate God cares for you now and God cares about you making it through today as much as the next however many years and eternity. And it's not something I understood at all, I don't think, until I came to the food bank.

Second, these changes in the volunteers point Williams to another issue that can be under-represented: the agency and power of food bank clients to shape encounters and foment change. Admittedly constrained by the need to maximize the chance of receiving aid and conform to the intuited norm, food bank users still nevertheless sometimes refuse to be typecast as 'somehow responsible for their plight' or as 'victims of personal misfortune'.[89] Williams found food bank users 'sought to give volunteers insight into the lived experience of systemic processes of labour and housing market insecurity, for example, or the Kafkaesque system welfare recipients must increasingly negotiate'.[90] These changes in both clients and volunteers give Williams hope that food banks might 'rework, reinforce and generate new and progressive political sensibilities among food bank volunteers and clients' and become spaces that 'help catalyse wider food justice campaigns that seek to address deeper inequalities in the food system'.[91] There are also many important, small ways in which 'both clients and volunteers frequently adopted a range of strategies seemingly designed to reduce inequalities of power between them': humour, prayer, conversations about shared interests, meeting up after the food bank, ways in which the hierarchy of giver and receiver are broken down in everyday and ordinary encounters.[92]

In theological terms, the transformation of the volunteer and the agency of the food bank client suggest that God is inclined to take surprising forms. The Hebrew Bible is replete with stories of the holy people's dependence on the alien, as the Anglican theologian Sam Wells notes:

It is Melchizedek who brings out bread and wine and blesses Abraham. It is Pharaoh whose 'fat cows' sustain Jacob's family in times of hardship. It is Balaam who blesses Israel in the sight of her enemy Balak. It is Ruth who demonstrates the faithfulness and imagination that Israel will need under her descendant David. It is Achish of Garth who gives a safe home to David and his followers when they are pursued by Saul ... Israel depends on these strangers. Strangers are not simply a threat. They are not all characterized by the hard-hearted hostility of Moses' Pharaoh, of Goliath of Gath ... Time and again strangers are the hands and feet of God, rescuing, restoring, and reminding Israel as elsewhere God does himself.[93]

In twentieth-century theology it is the Liberation Theology movement which began in South America that has most faithfully defended this insight and born witness to God's commitment to, presence with and mediation through the words and deeds of the poor. Reflecting on the poor's call for freedom from poverty and the church's growing responsiveness to this, Gustavo Gutiérrez writes that 'the breakthrough of the poor in Latin American society and the Latin American church is in the final analysis a breakthrough of God in our lives'.[94] When the poor call for fullness of life and justice Gutiérrez hears God's word being spoken. The appropriate response to the actions of God brought close by the testimonies of the food bank client is 'conversion': 'the change called for is not simply an interior one', Gutiérrez says, 'but one that involves the entire person as a corporeal being ... and therefore also has consequences for the web of social relation of which the individual is a part.'[95] In the Hebrew Bible God works through the alien; on the road to Emmaus Jesus comes to his own followers as a stranger; for Lydia and Victoria the food bank's users had brought them something divine.

## Conclusion

Food banks are contradictory spaces: relational but hierarchical, participatory but predicated on kinds of marginalization, inclusive but not in socially legitimate ways, distributive but extractive, hospitable and stigmatizing. Those who have been to the gym will be familiar with running very fast but going nowhere on the treadmill; those who have had children with the hard work of walking up and down in the same dark room with a baby in one's arms in order to facilitate the nothingness of sleep; those who have seen a spinning top know that it is its speed that keeps it stationary; a similar conscientious futility marks charity in neoliberal times, as Berry himself has noted.[96] The problem is not simply that neoliberalism will undermine any form of participation that inhibits participation in the market: even using hunger as a disciplinary tool (denying to the poor even the peace of being one with, or participating in, their own body). Neoliberalism is also insidious enough to shape our perceived solutions to the problems it itself generates, in this case food banking.

In relation to the question of food banks' cause it is difficult to identify categorically a primary agent. It maybe, as Berry says, that the problem is deeper and more troubling than the level of policy and government, that it resides in a human at variance with itself. Berry writes 'too much that we do is done at the expense of something else, or somebody else. There is some intransigent destructiveness in us.'[97] And he goes on to say that 'it is not from ourselves that we will learn to be better than we are'.[98] In an essay written the same year, 1968, which chimes in with much of the UK's political present, Berry says:

> I am struggling, amid all the current political uproar, to keep clearly in mind that it is *not* merely because our policies are wrong that we are so destructive and violent. It goes deeper than that and is more troubling. We are so little at peace with ourselves and our neighbours because we are not at peace with our place in the world, our land ... Until we end our violence against the earth – a matter ignored by most pacifists, as the issue of military violence is ignored by most conservationists – how can we hope to end our violence against each other?[99]

Articulating a frame in which this destructiveness can be, at least partially, resolved will be a major part of the next chapter.

Furthermore, one of the consequences of the analysis presented in this chapter is that the continuity of food banks and neoliberalism means that reforms within food banks themselves (such as removing food access conditionality or promoting the 'drop-in' model) will only have a limited effect on the problem of hunger and ecological regeneration. Food banks cement and institutionalize the point at which violence to the land and to other people hold hands. Taking food banks seriously means looking at what lies around them. For Allen, instead of food aid, the church should focus on radical hospitality.[100] Rather than make repeated claims for increased consumer spending power for the poor achieved through the means of manipulating the leavers of the welfare state, the church should restate publicly and act out visibly its own radical heritage.[101] The church should

> use its own vast and underused land wealth to create community allotments and encourage collective practices of cultivation in each of its parishes. It would also procure expertise, tools, materials, and seeds for urban agriculturalists that might otherwise lack the requisite knowledge and finance to successfully cultivate community allotments.[102]

He continues: as well as transforming its own land, a

> land activist church would note that food poverty in cities like Liverpool sits within walking distance of 'land banks' that were acquired by forcibly evicting poor families from their homes and that are now awaiting prestige development 'when economic conditions are right'. It would take the view that such a situation dishonours God's 'common treasury' and violates our memberships-in-creation. Like the Diggers and contemporary peasants' movements in Latin America, it would morally reclaim and physically occupy such land in order to create new collective food growing spaces, even though this would involve violating private property rights.[103]

The strength of Allen's essay, along with these sensible suggestions, is his attempt to situate Christian engagement with questions of food, justice and practice in the context of God's making and sustaining of the world. Like Allen, I see food banks as blemished by the imaginative, economic and political context in which they have been embodied and the norms of that context that they (sometimes) reproduce. Unlike his analysis, the evidence suggests to me that they have not been completely determined by the times in which they have occurred; Williams' account of their contradictory dynamics better suits my findings in County Durham and the available academic literature: that they partially but incompletely realized 'The Law of Return', the principle of participation. In addition to Allen's aforementioned article's suggestions and in accord with his own theological commitments to the whole world sharing in a 'communism of being', a more plausible articulation of the Christian worldview needs to include, I believe, the confronting and re-narrating of our imaginative, economic and political lives together. Sidestepping the entrenched neoliberalism of recent governments by focusing exclusively on the church or just reforming food banks' internal practices both leave the real problems in place. Facing up to the complexity of the food bank asks instead for the articulation and embodying of a viable alternative for the state, the market and the church, with the aim of making peace with each other and the land we have been given.

# 5

# Political, Ecclesial and Personal Participation

## Introduction

Before proceeding to ask 'What next for Christians concerned with British food insecurity?' it is worth pausing and taking stock of how this book has progressed so far and what this progress suggests for the final chapter. Chapter 3 argued that Christian communities have been inclined by their scriptures and history to see food as a sacrament, a means to know God. To call food sacramental is simply a technical way of saying that food is relational, it is an important part of how participation in the world and each other and the divine is made flesh. The potency of food lies, furthermore, in its ability to either obscure or disclose the Christian belief that the world is to be received humbly, attentively and conscientiously as a great gift. Wirzba summarizes this sentiment and the appropriate response when he writes that

> life is a miraculous, inexplicable gift. It exceeds all economies of exchange. We stand within it, beggar-like, unable to receive it fully or properly because whatever we would claim or take already exceeds our longing and comprehension. The best we can do is make our lives into an offering to others.[1]

The problem with food banks, as explored in Chapter 4, is that they are insufficiently sacramental. Food banks fall short of giving adequate expression to the multiple relationships in which the human is suspended. They have distinct positives, Christian action on food insecurity is theologically legitimate and food banks present a means for expressing this insight. Likewise, food banks can be places of profound encounter, exchange and transformation, and in a society in which isolation is endemic and people are often starved of sympathy these are crucial things to facilitate. But food banks can also be places where people feel profound shame and differences between volunteer and recipient are reinforced rather than broken down, in which status is extracted rather than given and responsibility is denied rather than recognized. In particular, food banks' dependence on an unsustainable and market-driven food industry that has little or no place for nature's intrinsic value is theologically unsatisfactory.

Food banks are a good example of how neoliberalism is chiastic, as the book's introduction suggested. On the one hand, UK food banks have been colonized by neoliberal ways of thinking and acting, pulled into the neoliberal totality as both 'solution' and agent of dissemination. On the other hand, combining the Conservative Party's narrative of civil society and the state working as distinct but complementary partners (discussed in the book's introduction and first two chapters) and Alexander Schmemann's rejection of the dividing of the world into discrete 'sacred' and 'profane' spheres, which in effect denies that the whole world has been taken up and transformed in Christ's eucharistic body (as discussed in Chapter 3), food banks are symptomatic of a tendency in modern Christianity to concede the completeness of Christ's reconciliation of the whole and sunder what should be held together. Neoliberalism, as the old adage goes, divides in order to rule and rules by further dividing.

For the church, then, the task is clear: to disclose more transparently that God has through the incarnation made all of creation the sign and means of God's presence. Thinking of the world as communion means elucidating a frame in which relationship with God, each other and the natural world are in complementary peace. So, what is the next step for Christians who are concerned with food insecurity? First, this chapter surveys the current solutions to the food bank upsurge and suggests, based on the analysis of precariousness developed in earlier chapters, that they fall short of being an adequate response to the complexity of the current labour market, while these solutions also retain invidious distinctions (like that between welfare and work, deserving and undeserving poor, and voluntary and paid labour) which make them theologically problematic. Increasing benefits to meet widely accepted minimum income standards and raising the minimum wage, the key demands of contemporary food activists, would be steps in the right direction but they still leave questions unanswered and problems unresolved.

Therefore, the chapter proceeds to explore three ways participation may be served, reciprocity incarnated and sacramentality furthered in British social, agricultural and ecclesiological life. First, the chapter examines an idea, popular across the political spectrum, called Universal Basic Income (UBI). Is UBI, enough money for dignified living, paid to everyone regularly, in perpetuity and unconditionally, a credible way to show that all people are individually valuable while also putting money into a positive feedback loop with the natural and social histories which are the necessary conditions of its occurring? The first part argues that it is. Second, recalling the contempt, the egregious neglect bordering on active maltreatment, shown by successive governments to the British poor recounted in the first two chapters of this book, the third part of this chapter asks whether it is possible in good faith for the Church of England to remain an 'established' church. The historical tendency for the plural and diverse Christian community to see the state as a useful institution (either in positive terms with Aquinas, as a way of realizing the common good, or in more cautionary terms with Augustine, as a way of limiting violence) does not absolve the current Church of England from submitting itself to a process of collective deliberation around this issue.[2] Asking whether this state, in its recent history, and these governments deserve a chaplain to wash their hands, or whether they would be better served, along with the people of this country and its natural habitats, by prophetic dissociation is the question raised in Part Three. Finally, the chapter closes by asking the agrarian question: what patterns of consumption and modes of agricultural production would allow us to live not just sustainably but restoratively within the territorial boundaries of the United Kingdom?[3] In particular, this part endorses agrarian permaculture and the return of the land to the people and the people to the land as a way to increase our food supply and simultaneously to lower our carbon emissions. Alongside this, the chapter concludes by suggesting that a critical engagement with the question of the Christian diet, reduced meat and dairy consumption or vegan and vegetarian diets, presents an important means for exhibiting Christian distinctiveness and publicly acknowledging thankfulness for life, concern for the poor and willingness to make space for the other.

## Part One: wages and benefits

A series of proposals have been put forward by members of parliament and civil society activists for addressing the current food insecurity crisis in the UK. In 2013, Frank Field MP and Laura Sandys MP launched the All-Party Parliamentary Group (APPG) on Hunger and Food Poverty, renamed the APPG on Hunger in 2015.[4] In the spring of 2014 an official inquiry into hunger was commissioned by the APPG, chaired by the Church of England Bishop Tim Thornton and Frank Field. The aim of the inquiry was to outline the spread of hunger in the

UK, its causes and possible remedies, along with how food insecurity fits into the UK's current 'food model'.[5] The team were also interested in charting the availability, sustainability and utility of the UK's emergency food bank network.[6] The initial report, *Feeding Britain*, made extensive recommendations and presented its findings on three key areas. First, that food banks are staying for the medium term, given that 'turning around ... those deep-seated economic forces that have so disadvantaged most, but particularly poorer families, [are not] going to be achieved in the short term'.[7] The second key area, they say, is 'minimizing demand', freeing food bank volunteers to 'focus instead on using food as a gateway to provide intensive care and support to individuals who urgently need befriending and whose lives are often most challenging' due to addiction, debt, social isolation and physical and/or mental health difficulties.[8] Third, the APPG's 'anger knows no bounds' when faced with current food waste when it could be used, the authors claim, to eliminate food insecurity.[9] The relationship between the medium/long-term need for food banks, the call for government intervention in the labour market through a 'higher national minimum wage', cuts to income taxes for lower earners and a 'fairer and more reliable benefits systems' are not fully worked out but should, we are informed, help lead to a zero hunger Britain, the authors' aim.[10]

These recommendations have been taken up both by End Hunger UK, a leading anti-hunger campaign group in the UK, and by the Trussell Trust. The demand for benefits reform and increased wages have traction with both religious and secular stakeholders and exhibit an adherence to the logic of participation. They are both legitimate if incomplete answers to the question: what is necessary for personal health and dignified involvement in public life? If realized (and even *Feeding Britain* is unsure of this), they would be significant improvements on our current arrangement and take us notably closer to a shared life that is in accord with Christian values and ideals. However, both suggestions – increased minimum wages and increased benefits – have limitations which require further discussion.

Leaving aside the lack of political will for more progressive welfare reforms and taxation, it has been asked whether increased minimum wages and benefits are an appropriate response for a highly precarious labour market. According to the Anglican Priest Malcolm Torry, who defends a Universal Basic Income as an alternative and Christian social policy, 'communication and information technology is dispensing with jobs of many different kinds; employment patterns are increasingly diverse and precarious; and family structures are increasingly diverse. Our benefits system, designed for a different era, is increasingly unable to cope.'[11] Increasing benefits is good but it still leaves the transitioning from benefits into work or back again fraught with risks, periods of destitution and, sometimes, very little financial gain (the issue of 'marginal deductions'). Furthermore, what about the relationship between our economy and the environment? Incorporating more workers or sharing the fiscal proceeds of an economy that is unsustainable is not a long-term solution; ecological limits need to be factored into these political solutions.

The result of the *Feeding Britain* report was Feeding Britain the charity, set up to co-ordinate the work of government, charities and businesses that are concerned with the issue of food insecurity. Feeding Britain, the campaigning group, have had some successes since their initial report in 2014. The most outstanding of these, led by Emma Lewell-Buck MP, was the government's agreement to include the United States Department of Agriculture's Household Food Security questions in the next Food Standards Agency's 'Food and You' survey.[12] However, even if Feeding Britain's most substantial policy suggestions were implemented, the work of Guy Standing suggests that they are not appropriate for our current economic and ecological circumstances. Standing says that increasing the minimum wage is likely to 'work well in an industrial labour market in which stable full-time jobs predominate' and there is full employment, with strong bargaining institutions for labour, but that in our times of precarious employment with people moving between jobs or suspended on zero-hour contracts a rise in the minimum wage is redundant for many of those most in need.[13] What use is it getting paid more per hour when you do not get any hours? For Standing, there are further problems with the proposal for minimum wage increases. He notes that enforcing the minimum wage has been difficult thus far,[14] that it fails to address the major issue of our current differentiation between work that is paid ('productive' labour, traditionally male) and work that is unpaid ('reproductive' labour, including volunteering, traditionally female), and can, counter-intuitively, even lead to reduced incomes for low-paid workers, as cleaners at the government's tax office (HMRC) found out in 2015.[15] That said, there is evidence that minimum-wage/living-wage increases have added significantly to the incomes of low-paid workers and that the overall price inflation associated with companies passing on increased costs to consumers has been exaggerated, the real concern, according to Giulia Giupponi and Professor Stephen Machin, is whether employers have compromised on quality by reducing hours.[16]

Raising the level of benefits to meet minimum income standards also has limitations as a long-term solution, though it would be welcome in the short term. Standing notes that benefits conditionality is very expensive to administer,[17] while Mark Fisher correctly observes that the neoliberal promise to increase freedom and reduce bureaucracy has never been fulfilled.[18]

> [W]ith the triumph of neoliberalism, bureaucracy was supposed to have been made obsolete; a relic of an unlamented Stalinist past. Yet this is at odds with the experiences of most people working and living in late capitalism ... instead of disappearing, bureaucracy has changed its form; and this new, decentralized, form has allowed it to proliferate.[19]

Do higher benefits levels mean sustained intrusions, questions, stipulations, forms, appointments, queues, documents, errors and (consequently) under-claiming that marks the experience of people currently depending on the benefits system?[20] Alongside Richard Titmuss saying that 'state benefits that are only for the poor are invariably poor benefits', there is also the theological question about how to appropriately institutionalize humans' participation in each other, the divine and the natural world.[21] According to the aim of instituting a kind of participation that is reciprocal and holistic, would these increased out-of-work benefits include conditionality and sufficiently empower people to give back substantially to the commons? Could you still be sanctioned for failing to attend your Job Centre Plus stipulated CV-building seminar and can Christians who believe in the unsolicited generosity of God support such correctives? Are starving people and making them homeless legitimate disciplinary tools for those who toil for Christ?

## Part Two: participating in people – Universal Basic Income

It is in part the limits of the suggestion that increased minimum wages and benefits are an adequate response to our current situation that recommends Universal Basic Income to Standing. UBI is an idea shared by a number of authors drawn upon in this book and is justified by divergent aims.[22] For Kotsko, 'our present political moment is the beginning of a struggle to withdraw consent from the neoliberal order by developing a new and more meaningful conception of freedom' and UBI is conducive to this task because it would 'free us from the compulsion to sell our labor power on the market' and marks a 'break with the basic premise of the capitalist system by decoupling income from labor for the entire population rather than for the capitalist class alone'.[23]

Srnicek and Williams write that 'drawing upon moral arguments and empirical research, there are a vast number of reasons to support a UBI: reduced poverty, better public health and reduced health costs, fewer high school dropouts, reductions in petty crime, more time with family and friends, and less state bureaucracy'.[24] Within the general context of offsetting fears around lost employment as new technologies are implemented in the economy, Srnicek and Williams highlight four reasons in particular why UBI is desirable: first, alienated from the means to provide their own subsistence, the poor are forced into the market to sell their labour, but a UBI gives the poor power to choose which work they take and at what cost.[25] Second, UBI retains labour flexibility but sheers it of its anxiety, it 'responds to this generalisation of precarity and transforms it from a state to be feared back into a state of liberation'; third, it would force us to consider the real value of different forms of work, essential work that is boring, hazardous and unattractive would no longer be forced on the poor as 'the *nature* of work would become a measure of its value, not merely its *profitability*'; fourth, they write that UBI is a 'fundamentally feminist proposal' because it 'recognises the contributions of unwaged domestic labourers to the reproduction of society and provides them with an income accordingly'.[26] With contrasting priorities, the American libertarian Matt Zwolinski and the London-based anarchist David Graeber converge on UBI as a way to reduce the remit of the state.[27]

Standing defines UBI as 'a modest amount of money paid unconditionally to individuals on a regular basis'.[28] First, then, it is 'basic': 'an amount that would enable someone to survive *in extremis*, in the society they live in'.[29] The minimum should include 'basic security in terms of being able to obtain enough to eat and a place to live, an opportunity to learn and access to medical care' and be set at either 'the highest amount that is sustainable, and as close as possible to an "above-poverty" level' or started 'at a low level and ... built up gradually, determined by the size of a fund set up for the purpose and the level and change in national income'.[30] For Torry and Standing, 'universal' means 'paid to everyone usually resident in a given community, province or country'.[31] It would be paid to individuals, unlike current means-tested benefits which are paid to households, with possible differences in payment between the old, young and those of working age.[32] By 'unconditional', Standing means (1) 'there would be no income conditions', it is for the rich and the poor; (2) there 'would be no spending conditions'; (3) 'there would be no behavioural conditions ... such as taking jobs or particular types of jobs, or being willing to do so in order to qualify for the basic income'.[33] It would furthermore be regular and non-withdrawable, an economic right that could be relied upon and would reduce the uncertainty of the current labour market and benefits system.[34]

Torry and Standing note a series of other strengths to UBI. First, a UBI would help reduce food insecurity. There is evidence from pilot schemes that 'shows that cash payments improve nutrition and health, particularly for babies and children, but also for the frail and disabled'.[35] In a study carried out in Canada, 'the prevalence of food insecurity was cut by nearly 50% among low-income single-person households who were food insecure after the age of 65'.[36] In its 2015 annual report, on the back of growing food bank use following the 2008 economic crash, Food Banks Canada put a UBI as their number one policy suggestion.[37] In research carried out for the World Food Program (WFP), researchers for the International Food Policy Research Institute found that in three out of four cases cash transfers were more effective than food aid (in the fourth, lack of food availability and price predictability meant food recipients rather than cash recipients fared better).[38]

Second, unlike the current tax and spend system which is partially participatory in soliciting funds and distributing them, UBI includes the allocation of dividends to everyone. Participation, ecological and theological, is a feature of UBI that can be seen in a founding essay of the movement, *Agrarian Justice* by Thomas Paine. The radical eighteenth-century democrat begins by distinguishing between two forms of property that overlap but cannot be fully conflated. He writes:

> There are two kinds of property. Firstly, natural property or that which comes to us from the Creator of the universe – such as the earth, air, water. Secondly, artificial or acquired property – the invention of men.[39]

On this first kind of property, our dependence on the gift of creation, Paine says:

> It is a position not to be controverted that the earth, in its natural uncultivated state was, and ever would have continued to be, *the common property of the human race*. In that state every man would have been born to property. He would have been a joint life proprietor with the rest in the property of the soil, and in all its natural productions, vegetable and animal.[40]

For Paine, to recognize and institutionalize this basic common ground, everyone who owns a part of the land should pay a 'groundrent ... for the land which he holds' because 'man did not make the earth, and, though he had a natural right to *occupy* it, he had no right to *locate as his property* in perpetuity any part of it; neither did the creator of the earth open a landoffice, from whence the first title-deeds should issue'.[41] From this groundrent, Paine goes on to argue that a fund should be created that pays out to each individual when they reach 21 and yearly thereafter, as a human right, not an act of charity.[42] Paine's argument has a positive ecological logic to it: wealth shared stems from an earth shared, and future wealth in which all are invested depends on the health and sustainability of the earth.[43] Second, Paine says there should be a second tax on wealth to complement the first on land. Paine does not deny the right to private property, but does contend that all wealth depends to lesser or greater degree on the aggregate achievements of past generations.[44] All productivity has social and historical elements: 'personal property is *the effect of society*; and it is as impossible for an individual to acquire personal property without the aid of society, as it is for him to make land originally'.[45] Our failure to retain in our minds the intimate links between state innovation and private profits, along with our liability to sustain the fallacy that the state impedes business, is indicative of the pertinence of Paine's points and our need to hear him again.[46]

For Paine a UBI is an individual right and a due given our sociality as creatures and embeddedness in history. Paid to every person it honours what we have in common while also partially helping to 'prevent invidious distinctions' between social groups.[47] Paine asks: rather than 'make some provision for persons becoming poor and wretched ... would it not, even as a matter of economy, be far better to adopt means to prevent their becoming poor?'[48] Poverty is detrimental to the poor and the rich, Paine continues, for it is 'impossible to enjoy affluence with the felicity it is capable of being enjoyed, whilst so much misery is mingled in the scene'.[49] 'The sight of misery and the unpleasant sensations it suggests', which, though 'they may be suffocated cannot be extinguished', is a greater burden on the rich than the proposed amount the rich would have to contribute.[50] In sum, 'he that would not give the one to get rid of the other has no charity, even for himself'.[51]

George Monbiot reiterates aspects of Paine's thought, writing that 'the idea of building a national social wealth fund from the fees charged to those who use assets they did not create is appealing for several reasons'.[52] Building on the work of the land activist Martin Adams, he suggests that those who use the land should pay a 'community land contribution' (scaled according to land value).[53] This is not a tax, Monbiot says, but a 'fee for services rendered: a return to the public of the benefits we have donated to the landlords'.[54] Held by local or national government, these funds (potentially supplemented by tax reforms, a tax on financial transactions, or a tax on shareholding) could be used to launch a national social welfare fund which pays out a UBI to all citizens.[55] However, Monbiot rightly warns that value 'does not always divide neatly between "natural" and "acquired" property, to use Thomas Paine's distinction' and that 'to determine which community should fairly benefit from a natural or common resource, who qualifies as a member of this commons, and how they should best be compensated for the use of their resources' will not be an easy task.[56] He continues, 'whatever we do to create a fairer, more inclusive system will be messy, incomplete and subject to constant negotiation', and notes that even if a UBI were instigated it could be used as a means to either supplement low wages or justify the removal of social services.[57]

Critiquing UBI on the grounds that payments given to individuals will undermine the family,[58] or that providing people enough to feed and house themselves will diminish their desire to work,[59] are difficult to plausibly sustain given the current benefits arrangement, the account of human enjoyment at being 'the cause' as discussed in Chapter 1, and the (admittedly piecemeal) evidence that has been garnered from the (very divergent and often not complete) UBI trials that have been carried out. Malcolm Torry observes that in the current system 'means-tested benefits are withdrawn as earned income rises', which means that 'additional earned income can result in very little additional disposable income. A payment that is not withdrawn does not have this effect, and so increases employment incentives.'[60] Torry is talking here about 'marginal deductions', the amount one loses of all new earnings when one transitions from benefits to paid work but loses money to income tax and National Insurance.

> A particular problem imposed by means-tested benefits is that if the claimant gets a job, or if their earnings rise, then their benefits reduce in value. For too many households, the withdrawal of benefits, at the same time as Income Tax and National Insurance Contributions have to be paid, results in a total withdrawal rate of 96 per cent, so that for every extra £1 earned, the household's net income increases by just 4p. Universal Credit will reduce the withdrawal rate to 76 per cent, but that still provides little financial incentive.[61]

Marginal deductions have direct links to current thinking on child hunger alleviation strategies. Feeding Britain have been focusing on the issue of holiday hunger, and have been promoting schools working in conjunction with food banks to provide free schools meals (FSMs) for children in danger of hunger during the holidays. Like other forms of means tests assistance, the threshold at which support is given means that anyone crossing the line loses support. In relation to FSMs, Feeding Britain say that they have 'concerns that the earnings threshold at its current level will result in a certain number of children from low income working families not receiving FSMs, and the cliff edge could disincentive some low income workers from extending their hours as this would result in a loss of FSMs'.[62] Torry compares this to the disposable income available to the wealthiest when they improve their incomes. The current tax regime means that the wealthy 'can improve their financial position by at least 53p for every extra £1 that they earn ... It is not a just society.'[63] Our anti-poverty policies disincentivize the very pro-self-help, self-sufficiency and independence they are supposed to achieve. The current system is inadequate even when considered in relation to its own criteria of success.

But the criteria for adjudicating legitimacy that has been taken from Christian theology (reciprocal participation) is not the criteria that has been identified in neoliberalism. Monbiot writes that 'the era [that] our intellectual forebears anticipated, in which the majority of humankind would be equipped with enough education and leisure to permit a general engagement with the great questions of life, has not materialised, and shows no sign of doing so'.[64] Instead of creating the economic conditions necessary for widespread deliberation over the nature of the good life, the speed, ethos of competition and economic insecurity that mark our current arrangement have contributed to declines in almost all forms of civic participation. As the London-based geographer Jane Wills says: 'data about political participation at the national scale shows a decline in almost all forms of political and civic activity'.[65] She goes on: 'data that explicitly explores feelings about civic engagement shows significant declines in both perceived influence and aspirations to shape local political life.'[66] Membership of religious organizations is down from 21% in 1981 to 4.8% in 1999, those providing welfare services for the elderly down from 8.6% to 6.8%, trade unions 19.9% to 7.3%, political parties 4.7% to 2.6%, youth work organizations from 7.6% to 5.5%.[67] For the sake of their own long-term existence, food banks and churches have a vested interest in securing an alternative economic arrangement that gives a greater sense of security.

But the rationale for UBI found in Christian defenders of the positions like Malcolm Torry's is not the longevity of the church. Torry says:

wealth is God's gift, and it is intended for the common good, and not for accumulation by a few to the exclusion of the many: so if we find that the gift has not been shared out as originally intended, then surely it is our responsibility to ensure that it should be, which means collecting resources from those who have benefited disproportionally from their position in the economy in order to pay to every individual a share of the wealth that properly belongs to everyone. A similar secular argument can be made. The physical and social capital from which we all now benefit has been built up by many generations of hard work, and it belongs to all of us, not just to a few.[68]

Torry goes on to develop analogies between (his preferred title) a 'citizen's basic income' and recurring principles in Christian theology: forgiveness, a mix of reciprocity and interdependence, universality, a blend of equality and individual dignity, a preferential option for the poor, and a valuing of work and co-creation alongside God.[69] The question of affordability is not insurmountable;[70] the claim that a UBI would lead to runaway inflation neglects both the possible impact a UBI would have on demand in the economy[71] and the current difference between productivity in the economy and the amount of money paid out in wages.[72] Standing summarizes the current affordability debate:

> The affordability issue essentially comes down to two sets of choices – how high should the basic income or social dividend be, and what are society's fiscal priorities? There is nothing sacrosanct about existing tax systems, most of which are excessively complex and highly regressive. And this is without counting the enormous sums that are lost to Government coffers through tax avoidance and evasion.[73]

The current tax regime and labour market is complex, inefficient and incoherent. It also fails to satisfactorily substantiate our participation in God, in the gift of grace that is the world and each other. Returning to story of Jesus feeding the 5,000 in the Gospel of John, it is worth recalling that Philip says that the disciples do not have enough between them to feed those who come to Christ and are hungry. Developing Chapter 3's argument that Jesus discloses both God's character and creation's nature, the issue here is not so much that Philip has failed to see who Jesus is but rather that he has failed to perceive nature's fecundity.

A significant part of why the limited UBI trails that have been carried out are so interesting is that the fiscal confidence UBI provided led to increased economic activity, with more people starting their own small businesses, retraining or going back into education.[74] Unlike current welfare that holds people in demeaning, dependent relationships, UBI could help facilitate a flourishing of our civil, political and economic lives, instituting reciprocity. Would UBI mean that the 'the streets would fill up with bad poets, annoying street mimes, and promoters of crank scientific theories', as Graeber asks?[75] Potentially, yes. But whether that is worse than the 37% to 40% of people who already feel that they have pointless ('bullshit') jobs that offer nothing back to society and the millions more who live in damp homes without enough money for good food is contestable.[76]

For Paine, a UBI offers a way to practise reception: the reception of creation as a gift from God, the denial of which is, fundamentally, the alienation of the person from the land and from God its maker. Torry says that 'if "grace" is at the root and centre of the Christian tradition, then a society will be "Christian" to the extent that it is a grace-centred society, that is, a society that forms its social policy on the basis of grace, on the basis of unconditional giving.'[77] Christianity has shaped the culture and identity of many nations, including the UK. If the UK wishes to remain in continuity with this aspect of its past, it should consider UBI. If not, it may be time for a more substantive reassessment of the relationship of the church and government, a particularly complex area for members of the Church of England given the nature of establishment.

## Part Three: participating in the church – disestablishment

Given its recent history, trusting the government to solve the issue of food insecurity is as prudent as giving all the monkeys at the safari drive-through coffee shops, spanners and mechanics' overalls and putting them in charge of windscreen wiper repairs.

In February 2014, 43 Christian leaders including 27 Anglican bishops wrote to the then Prime Minister David Cameron saying that 'as a society' we must 'face up to the fact that over half of people using food-banks have been put in that situation by cutbacks to and failures in the benefit system, whether it be payment delays or punitive sanctions'.[78] These Christian leaders assert that 'there is an acute moral imperative to act' and call on the 'Government to do its part: acting to investigate food markets that are failing, to make sure that work pays, and to ensure that the welfare system provides a robust last line of defence against hunger'.[79] Evidently, the last three governments have not in any substantial sense taken up this challenge and it follows that the onus falls once again on the church to consider the available means whereby it might escalate its actions and reiterate its demands.

Historically, one means by which the church has engaged pressing social and political problems is to produce a *status confessionis* (a statement of confession).[80] Recognizing the legitimate diversity and differences sustained under the banner 'Christian', an issue still remains as to whether indifference to the welfare of the poor is so manifest a failing that it places one beyond the boundaries of the Christian community. Is neglected responsibility in this area 'a theological position that threatens the heart of the gospel of reconciliation in Jesus Christ' and therefore beyond a 'statement of confession' by the church?[81] Karl Barth's assertion that 'in the relations and events in the life of his people, God always takes his stand unconditionally and passionately on this side and on this side alone: against the lofty and on behalf of the lowly; against those who already enjoy right and privilege and on behalf of those who are denied it and deprived of it' suggests that any policy that exasperates poverty cannot be legitimately defended (theologically or otherwise) and that, consequently, disestablishment may be mandated by fidelity to the gospel.[82] Gutiérrez endorses a similar kind of logic when he quotes from a document produced by the Latin American churches that states:

> We believe that today more than ever before the mission of the church on this continent requires the active presence of religious communities as authentic living sacraments (signs and instruments) of the reign that God exercises in favour of the poor. To this end it is urgent that [the] religious effectively dissociate themselves from the injustices of the prevailing system; that in whatever environment they find themselves they give a clear witness to evangelical poverty by their spirit, their manner of life, and their structures.[83]

Before continuing, we must first ask: what is establishment? The Church of England is an established church, with links both to how the nation is governed and to the monarch. For David Fergusson, a Scottish theologian, establishment refers historically to a variety of partnerships 'between church and state that recognise the integration of civil and church life'.[84] So, the established church may receive special privileges in exchange for services offered. The church provides ministers and ceremonies for occasions of state, births, marriages, funerals and chaplains for prisons, hospitals and schools while the state makes the church exempt from aspects of legislation, taxation or certain payments.[85] Furthermore,

> Some decisions of the church may require to be ratified or at least acknowledged by the state. The office bearers of the church may require the approval of the state in holding their appointments. The head of state may stand in ceremonial relationship to the courts and services of the church.[86]

The relationship between church and state runs both ways: with the state given a role in the life of the church, and the church in the life of the state. In England, state and church find a unity in the monarch who integrates these distinct realms. The 'Lords spiritual', 26 bishops of the Church of England who sit in the UK's second, unelected house, the House of Lords, have a role in critiquing, amending and passing government legislation. Conversely, the state has a role in the appointment of the church's leaders. The Crown Appointments Commission (CAC), working under the General Synod (the Church of England's leading group), hand the Prime Minister two possible episcopal or archiepiscopal names as the shortlist for the highest office – Archbishop of Canterbury – from which the Prime Minister chooses the final appointment. A cooperative election makes sense if society and church are intermingled in the overlapping of civil and spiritual realms[87] but is very problematic if these jurisdictions are divergent or the Prime Minister goes against the CAC recommendation and makes an alternative appointment (as is reported to have happened twice under the Prime Ministership of Margaret Thatcher and once with Tony Blair).[88]

In his book *Between Kin and Cosmopolis: An Ethic of the Nation*, the Oxford-based Christian ethicist Nigel Biggar argues that Christians should be loyal to the nation-state to the degree that it realizes and defends the good.[89] He writes, 'Insofar as a nation-state has a record of virtuous action internally and externally, shaping life well within and without its borders, it deserves a measure of affection, loyalty, and gratitude as much as any beneficent family or global charity.'[90] In an earlier text, *Good Life*, Biggar develops a series of reflections on Britain's social, moral and political life. Giving a partial defence of Margaret Thatcher on the grounds that she did intend to invigorate British communal life, he goes on to note that her 'policies have back-fired – as she was warned they would. In particular, the contraction of certain kinds of welfare provision, intended to activate the indolent, has often had the effect of rendering the poorest members of society even more helpless and desperate.'[91] 'It is one of the state's proper functions to ensure that aid is distributed *fairly* to *all* needy groups and areas within its jurisdiction,' Biggar says.[92] In his view, it is possible that 'the paternalist welfare state weakens the individual's inclination to take responsibility for the consequences of their actions' but it is still right for the state to take an active role in investing in youth workers, pro-bation services, day care facilities and family centres.[93]

Given that these services have been adversely affected by recent government cuts and the living standards of the British poor are as bad as they were in the 1980s, it follows logically that Biggar would be very concerned about a close link between the state and the church, but this does not appear to be the case when he turns to the issue of establishment.[94] Writing in a collection of essays called *The Established Church: Past, Present, and Future*, Biggar defends establishment and says that 'against establishment there are two main arguments, both of them moral, one emanating from secularists and the other from within the churches themselves'.[95] The church critique, Biggar goes on, is that establishment 'corrupts the church, constraining its freedom to speak truth to power'.[96] Biggar says that this is not a very 'considerable' prob-lem.[97] He gives three examples of when the church has distanced itself from the state despite being established:

> criticism of the Thatcher government in *Faith in the City* in 1985. Nor did it prevent the Archbishop of Canterbury (Rowan Williams) from publicly dissenting from Prime Minister Blair's decision to go to war against Iraq in 2003. Nor did it stop him from warning the current Coalition Government against using the 'Big Society' as a fig leaf for dismantling welfare provision.[98]

Biggar argues that there are good reasons for maintaining the current arrangement. He says that the 'tying of [the church's] prophetic tongue is only one situation the church should strive to avoid'; another is the refusal to accept the demanding responsibility of ruling.[99] Biggar says 'establishment in the form of episcopal participation in the work of the House of Lords helps to keep at least one major civil social body sensitive to the difficulties and complexities of the necessary tasks of government'.[100] Biggar argues that establishment safeguards the integralist, Christian vision of the natural and the supernatural participating harmoniously in each other, along with the public character of Christian confession. William Whyte, in the final chapter of *The Established Church*, puts forward the same argument when he say that establishment retains legitimacy by 'symbolically asserting the State's spiritual dimension'.[101] Establishment substantiates the principle, in the words of Biggar, that 'contrary to the populist orthodoxy that prevails among us, the moral legitimacy of government issues primarily from its faithfulness to the *given* principles of justice, and *not* from its reflection of the popular will'.[102] Furthermore, Whyte argues that part of the value of establishment is that it is at odds with the modern tendency to see 'the public sphere ... as wholly secular and religion ... as a matter of purely private concern'.[103]

In response to the secular argument 'that, since we now live in a liberal, plural society, it is unfair for any one religion to be privileged; and that public institutions and rituals should therefore be "neutral" with regard to rival views of the world', Biggar responds by saying that it is the liberal, Anglican commitment to the principle of humanism that guarantees the diversity and decency of the polity.[104] Building on the work of one of the most influential political theorists of the twentieth century, the American liberal John Rawls, Biggar writes that privileging the Church of England is legitimate for three reasons:

> First, [Anglicanism] represents a worldview that is supportive of a liberal humanist ethos; second, that its particular form of establishment has not involved civil and political penalties for non-Anglicans for well over a century; and third, that its public orthodoxy can contradict the worldviews of some citizens without offending against their equal dignity.[105]

Counter-intuitively, it is suggested with reference to a quote from Tariq Modood that an established church is good for minority religious identity: 'the minimal nature of the Anglican establishment,' Modood said, 'its proven openness to other denominations and faiths seeking public space, and the fact that its very existence is an ongoing acknowledgement of the public character of religion, are all reasons why it may be far less intimidating to the minority faiths than a triumphal secularism.'[106] Biggar's article musters a range of defences for establishment, combining theological logic, liberal commitments and attention to minority or dissenting opinions which, to be engaged fully, would take us far afield of our current concerns.

Nevertheless, the analysis of recent governments presented in the first two chapters of this book, compounded by the longer-term record of failure by the British state to address either poverty or environmental catastrophe in proportionate terms, suggest that there is a third reason why establishment may be illegitimate: the Church of England may be humanist but recent governments palpably are not. Comparing mortality rates between 2001 and 2010 with those between 2011 and 2014, for example, academics working for BMJ Open argued that approximately 45,000 people had died because of austerity spending cuts.[107] Unlike Biggar, Fergusson is more receptive to what he calls 'prophetic' rationales for disestablishment. Mirroring Biggar's first argument, Fergusson says that disestablishment advocates 'have claimed that the church's responsibility to engage in prophetic criticism of society and the government will inevitably be blunted by state involvement in the appointment of its leaders, or indeed the granting of any privileges or status by the state to the church'.[108] For Fergusson, 'the coopting of church representatives by vested interests has not ceased to be an unfamiliar problem'. He goes on to quote from an essay on the topic by the theologian Donald MacKinnon:

> Where England is concerned, the passing of Establishment as we have known it would surely lead to a day in which episcopal lawn sleeves would cease to flutter in the breeze as their wearer bestowed the diocesan benediction upon the latest Polaris submarine. Here we should find sheer gain without any loss at all.[109]

Earlier in the same book, Fergusson talks about how radical Christian groups contributed to general culture by being contrast societies. Fergusson says that some Christian radical movements in their 'discipline and community structure bear witness before the rest of society to the moral possibilities of Christian life and polity ... In their economic and social ties' groups like the Desert Fathers (discussed in Chapter 3) or the radical reformers (anabaptists) 'offer a glimpse of an alternative community under the Word of God. By doing so, they provide a critical standard by which the world can measure itself.'[110]

Returning to the argument that establishment safeguards an integralist overlapping of the spiritual and the material, or the public nature of religious profession, plausible alternative conclusions can be drawn on both these fronts. Governments that shape the institutions and laws of the state in their own image and refuse social participation to a significant proportion of its most vulnerable citizens can viably be seen to have themselves refused participation in the good and the reality of the supernatural. So, too, a state that fails to recognize the integrity and subjectivity of the earth and God's concern for it could viably be seen to deserves no church.[111] If this book is right in arguing that successive governments have set the nation against itself and the people against their land, then it is plausible to contend that being a national church can only be achieved by separation from the institutions of such people. Concerning the claim that establishment arrests the division of spheres into a secular public realm on the one hand and a private spiritual area on the other, the converse is just as imaginatively possible: religion is today primarily a private matter because the public sphere is already fine, as symbolically demonstrated by the bishops' ongoing and apparently unproblematic participation therein and the Queen's rule thereover. To raise the question of disestablishment again is entirely conceivable as a means to assert Christian concern with the material and political worlds and deny the privatization of the gospel. According to Iain McLean and Scot Peterson:

> A relatively simple bill could be proposed, which would (1) remove the bishops from the House of Lords; (2) abolish lay patronage, as was done in Ireland in 1869, in Scotland in 1874 and in Wales in 1920, authorizing the Church to select its own clergy and dignitaries … (3) repeal the Enabling Act and authorize the Church of England to pass measures without reference to parliament … (4) abolish the nineteenth-century offices of Church estate Commissioners, replacing them with trustees responsible for all assets of the Church.[112]

MacKinnon, a recurring authority on the question of disestablishment in the writings of Fergusson, acknowledges that disestablishment would take the British people and their churches into uncharted territory.[113] Nevertheless, MacKinnon says that 'the imperative is clear to go forward, not clinging to external protection but embracing insecurity, and to go forward in hope … It is a hope big with the promise of a more inclusive, if much costlier, charity, and I would insist that, for myself, I see the future as likely to bring more gain than loss, provided we are bold enough and sufficiently freed from bondage to the false imagery of the past, to rise to the extent of its opportunity.'[114] 'Loss of security', he continues, 'will not be as frightening a thing in actuality as it is to many in prospect; exclusion from a traditionally accepted place in the ancient structure of our society is likely to prove a means of presence rather than withdrawal.'[115] Elections bring new governments which in turn impose new priorities on the institutions of the state. The range of government functions (defence, education, law, crime, punishment/rehabilitation and health) adds further variables into the deliberation. Nevertheless, should food bank use stay stable or increase and the Church of England reach the collective conclusion that alleviating poverty is integral to the ministry of Christ's church and Christ's returning of the whole world back to God then discussing disestablishment becomes a pressing theological necessity.

## Part Four: participation in the earth – production and consumption

MacKinnon's suggestion is that disestablishment presents a way for the church to form more substantial and intimate relations. Counter-intuitively, the logic of the argument is that a form of disassociation (from the historical privileges of close ties to the state) is a means to more proximate relationships (with those in need). Similarly, it is equally plausible that engaging with our potential power as consuming *individuals* can be a means to take responsibility for our *dependence* on and entanglement in the earth and its processes.

In a small but still significant way engaging the question of diet is directly relevant to the lives of food bank users. Producing meat in enough quantities to meet the demands of western patterns of consumption is land, surface water and food stuffs intensive (discussed further below). Reducing the amount of meat and dairy one eats has a multiplier effect on the amounts of food basics available in the global food market (soy and cereals, in particular, are needed in large amounts to grow animals), which in turn increases the available supply of basic food stuffs in the global food system and reduces food prices. Reducing meat consumption increases the purchasing power of the food insecure at home and abroad. However, as this book has already suggested, food prices need to be higher not lower, for a number of reasons (see Chapter 2). So, why is the consumption of meat and dairy a food bank issue? First, reducing our levels of consumption of high-energy input foods is important because it allows us to transition hunger from an individual to a social problem, it makes it possible to nationalize food insecurity. What does this mean? Currently, the UK has a food footprint twice the size of its agricultural area, but there is evidence that the UK could become a net food producer and provide safe, equitable, healthy food for its own population and others.[116] However, as Simon Fairlie suggests, the UK living within its agricultural territory while keeping space for wildlife, woods and homes, means adjusting what we eat. Eating less meat is the necessary condition of possibility for thinking an equitable, sustainable, sovereign food system in the UK. Second, the same issue holds globally. The demands on the earth that come from the diets and lifestyles of people in western societies discredit the idea that UK food insecurity can simply be dealt with by increasing food availability (through food aid) or increasing the spending power or remit of consumer discretion of those who use food banks (through increased benefits or wages). A larger number of people living unsustainably is, arguably, more 'just' in the short term, but also accelerates catastrophe (not merely climate change but soil deterioration and biodiversity loss) in the medium and long term.[117] A part of the appeal of food banks is that they are perceived to deal with two problems simultaneously: food waste and hunger. But the evidence drawn on in this book suggests that they solve neither and add to a third problem: environmental catastrophe. Hunger, agriculture and ecology cannot be separated, as Berry says: 'the future of food is not distinguishable from the future of the land, which is indistinguishable in turn from the future of human care'.[118] Being willing to address the question of what we eat, hard as it may be, makes new options possible which are otherwise unthinkable and shows, more in symbolic terms than in actuality, admittedly, a commitment to making space for and taking seriously the needs of the other.

Returning to the writings of Berry, a better frame, in which the interests of the natural world and her people are compatible and not conflicting, needs to be articulated and acted upon. Berry grasps this and as a first step in that direction claims that he aims to 'live in protest'.[119] Along with marching in the street, community organizing and civil disobedience, he goes on to say:

> Another possibility, equally necessary, and in the long run richer in promise, is to remove oneself as far as possible from complicity in the evils one is protesting, and to discover alternative possibilities. To make public protests against an evil, and yet live in dependence on and in support of the way of life that is the source of the evil, is an obvious contradiction and a dangerous one. If one disagrees with the nomadism and violence of our society, then one is under an obligation to take up some permanent dwelling place and cultivate the possibility of peace and harmlessness in it. If one deplores the destructiveness and wastefulness of the economy, then one is under an obligation to live as far out on the margin of the economy as one is able: to be economically independent of exploitative industries, to learn

to need less, to waste less, to make things last, to give up meaning-less luxuries, to understand and resist the language of salesmen and public relations experts, to see through attractive packages, to refuse to purchase fashion or glamour or prestige. If one feels endangered by meaninglessness, then one is under an obligation to refuse meaning-less pleasure and to resist meaningless work, and to give up the moral comfort and excuses of the mentality of specialization.[120]

For Berry, as far as 'one is able' meant going out into the countryside and making a 'home there in the fullest and most permanent sense: that is live on and use and preserve and learn from and enrich and enjoy the land'.[121]

The agrarian commitment to live responsibly from the land crops up again in the writings of Simon Fairlie, farmer and editor of *The Land* magazine. Fairlie, repeating a plausibility study undertaken in the 1970s by the Scottish ecologist Kenneth Melllanby, asks:

if suddenly we had to shoehorn [our environmental footprint] into the 22 million hectares of non-urban land we have in this country, how would we cope? Could this be done organically, whilst keeping a reasonable amount of meat in our diet for those who wanted it, and ensuring that a reasonable proportion of the country is reserved for wildlife?

Fairlie's answer is yes and he provides a number of different models for this (chemical, organic and permaculture systems). His preference is for permaculture, as organic models require significantly larger amounts of land to produce the same amounts of food, though they require less human labour (chemical agriculture requires less labour but is highly dependent on synthetic fertilizers).[122] When he refers to permaculture, Fairlie has a number of factors in mind:

These include: feeding livestock upon food wastes and residues; returning human sewage to productive land; dispersal of animals on mixed farms and smallholdings, rather than concentration in large farms; local slaughter and food distribution; managing animals to ensure optimum recuperation of manure; and selecting and managing livestock, especially dairy cows, to be nitrogen providers rather than nitrogen stealers. These measures demand more human labour, and more even dispersal of both livestock and humans around the country than chemical or vegan options. Effective pursuit of livestock-based organic agriculture of this kind requires a localized economy, and some degree of agrarian resettlement.[123]

The kind of self-sustaining Britain that Fairlie imagines, one that also produces its own timber and textiles and also keeps significant wildlife spaces open, is possible. But this kind of Britain 'is a society in a state of energy descent, with increasing dependence upon renewable resources and (consequently) a localized economy, more integrated with natural processes'.[124] There would still be meat, around 83 grams of red meat a day, or enough for a 5lb joint for a family of four on Sunday. Half the level of consumption of fish, but an increase in the consumption of pork to compensate. This is a country growing its fruit and vegetables intensively on allotments, in urban spaces, and maintaining pigs and chickens to recycle food wastes, and cattle for maintaining nitrogen cycles in larger crops. It includes a distribution of the population across the country to live and participate in high-labour local farming permaculture practices.[125]

The kinds of small farms and locally responsive agricultural practices that Berry and Shiva advocate are both more productive and a sink for greenhouse gases.[126] Analogous to the contrast between theology and neoliberalism developed in this book, Shiva says that agriculture is undergoing a 'conflict and contest between the two systems – one based on eco-imperialism, bio-imperialism and eco-apartheid, the other on earth democracy and bio-democracy'.[127] Tragically, 30,000 small farms have closed in the UK in the last ten years.[128] The excellent *A People's Food Policy: Transforming Our Food System* says that pressures on farmers and fishers have been 'compounded by narrow government policy', changing diets and the 'excessive power of supermarkets over the food supply chain'.[129] The industrial model of farming, still widely practised in the UK, adds to 'ecological deterioration in terms of soil depletion, environmental contamination from agrochemicals, disease and antibiotic resistance, biodiversity loss, high GHG emissions, and huge amounts of food waste'.[130] Important improvements, like local farmers' markets, community cooperative buying arrangements, and direct purchasing from farmers, are marred by the reality that 'the growing number of local food distribution networks are almost exclusively found in affluent areas of the country'.[131]

If the transformation of British food production and distribution is the medium-term goal, then vegetarian, vegan or reduced meat diets, according to a number of contemporary theologians, are a way to responsibly enact our dependence on the earth now.[132] In the area of food consumption, the energy intensity of meat production has led to an increase in the numbers of those living vegetarian or vegan lives. Van Wieren identifies 'four key areas of ecological concern when it comes to global animal production – land degradation, atmosphere and climate, water and biodiversity'.[133] In all four of these, current levels of meat production and consumption are problematic. Van Wieren writes: 'Eighteen percent of total global greenhouse gas emissions, one tenth of carbon emissions, more than one third of methane emissions, and nearly two thirds of nitrous oxide emissions come from [livestock production] alone.'[134] Animals, especially when kept in concentrated animal feeding operations, require large amounts of food – 'ninety percent of all soy and half of all corn [in the United States] – one third of the world's cereal harvest – is used to feed animals on industrial farms'.[135] By the year 2000, the biomass of domesticated animals 'exceeded that of all wild land mammals by 24 times'.[136] When the biomass of chickens is three times that of all other birds you need a lot of land and water to sustain them.[137] But often that land could be more efficiently used; Lang writes that '85% of the UK's total land footprint is associated with meat and dairy production, but only 48% of total protein and 32% of total calories derive from livestock'.[138] Alongside the ecological consequences of high levels of meat consumption, factory farming is the cause of extensive animal suffering and can be a contributing factor in a number of human health problems.[139]

Combined with the notable Christian heritage of vegetarian practices, the ecological consequences of meat consumption make it an obvious topic for public deliberation by the church. Grumett and Muers write about the 'strong Christian tradition of meat abstinence' along with the history of 'persistent association between dietary abstinence, particularly meat avoidance, and cultural protest'.[140] The Christian scriptures state that God made, has compassion on and provides for every living thing, that God is aware of every sparrow.[141] Norman Wirzba asks a number of questions at the end of *Faith and Food* about what Christians eat:

> Does the food we are about to eat reflect production practices in alignment with Christ's desire that creatures be whole and well? Were food providers honoured for their work? Were they able to work in creative ways with the world? With respect to the food itself, we will ask if the soil and water from which our plants grow are healthy and clean. Are biological rhythms and ecological integrity observed? Were the animals respected and treated with care? And with regard to the eating practices, we will ask if the food eaten is distributed in an equitable manner. Does the eating we enjoy deprive others of the ability to eat well? Is food being grown and distributed in a way reflective of God's desire that all be fed?[142]

He goes on to say that he is aware that these are hard questions to answer, and suggests that each church begin by ensuring that its communion bread and wine (and what Christians donate to the food bank) meet these criteria.[143]

The complexities of the current moment of food, farming and politics are summarized well by Tim Lang, Professor of Food Policy at London University: 'The Food Brexit process raises real interconnected vulnerabilities by withdrawing from a highly integrated food marketing and regulatory system at the very time that the UK already faces growing systemic food vulnerabilities.'[144] The UK food system is 'highly vulnerable to the rising costs of diet-related ill health, ecosystem damage, economic dependency, and social reliance on migrant and relatively low-waged labour.'[145] Despite hunger and the rising percentage of incomes spent by people on food by the poorest, our food is still priced too cheap because 'food prices do not include the full costs of production, especially in terms of resource depletion and environmental pollution. Also, externalized costs to public health … are not properly reflected in consumer prices. In particular, cheap food prices have depended on cheap labour.'[146] According to the Office for National Statistics, 'the accommodation and food sectors have the highest number of zero-hour contracts of any sector', the issue of precariousness, and yet 'the UK's big food companies feature in the High Pay Centre's catalogue of vast pay to CEOs'.[147] The top-paid CEOs get an average person's yearly salary by 4 January each year, at a ratio of 129:1.[148] While the profits for farmers and supermarkets are tight, bottlenecked supply, low wages and international supply chains are generating high profits for the food megacorporations.[149] There is, as the economist Will Hutton argues, also the pressing need to look again at British corporate law if a sustainable, modern, equitable food system is to be realized.[150]

## Conclusion

Feeding Britain's proposals for a higher minimum wage and benefits reform are aimed at reducing food bank usage and food insecurity but not eliminating them. They have put forward a way of managing the problem and policies consonant with that aim. What are the aims suggested by theology, and how should they be interpreted by Christians at the personal, ecclesial and political levels? For Christians who seek to shut down the food banks they once opened up, the issues of precarious labour and a vulnerable and unsustainable food system need to be addressed and more wide-reaching programmes discussed. For Wirzba, the issues of ecological deterioration and economic inequality meant that 'a broad-based discussion on the nature of responsible freedom should be our highest cultural priority'.[151] How can one be at once responsible and free? To give money to individual citizens as a way of enacting their dependence on the whole; by the Church of England separating off from the state in order to show that it is a church for everyone; to consume as a conscientious, self-possessing creature in deference to one's complicity in the totality and where possible to take responsibility for growing one's own food – these were the answers this chapter suggested.

For Berry, there are answers in history to the problems we face now. He affirms the simple idea, taken from Thomas Jefferson's letters, that 'as many as possible should share in the ownership of the land and thus be bound to it by economic interests, by the investment of love and work, by family loyalty, by memory and tradition'.[152] He finds in the writings of the US founding fathers that an 'independent, free-standing citizenry' with their own piece of the earth to work may be 'the surest safeguard of democratic liberty'.[153] While this chapter has been concerned with thinking through the issues raised by food banks' existence within the parameters of the Christian imagination and has defended the proposals here as a way for thinking within the trajectory of that tradition, the invitation to join the church in this endeavour and learn to think within the parameters of its story stands open to anyone. Both the British food crisis, and the world's ecological crisis, are multivariant problems which will require reflections and contributions from many diverse traditions of thought and practice; this chapter adds a little to that task by taking it up from within the parameters of Christian thought.

# Conclusion

Mark and Joe looked tentative when they entered Durham City Foodbank. They took a seat together at the table closest to the door, Joe holding a red food bank voucher indicatively in his hand. It was rare, in my experience, to see young men in their late teens or early twenties come to the food bank. I approached them and asked if they wanted a tea or coffee and if I could check their voucher. As we talked they relaxed and told me more about their lives in the lead-up to this food bank visit. Mark first:

> Yea, I'm from this area. My family is close, my Mum is in a care home in Chester-le-Street. My Dad died when my Mum was pregnant with me. I've got three brothers: nine, 11 and 16 and a sister, all us brothers are from different fathers. Like me, my Mum has mental health issues, more than I can help her with. It was hard living together, and I ended up moving out. That was when I started sleeping rough for a bit and some homeless people were looking after me for a while.

Joe joins in and continues the story:

> We met at the hospital. My Dad had made me homeless as well and I was in the hospital at this time, they'd been giving me antidepressants. I'd been living in different places, moved from Lancaster to Middleborough to Darlington and Durham. In March (2018) I'd attempted suicide, had a breakdown and was hospitalized. That's where we met each other, in the ward.

Joe had dropped out of university and since then worked in a number of different jobs. His most recent employment at a supermarket had ended when his anxiety became unmanageable and now both Joe and Mark were on unemployment benefit. Since they left hospital in the spring they have been living together in the flat that Joe gets from the council and are excited about the food parcel that they are getting from the food bank. Mark:

I have a psychologist meeting tomorrow which I have to go to. It's worst when you get lonely, its great having Joe for company. When you're on your own and lonely your thoughts go onto the negative things. We share what we have, this food parcel from the food bank and play Fortnite on the Playstation.

Fortnite is a free and popular computer game. I ask them if they are any good at it and they chuckle and say no, but that they play it because it's free and they can't afford to buy any other games. Both of them hope that they will be able to get work soon and that their mental health improves. Joe says:

If my mental health improves, I can get a job, fit back into society. Staying on the sick, it's not a good lifestyle, I don't want to do it, too much free time, it isn't good.

I ask them in the interview about what they think about the food bank and whether they have had any experiences of religion or spirituality, or views on the links between Christianity and the food bank. They tell me that they like the food bank and think that the volunteers here are friendly and have good hearts. They say they are interested in volunteering themselves and would like to return something for what they've been given. Joe says he does not think that religion is a real thing but that sometimes when he's survived bad things and looks back he has asked himself whether there is someone who might be looking out for him. His granddad was a Christian and we wondered if this was where he got this feeling. For Mark, a similar sentiment has taken on a more explicit form.

Mark told me that when he left his mother's home, he got a job moving chickens. He showed me the scarred scratches that cover both of his hands and run up his arms to the elbow as he talked. During this period and before his second hospitalization, the one in which he met Joe, he was homeless for a period of two months and living in the woods. I asked him how this felt and he said:

Terrible, embarrassed that it was like this, I felt ashamed. I had a job, working as a chicken catcher but also I had these mental health problems, so I went to Citizens Advice Bureau (CAB) and they said I need to go to the hospital to get some help with this. They [the hospital] gave me anti-psychotic drugs, medication, because I thought I was hearing things. Rough sleeping was really difficult. I smoked weed at that time (cannabis), that used to help me sleep.

The hospital moved him to another location and then released him. It was after this release that he tried to take an overdose and it was during this overdose that he told me:

> I had a vision, when I'd overdosed. It was a second chance. I remember after I had taken the drugs there were these words, a voice that said to me that I thought I was a bad person and that I'd done bad things but that I shouldn't try and kill myself, that I should keep living and go on. When I woke up I was in the hospital. The medics had moved me there, they told me that they thought I wasn't going to make it when they found me.
>
> *That's an amazing story. Have things been different since then? Do you think this vision has had an impact on you?*
>
> It's had an impact on me I think, I now give money to the homeless, I wouldn't have done that before. The overdose, after that they took me to the hospital and when I woke up I went to the chapel in the hospital and prayed. I've been christened now but I've not got any experience of church or Christians in the family or anything like that. One other thing after the vision that's different, I'm more open on mental health, sharing my mental health issues with people. You shouldn't keep it to yourself. People think that mental health problems aren't real problems but they are and they need to be talked about.

The reasons for Christian charity are various and complex. Part of why food banks have been seen as a legitimate intervention and plausible solution, and consequently grown so quickly, resides in their compatibility with received ways of thinking. This is particularly evident in the vouchers system, the inclination towards charitable rather than political solutions and the food bank's protocols for minimizing dependency, all of which carry with them a series of commitments to ideas of deservingness, choice, responsibility and freedom, classic facets of contemporary neoliberalism. In short, food banks have either internalized or flourished within the parameters of neoliberal definitions of success.

But this is only one of food banks' faces. They are equally animated, for many, by the belief that God is for life, the lives of others in all their fullness.[1] One of the primary aims of this book is to render more explicit and satisfactory Christian engagements with British food insecurity and emergency food aid and compare it with the modes of thinking that are currently dominant. In the lives of those who come to the food bank it is possible to see how little neoliberalism values the lives of those perceived to be different; there is no place in neoliberalism for what does not make profit, for Joes and Marks. It is in continuity with the logic of neoliberal ways of thinking that even people are liable to be treated instrumentally because they are vassals of the market and not inhabitants of the Kingdom. When labour and employment are discussed primarily in the context of the needs of the economy, then oscillating between surplus populations being either annihilated or incorporated and workers being disposable or interchangeable are simply the outworkings of common sense. When nature too has no inherent value but is priced only according to the labour that is put into it and the desirability of the product that can be extracted from it, then nature is rendered mute and invisible.[2] The existence of hundreds of thousands out of work and millions in precarious labour isn't an aberration, neither is the distinction between deserving and undeserving poor, nor the pollution, degradation of homogenization of nature. All are endemic in contemporary neoliberalism running smoothly, rather than failures or oddities in the system.

To respond to the rise of food bank usage in the UK by saying that 'you will always have the poor with you' is insufficiently nuanced and attentive to Christ's presence with the poor. Chris Allen quotes Wirzba in his essay on theology and British food insecurity:

The gospels frequently show Jesus eating with people because table fellowship is among the most powerful ways we know to extend and share in each other's lives. Jesus eats with strangers and outcasts, demonstrating that table fellowship is for the nurture of others and not simply for self-enhancement. Jesus rejects the social systems of rejection and exclusion by welcoming everyone into communion with him. Table fellowship makes possible genuine encounter with others ... By freely eating with everyone [Jesus] breaks and challenges all the social taboos that keep people apart.[3]

Theologically, I have argued that the reason Christians are inclined to commit themselves to charity reside in fidelity to the belief that God is for life as water is for running downhill. By stressing Christian theology's simultaneous belief in the dependence of the world on God *and* its difference from God, this book has suggested that Christian theology has the resources to articulate a vision of the human place in the world that is at once compelling and counter-intuitive. A tradition of thought that draws from a range of religious traditions and secular thought and has strong affiliations with the kind of Christianity this book has explored, and is directly applicable to issues raised by the phenomena of food banking, is contemporary 'agrariansim'.

Wirzba defines agrarianism as 'learning to take up the responsibilities that protect, preserve, and celebrate life'.[4] Life, the Christian tradition teaches, is a gift from God. St Thomas Aquinas, the most influential theologian of medieval Christianity, wrote that 'all things other than God are not their own existence but share in existence'.[5] Christians have historically said not only that God made the world out of nothing but that God is constantly willing the world to be and it is on this desiring that the world depends. This does not mean that the world has no legitimacy of its own, God always wills the world into being as something distinct from God's self.[6] For Christians, the world and the self are thus a gift from God and inherently relational things: 'Everything other than God receives its being from the Creator as a gift,' writes theologian David Burrell.[7]

Consequently, and unlike neoliberalism, it can be reasonably argued that Christianity is for the different. Giving this a technical name, creation, some Christian theologians have argued, has a 'kenotic' shape. The Christ event, in which Jesus 'who, though he was in the form of God, did not regard equality with God as something to be exploited, but emptied (*ekenōsen*) himself, taking the form of a slave, being born in human likeness', is a giving up of the self that the other may thrive.[8] Likewise, in creation, God makes a space for the other without ever ceasing to be in fundamental relationship to it; the crucifixion and resurrection paradigmatically reiterate and exemplify the nature of God's creation and how God acts towards it. 'I am the good shepherd. The good shepherd lays down his life for the sheep' says something about shepherding and the divine at once.[9] As Jesus' ministry comes to its climax, his apostle John writes that Jesus knew that the hour of his death was coming and that 'having loved his own who were in the world, he loved them to the end (*eis telos*)'.[10] What is lost from the English translation of Jesus' final words on the cross, 'it is finished (*tetelestai*)', is the reader's awareness of the repetition of this same root word, *telos*, in these two crucial moments. Presuming for the moment that John's comment in 13.1, along with the prominent interlinking of death, love and food in the Gospel, are meaningfully, or thoughtfully, done, it is a legitimate possibility that in Jesus' words 'it is finished' John heard from the one he loved: 'to the very end, I loved you'.

The Christian question to society and government is: how will it substantiate life lived for the other, loving kenotically? The first answer this book suggested, with the aim of drastically reducing food insecurity, is a universal basic income. Ecclesiologically, the question is how the church is going to release and put into practice this commitment to loving the other. First, this book suggested that the church should critically interrogate the relationships it is already in, primarily its overlaps with the state, and to this end I've suggested a renewed conversation in the Church of England around disestablishment. Second, following Chris Allen, a land activist church that supports small-scale growing projects and turns its own properties into food-producing communities is desirable as it puts the church into the service of the populous and our local places simultaneously. Individually, how are Christians to live it in their day-to-day lives? Part of the answer here is a more stringent, critical Christian engagement with habits of consumption, particularly of foods that require high resource inputs for low calorie outputs.

For food banks in particular, how to realize participation that affirms the value of the other is of crucial importance. Volunteering can be seen to partially realize this narrative of life lived for the other (as de Souza suggested) but it is also problematic because of its inclination to deny to the other the kinds of dignity that are perceived to be valid (both, though they are distinct, in neoliberal terms as worker, consumer, chooser, and in theological terms as a person who is loved by God, has inherent value, and brings to us something of the divine). The aim, as has been classically expressed by food bank volunteers since their first inauguration in the United States in the second half of the twentieth century, is not giving up time to volunteer but how, responsibly, to give up volunteering entirely.[11] Peter MacLellan noted this in my interview with him when he said:

> We've seen these waves of social action projects. Street pastors went from nothing to all across the country fairly quickly and is now potentially stalling. Some are struggling, some are thriving, it's past the crest of the wave, the wave has broken and it's seeing what comes out of it. Will food banks follow that same pattern? Interesting question. Clearly the big growth in them is now done, that meteoric rise in the numbers. We [County Durham Foodbank] go up and down one or two distribution points typically in a year but basically we are what we are now and unlikely to change very radically, until such a time as the need declines. Will people still have the enthusiasm and be invested in it, or will they be looking for the next volunteering opportunity, the next sexy topic to get involved in, whether that be in church circles or others. Interesting question, which I don't know.

He continued, reflecting on the future of County Durham Foodbank:

> I think food banks have sustained very well. Certainly, we haven't seen any donor fatigue, which is nice, to say the least, very happy with that. But will that be the case in five years' time? People can understand

responding to a crisis, austerity, government cutbacks etc. etc. The whole narrative has been about people struggling because the government stepped back because we can't afford things. How long can that narrative go on for? Now, potentially with Brexit, and depending on what comes out of that, there could be another crisis that people are responding to with fresh impetus, or it may not be a crisis, which would be great. But how long are people going to accept austerity for? That's an interesting political question apart from anything else ... It may be that the need goes away, in which case we should celebrate these projects and say 'didn't it do a good job, wasn't it wonderful, it's no longer needed, let's celebrate everything that happened through it and the people who were involved in it and shut it'. That's a really tough thing to do.

The prospects for closing down County Durham Foodbank in the imminent future seem bleak. Neoliberalism, which 'brought unparalleled wealth and affluence to powerful elites' in both the developed and developing world and 'deepening inequality, increasing income poverty and food deprivation for many', has entered a more punitive phase since the great recession of 2008 but still shows little sign of being replaced by a more participatory and genuinely liberating order.[12] Its entrenchment in our imaginative and material infrastructures is still strong, so strong as to render its causes and consequences almost invisible.[13] In their review of media reporting of food banks, for example, the academics Wells and Caraher found a general absence of coverage of poverty in the mainstream UK papers and that when it was covered 'explanations of the causes of poverty' were 'particularly absent'.[14] They went on to note that 'there was a conspicuous absence of the voices of those in poverty themselves from much of the reporting'.[15]

Neoliberalism's reach is so long it shapes the answers that are given to the problems it generates, as we see with food banks and parts of the climate change debate. The widely circulated hopes for technological solutions to our ecological predicament seem ill placed given that British society is going through a crisis of meaning and production of aims, as some commentators on the rise of food banks have argued. Berry says that it is now inconceivable

to tag along with the fantasists in Government and industry who would have us believe that we can pursue our ideals of affluence, comfort, mobility, and leisure indefinitely. This curious faith is predicated on the notion that we will soon develop unlimited sources of energy: domestic oil fields, shale oil, gasified coal, nuclear power, solar energy, and so on. This is fantastical because the basic cause of the energy crisis is not scarcity; it is moral ignorance and weakness of character. We don't know *how* to use energy, or what to use if *for*. And we cannot restrain ourselves. Our time is characterised as much by the use and waste of human energy as it is by the abuse and waste of fossil fuel energy.[16]

Or, in the words of the song 'Ocean Breathes Salty' by the band Modest Mouse, 'you wasted life, why wouldn't you waste the afterlife?' But there are alternatives, tentatively but importantly realized already in history and contemporary practice, and agrarianism is one of them.[17] Agrarianism is 'the sustained attempt to live faithfully and respon- sibly in a world of limits and possibilities'.[18] It is 'a compelling and coherent alternative to the modern industrial/technological/economic paradigm'.[19] It is stridently secular in its iconoclastic refusal of the 'faiths' of modern economics, industry and technology and in its com- mitment to learn from history and nature.[20] And yet agrarianism is also deeply religious in its refusal to treat the world as a purely malleable and material thing, subject solely to varying degrees of human mastery.[21] Its morality, inferred above by Berry, is not 'constructing blueprints for action, particularly if these blueprints are drawn up by a disembodied or disembedded mind' but taking up collectively the task of 'immedi- ate clarification with regard to a foundation of life that is absolutely genuine (as opposed to optional, arbitrary, or conditional), and utterly beyond artifice or manipulation'.[22] There is no room for complacency here, as Christianity has been fertile ground for forms of 'otherworld- liness' that advocate flight from this fallen world into a pure afterlife.[23]

For Wirzba, and Berry before him, agrarianism's advocacy of a stance in the world akin to faithful awe or childlike wonder is not 'simple adherence to dogma, as if faith were finally or maximally a matter of intellectual assent to a series of religious propositions' but lodged instead in the suggestion that we should 'trust and accept responsibility for the gifted and graced character of experience', 'immerse ourselves into the flow of experience' and stay open to the possibility that we 'there find ourselves maintained by meaning and love that we do not control and, for the most part, do not deserve'.[24] Mark's experience of a voice that addressed him and called him to life as he came to the end of his own capacity to give and find meaning in the world and himself is at once the authentic heart of the food bank movement and the Christian ·calling.

# Notes

## Prologue

1 For examples of 'multi-criteria' approaches to the problems present in the British agricultural sector/food industry and in theological responses to climate change, see Tim Lang, Erik Millstone and Terry Marsden, *A Food Brexit: Time to Get Real* (University of Sussex Science Policy Research Unit, 2017), www.sussex.ac.uk/webteam/gateway/file.php?name=foodbrexitreport-langmillstonemarsden-july2017pdf.pdf&site=25 (accessed 30 May 2018); and Willis Jenkins, 'After Lynn White: Religious Ethics and Environmental Problems', *Journal of Religious Ethics*, Vol. 37, No. 2 (2009), pp. 283–309.

## Introduction

1 'We grow enough food today to feed 9.3 billion people. It is just that a lot is wasted and a lot more is diverted towards animal feed and biofuels. This is why it is so shocking that 870 million people still go hungry' (Paul McMahon, *Feeding Frenzy: The New Politics of Food* (London: Profile Books, 2014), p. 95). According to the Food and Agriculture Organization of the United Nations the number of undernourished people in 2017 was 821 million (FAO, IFAD, Unicef, WFP and WHO, *The State of Food Security and Nutrition in the World: Building Climate Resilience for Food Security and Nutrition* (Rome: FAO, 2018), www.fao.org/3/I9553EN/i9553en.pdf, p. v (accessed 15 November 2019)). For a succinct account of issues around farming and food production in the UK, see Isabella Tree, *Wilding: The Return of Nature to a British Farm* (London: Picador, 2018), pp. 130–6 and Eva Gladek and others for the WWF, *The Global Food System: An Analysis* (Amsterdam: Metabolic, 2017), www.metabolic.nl/publications/global-food-system-an-analysis/, p. 4 (accessed 28 September 2019).

2 According to Owen Davis and Ben Baumberg Geiger, food insecurity since 2008 has risen across Europe, 2.6% between 2003 and 2011, from 6.1% to 8.7%, with significant national variation: 'the UK – an Anglo-Saxon welfare regime' which has 'adopted a stringent set of austerity policies in line with a free-market economic approach' has seen a 4.6 percentage points rise (from 4.2% to 8.8%), some of the worst in Europe despite having one of the strongest economies. See Owen Davis and Ben Baumberg Geiger, 'Did Food Insecurity rise across Europe after the 2008 Crisis? An analysis across welfare regimes', *Social Policy and Society*, Vol. 16, No. 3 (2017), pp. 343–60, at pp. 347, 351.

3 Niall Cooper and Sarah Dumpleton, *Walking the Breadline: The Scandal of Food Poverty in 21st-Century Britain* (Oxford: Oxfam, 2013), https://policy-practice.oxfam.org.uk/publications/walking-the-breadline-the-scandal-of-food-poverty-in-21st-century-britain-292978,p.5 (accessed 1 June 2018); www.trusselltrust.org/news-and-blog/latest-stats/end-year-stats/ (accessed 28 September 2019).

4 Stewart Lansley and Joanna Mack, *Breadline Britain: The Rise of Mass Poverty* (London: Oneworld, 2015), p. 210. According to Davis and Geiger, 'there is some support from qualitative research with frontline food bank staff' that this is a possibility 'and it is plausible that there is some interrelationship between supply and demand for food aid' (Davis and Geiger, 'Did Food Insecurity Rise?', *Social Policy and Society*, p. 345).

5 For an example of a media presentation of the food bank issue sympathetic to the Conservative position, see www.dailymail.co.uk/news/article-2606573/Food-bank-charity-misleading-public-Claim-1m-need-food-parcels-just-self-promotion.html (accessed 29 September 2019). On the proportion of debt to gross domestic product (GDP), which was lower in 2007 than in 1997 when Labour came to office, see Simon Wren-Lewis, *The Lies We Were Told* (Bristol: Bristol University Press, 2018), pp. 20–3. On the UK's high recent employment rates, see Matthew Taylor, Greg Marsh, Diane Nicol and Paul Broadbent, *Good Work: The Taylor Review of Modern Working Practices* (2017), www.gov.uk/government/publications/good-work-the-taylor-review-of-modern-working-practices (accessed 29 September 2019), p. 17.

6 All-Party Parliamentary Inquiry into Hunger in the United Kingdom, *Feeding Britain: A Strategy for Zero Hunger in England, Wales, Scotland and Northern Ireland* (2014), https://feedingbritain.org/wp-content/uploads/2019/01/feeding_britain_report_2014-2.pdf (accessed 19 July 2019). Moussa Haddad, Jane Perry and Mia Madfield-Spoor, *Emergency Use Only: Update 2017, Change is Possible* (London: Child Poverty Action Group, 2017), www.trusselltrust.org/wp-content/uploads/sites/2/2017/12/EUOII.pdf (accessed 29 September 2019). Jane Perry, Martin Williams, Tom Sefton and Moussa Haddad, *Emergency Use Only: Understanding and Reducing the Use of Food Banks in the UK* (Oxfam GB, 2014), www.trusselltrust.org/wp-content/uploads/sites/2/2016/01/foodbank-report.pdf (accessed 29 September 2019).

7 Within the civil service, the Department for Environment, Food and Rural Affairs' (DEFRA) report on food aid was reported to be suppressed by a government uncomfortable with its implications and analysis, though the final version of the report is tentative in drawing conclusions for UK food aid from lessons learnt in other countries and ambiguous about the link between welfare and food aid. While a House of Commons paper written in preparation for a debate in parliament on emergency food aid and food poverty noted that there has been no government since the 1960s that has undertaken an 'official empirical study of benefit adequacy' but that the common consensus is that the current level of out-of-work benefits are 'significantly lower than the amounts necessary for a minimum acceptable standard of living'. See Hannah Lambie-Mumford, Daniel Crossley, Monae Verbeke and Elizabeth Dowler, *Household Food Security in the UK: A Review of Food Aid, Final Report* (2014), https://assets.publishing.service.gov.uk/government/uploads/system/uploads/attachment_data/file/283071/household-food-security-uk-140219.pdf (accessed 29 September 2019), pp. 37, 46; Isabel Oakeshott, 'Ministers Hide Surge in Use of Food Banks', *Sunday Times*, 3 November 2013, www.thetimes.co.uk/article/ministers-hide-surge-in-use-of-food-banks-w59ondckf6d (accessed 29 September 2019); Emma Downing and Steven Kennedy, *Food Banks and Food Poverty* (London: House of Commons, 2014), http://researchbriefings.parliament.uk/ResearchBriefing/Summary/SN06657 (accessed 28 May 2018).

8 Perry et al., *Emergency Use Only*, p. 7. By freezing benefit increases at 1% when inflation exceeded 1% the Conservative government in effect reduced the spending power of those receiving benefits. The insufficiency of current benefits has been identified

as an inadequacy in the sitting government's welfare policies and programme. Loopstra and Lalor, *Financial Insecurity, Food Insecurity, and Disability*, pp. 23, 24, 25.

9 Lansley and Mack, *Breadline Britain*, p. 210.

10 Ibid., p. 210. www.mirror.co.uk/news/uk-news/foodbank-charity-threatened-clo sure-government-3682914 (accessed 29 September 2019).

11 Lansley and Mack, *Breadline Britain*, p. 213.

12 Kayleigh Garthwaite, *Hunger Pains: Life inside Foodbank Britain* (Bristol: Policy Press, 2016), p. 149.

13 Ibid.

14 Elizabeth Dowler, 'Food Banks and Food Justice in "Austerity Britain"', in Graham Riches and Tiina Silvasti, eds, *First World Hunger Revisited: Food Charity or the Right to Food* (New York: Palgrave Macmillan, 2014), p. 164.

15 Graham Riches, *Food Bank Nations: Poverty, Corporate Charity and the Right to Food* (London: Routledge, 2018), p. 11.

16 Riches, *Food Bank Nations*, p. 172; Dowler, 'Food Banks and Food Justice', *First World Hunger Revisited*, p. 175.

17 Lansley and Mack, *Breadline Britain*, p. 222.

18 See Guy Standing, *The Precariat: The New Dangerous Class* (London: Bloomsbury, 2016); Isabell Lorey, *State of Insecurity: Government of the Precarious* (London: Verso, 2015); Robert Castel, 'The Rise of Uncertainties', *Critical Horizons*, Vol. 17, No. 2 (2016), pp. 160–7.

19 The British government's review of labour in 2017, *Good Work: The Taylor Review of Modern Working Practices*, found that 'the proportion of employees saying that flexible working was important to them when they initially decided to take up their current job had increased over recent years' and that flexibility was especially important for 'careers, women, those with disabilities and older workers'. Matthew Taylor, Greg Marsh, Diane Nicol and Paul Broadbent, *Good Work: The Taylor Review of Modern Working Practices*, 2017, www.gov.uk/government/publications/good-work-the-taylor-review-of-modern-working-practices (accessed 29 September 2019), pp. 14, 15. For an excellent discussion on the relationship between corporations and precarious labour, see Will Hutton, *How Good We Can Be* (London: Abacus, 2015), pp. 40–2. On the ambiguity of the term 'precariousness', see www.metamute.org/editorial/articles/pre carious-precarisation-precariat (accessed 29 September 2019).

20 'Relations of production' and 'modes of production' are shorthand terms used in radical theory to describe the relationships between workers, bosses and owners, and, second, the types of work or industry done in different societies (feudal, industrial, post-industrial/precarious). Lorey, *State of Insecurity*, p. 9.

21 Mark Fisher, *Capitalist Realism* (Winchester: Zero Books, 2009), pp. 34, 35, 79.

22 The demise of Fordism is also related to racism in America, with black and minority groups perceived to be disproportionately dependent on cradle-to-grave welfare, hence the need for welfare reform as a racial project. On sexism, racism and what could have followed Fordism, see Adam Kotsko, *Neoliberalism's Demons: On the Political Theology of Late Capital* (Stanford: Stanford University Press, 2018), pp. 70–3, 143.

23 For Fisher there is an inherent link between the kind of economy that predominates and general levels of mental health. He quotes from Oliver James' *The Selfish Capitalist*: 'rates of distress almost doubled between people born in 1946 ... and 1970', with the number of those having 'trouble with nerves, feeling low, depressed or sad' going from 16 percent to 29 percent between 1982 to 2000 for women and from 8 percent to 13 percent for men. Oliver James, quoted in Fisher, *Capitalist Realism*, pp. 35, 36.

24 Lorey, *State of Insecurity*, p. 1.

25 Ibid., p. 2.

26 Ibid.

27 Ibid.

28 Perry et al., *Emergency Use Only*, p. 30.

29 Garthwaite, *Hunger Pains*, pp. 130–4.

30 GPs interviewed for *Poverty, Pathology and Pills* reported between a 10% and 50% increase in patients whose primary concerns were social or structural, related to poverty, 'rather than medical issues per se'. The number of antidepressants prescribed has increased 600% in 25 years, to 68 million items per year in England. *Poverty, Pathology and Pills: Destress Project Final Report* (2019), http://destressproject.org.uk/wp-content/uploads/2019/05/Final-report-8-May-2019-FT.pdf (accessed 17 November 2019), pp. 2, 11, 13–15, 18, 19.

31 Nick Srnicek and Alex Williams, *Inventing the Future: Postcapitalism and a World without Work* (London: Verso, 2016), p. 87.

32 Garthwaite, *Hunger Pains*, p. 159.

33 Hutton says that 'household debt was a tiny 15 percent of national output in 1964; today that has increased nearly nine times to stand at 140 percent of GDP.' Lansley and Mack report that 'in the UK, levels of personal debt rose from forty-five percent of incomes in 1981 to 157 percent in 2008'. Cumulatively, the unsecured proportion of this debt (that owed on credit cards, current accounts and to other lenders) is £428 billion, well above the £286 billion UK households owed before the 2008 great recession. Hutton, *How Good We Can Be*, p. 8; Lansley and Mack, *Breadline Britain*, p. 186; www.theguardian.com/business/2019/jan/07/average-uk-household-debt-now-stands-at-record-15400 (accessed 15 November 2019).

34 Standing, *The Precariat*, p. 174.

35 Lansley and Mack, *Breadline Britain*, pp. 34, 38.

36 A young man who was a regular drop-in visitor to County Durham Foodbank, to the degree that he would help make toasties for others coming to use the service, once described to me the way he went from food bank to food bank getting free goods in Darlington. In our interview, he reflected on the way he was manipulating Darlington's food banks and said he was 'taking the piss' and depriving those who really needed the help of the service. A second, older man in a village food bank outside Durham described himself to me as a 'beggar' and a scrounger and that he only deserved little because 'beggars can't be choosers'; 'sponging,' he said, 'it's in my nature'. An American libertarian, Lawrence Mead, who visited the British government in 2010, held the view that 'Governments must persuade [welfare claimants] to *blame* themselves.' It is legitimate to say that the aforementioned moments of personal culpability can be seen as indicative of individual failure or political success. Mead, quoted in Standing, *The Precariat*, p. 168.

37 Developing a centre-right, Conservative defence of the status quo, or Conservative programme for reforms, which reduces food bank use is made much harder by the lack of direct and sustained engagement with the issue of food banks. During the course of this research, the works of the think-tanks the Institute of Economic Affairs, the Adam Smith Institute, Bow, the Centre for Policy Studies, the Centre for Social Justice, Policy Exchange and the Social Market Foundation were surveyed for engagements with the issue of food banks. The Centre for Social Justice mentioned food banks four times in a document 'Signed on, Written off', three of which were in a case study from Rochdale. Food banks were mentioned incidentally in two blogs on the Policy Exchange website in 2014 and twice in their 'Smarter Sanctions' policy document. The think-tank Bow

mentioned food banks once in a quote lifted from the Conservative Party 2015 manifesto, affirming the ongoing need for a robust civil society. No reference to food banks could be found in the Institute for Economic Affairs, the Adam Smith Institute, or the Centre for Policy Studies' work over the last nine years. Centre for Social Justice, *Signed On, Written Off* (2013), www.centreforsocialjustice.org.uk/library/signed-written-off-inquiry-welfare-dependency-britain (accessed 14 November 2019). Policy Exchange, *Smarter Sanctions* (2014), https://policyexchange.org.uk/wp-content/uploads/2016/09/smarter-sanctions-1.pdf (accessed 14 November 2019).

38 Church Urban Fund, *Hungry for More* (2013), www2.cuf.org.uk/research/hungry-more (accessed 30 September 2019), pp. 2, 4, 20. *Faith in Foodbanks?* (2014), www.jointpublicissues.org.uk/wp-content/uploads/Faith-in-Foodbanks-Report.pdf (accessed 30 September 2019), p. 44. Cooper and Dumpleton, *Walking the Breadline*, p. 1. Anne Richards, *Liberation and Entrapment Project, Mission and Food Banks* (2017), www.churchofengland.org/sites/default/files/2017-11/MTAG%20Mission%20and%20Food%20Banks.pdf (accessed 29 September 2019), pp. 9, 10, 30.

39 Church Urban Fund, *Hungry for More*, p. 4. *Faith in Foodbanks?*, p. 8. Cooper and Dumpleton, *Walking the Breadline*, pp. 3, 8, 9, 12. Richards, *Mission and Food Banks*, pp. 5, 34.

40 Church Urban Fund, *Hungry for More*, p. 1. *Faith in Foodbanks?*, p. 4, 21, 34, 43. Richards, *Mission and Food Banks*, p. 7, 12.

41 Church Urban Fund, *Hungry for More*, pp. 1, 2, 10. *Faith in Foodbanks?*, pp. 4, 27.

42 Cooper and Dumpleton, *Walking the Breadline*, p. 6. Church Urban Fund, *Hungry for More*, p. 2. *Faith in Foodbanks?*, pp. 10, 11. Richards, *Mission and Food Banks*, p. 17.

43 Richards, *Mission and Food Banks*, pp. 16, 23. *Faith in Foodbanks?*, pp. 4, 19–34.

44 Church Urban Fund, *Hungry for More*, pp. 3, 12, 20. *Faith in Foodbanks?*, pp. 7, 35, 36. Richards, *Mission and Food Banks*, pp. 10, 11, 14, 26, 32.

45 Richards, *Mission and Food Banks*, pp. 25–35.

46 For example, the Bishop of Truro, Tim Thornton, who has challenged Lord Freud on the issue of food banks in the house of Lords and was co-chair of the 'Feeding Britain' APPG on hunger, says that 'it is time to look again at the state of our country and to review the fundamental values that led to the creation of our welfare state', while also reproducing verbatim the government's logic for dismantling the welfare state: 'we are living at a time of difficult financial circumstances. The Government has to make hard choices with limited resources.' All-Party Parliamentary Inquiry into Hunger in the United Kingdom, *Feeding Britain*, p. 5. For a fuller account of this issue through a particular discussion of Anglican responses to the August riots of 2011, see Charles Pemberton, 'August Rioters, Rough Sleepers and Anglicans in a Psychoanalytic Lens', in Ben Wood, ed., *Renewing the Self: Contemporary Religious Perspectives* (Newcastle-upon-Tyne: Cambridge Scholars Publishing, 2017), pp. 179–200.

47 Richards argues that a Christian approach to the economy should be predicated on belief in the world and all its inhabitants as the receivers of the gift of creation; this, for Richards, cuts against the logic of a world based on ownership, property and individuality. However, Richards goes on to say the gift economy (though primary) should 'not replace the trade economy, but through the food bank, the gift economy could work towards making the trade economy function more effectively and in everyone's interests, especially those who live in poverty' without, unfortunately, specifying what this in practice means. Richards, *Mission and Food Banks*, p. 28.

48 Church Urban Fund, *Hungry for More*, pp. 10, 18, 19.

49 On the links of Christian beliefs and practices and food banks, see Dowler, 'Food Banks and Food Justice', *First World Hunger Revisited*, p. 170. Garthwaite notes the importance of Christian beliefs for the volunteers at one of the food banks she works at, along with the tendency of Church of England members to vote Conservative, and links volunteers drawn to texts like Matthew 25.35–37, but makes no more observations than this. Garthwaite, *Hunger Pains*, pp. 25–9. Riches notes how important international Roman Catholic networks have been for the spreading of the food bank model and how they fail to meet the standards for social change articulated by modern Pontiffs and parts of the tradition of Catholic Social Teaching, but he gives no reason why Christians would be against 'individualism, egocentrism and materialistic consumerism' which 'weaken social bonds' and for 'fraternity' and a 'culture of solidarity'. Pope Francis, quoted in Riches, *Food Bank Nations*, p. 119.

50 The exception here is the American sociologist Rebecca de Souza who does draw associations between the American Evangelical church and neoliberal economics. She argues that American Christianity and neoliberalism share a bias towards individualism, entrepreneurialism, emphasizing morality, debt and choice and actively build distinctions between the world and the church or civil society and the state, but eschews asking whether this is a legitimate link or in continuity with the best of the Christian tradition. See Rebecca de Souza, *Feeding the Other: Whiteness, Privilege and Neoliberal Stigma in Food Pantries* (London: MIT Press, 2019), pp. 8, 45, 153, 154, 166. More broadly there is also the work of Justin Beaumont and Paul Cloke, whose focus on the term 'postsecular' has been married to an engagement with theological ideas. See Justin Beaumont and Paul Cloke, eds, *Faith-Based Organisations and Exclusion in European Cities* (Bristol: Policy Press, 2012).

51 Jacques Maritain, 'Introduction', in United Nations Educational, Scientific and Cultural Organization, *Human Rights: Comments and Interpretations*, 1948, https:// unesdoc.unesco.org/ark:/48223/pf0000155042 (accessed 29 September 2019), p. 1. The human rights perspective which marks the work of those like Graham Riches and Hannah Lambie-Mumford has the significant advantage of holding governments, like the UK's, responsible for meeting the requirements of international conventions like the United Nation's International Covenant on Economic, Social and Cultural Rights which the UK ratified in 1976. There is also data to suggest that UK focus groups feel strongly about their right to a decent standard of living, and that some political parties in England and Scotland are explicitly endorsing a human right to food approach as they go forward. See End Hunger UK, *Why End Hunger?* (2019), www.endhungeruk. org/2019/11/06/whyendukhunger/ (accessed 14 November 2019), pp. 13–15; Graham Riches, *Food Bank Nations*, pp. 170–1. While I am broadly receptive to theological engagements with human rights, and see them as being as social as they are individual, the primary aim of this book is to position food banks in a theological frame and explore what is disclosed and suggested by such a perspective. For a theological engagement with human rights, see Lisa Sowle Cahill, *Global Justice, Christology and Christian Ethics* (Cambridge: Cambridge University Press, 2013), pp. 247–89. For an excellent history of human rights' emergence as a social construct, see Peter de Bolla, *The Architecture of Concepts: The Historical Formation of Human Rights* (New York: Fordham University Press, 2013).

52 A body of literature has emerged in the last 30 years in theology, and in some parts of the political sciences and sociology, which draws close links between the ideas we inhabit and the habitats we construct. This literature is broadly called 'communitarian' or 'postliberal'. These writers see religions as cultures or languages, as 'lenses

through which human beings see and respond to their changing worlds, or the media in which they formulate their descriptions'. George A. Lindbeck, *The Nature of Doctrine* (Louisville: Westminster John Knox Press, 1984), pp. 33, 83. Other key texts in this school of thought include Alasdair MacIntrye, *After Virtue* (London: Duckworth, 2007); John Milbank, *Theology and Social Theory: Beyond Secular Reason* (Oxford: Blackwell Publishing, 2006); Charles Taylor, *Sources of the Self: The Making of Modern Identity* (Cambridge: Cambridge University Press, 1992). An essay which brings a number of these insights together and puts them into conversation with the field of ethnography is the important piece of work by Nicholas Adams and Charles Elliott, 'Ethnography is Dogmatics: Making Description Central to Systematic Theology', *Scottish Journal of Theology*, Vol. 53, No. 3 (2000), pp. 339–64.

53 The British public theologian Elaine Graham has called the need for 'bilingualism' in religiously sourced contributions to public life. Public theology, Graham says, must be 'capable of being understood by those outside its own boundaries' and that this may 'involve a process of "translation" from confessional or dogmatic language into commonly understood concepts and values'. Graham can offer strong theological reasons for taking this stance, not least God's 'self-revelation and salvific grace' beyond the boundaries of the institutional and self-proclaiming church. Elaine Graham, *Between a Rock and a Hard Place: Public Theology in a Post-secular Age* (London: SCM Press, 2013), pp. 232, 103.

54 Wendell Berry, *The Unsettling of America: Culture and Agriculture* (New York: Avon, 1978), p. 19.

55 Ibid.

56 Ibid.

57 Ibid.

58 Ibid., p. 21. Robert Song rightly asked when he read through this text whether Berry could be questioned here for neglecting the interdependence that characterizes modern societies. Emile Durkheim counter-intuitively called modern societies 'organic' and pre-modern societies 'mechanical', he noted. In Berry's defence, the change from a 'mechanical' to 'organic' society was accompanied by major changes in the ways people thought about themselves, from 'porous' to 'buffered' selves, in Charles Taylor's terms. Nevertheless, Berry's observation does need a more precise expression. A more satisfactory presentation of Berry's point, accommodating Song's observation, is that modern specialization is problematic to the degree that it refuses to recognize the tapestry of relations in which it is suspended, and that faults in the knitting of the social garment can lead to the unravelling of whole sections. The failure to recognize the social character of wealth, the importance of the state for innovation and technology and our dependence on the land, as discussed in Chapter 5 of this book, are examples, I believe, of exactly this kind of elected neglect. Emile Durkheim, *The Division of Labour in Society*, trans. George Simpson (New York: The Macmillan Company, 1960). Charles Taylor, *A Secular Age* (Cambridge, Massachusetts: Harvard University Press, 2007).

59 *Faith in Foodbanks?*, p. 4.

60 Italics in original. Gary A. Anderson, *Charity* (London: Yale University Press, 2013), p. 4.

61 Ibid., p. 32.

62 For a good introduction to the relationship between Christianity and charity in the United Kingdom, see Frank Prochaska, *Christianity and Social Service in Modern Britain: The Disinherited Spirit* (Oxford: Oxford University Press, 2006). On British Christian humanism, see Nigel Biggar, 'Why the Establishment of the Church of England

is a Good for a Liberal Society', in Mark Chapman, Judith Maltby, William Whyte, eds, *The Established Church: Past, Present and Future* (London: T & T Clark International, 2011), pp. 1–25.

63 Christopher J. H. Wright, *God's People in God's Land: Family, Land and Property in the Old Testament* (Grand Rapids: William B. Eerdmans Publishing Company, 1990). Ellen F. Davis, *Scripture, Culture and Agriculture: An Agrarian Reading of the Bible* (Cambridge: Cambridge University Press, 2008).

64 Angel F. Méndez-Montoya, *The Theology of Food: Eating and the Eucharist* (Chichester: Wiley-Blackwell, 2012). David Grumett and Rachel Muers, *Theology on the Menu: Asceticism, Meat and Christian Diet* (London: Routledge, 2010).

65 Norman Wirzba, *Food and Faith: A Theology of Eating* (Cambridge: Cambridge University Press, 2011). Alexander Schmemann, *For the Life of the World* (New York: St Vladimir's Seminary Press, 1973).

66 Wirzba, *Food and Faith*, p. 4.

67 Ibid., p. 156.

68 Galatians 2.20: 'It is no longer I who live, but it is Christ who lives in me. And the life I now live in the flesh I live by faith in the Son of God, who loved me and gave himself for me.' Quoted in Wirzba, *Food and Faith*, pp. 156–7.

69 Peter Scott, 'Creation', in Peter M. Scott, William T. Cavanaugh, eds, *Political Theology* (Oxford: Blackwell Publishing, 2007), p. 337. On the paradoxes of Christian theology, see John Milbank, *Being Reconciled: Ontology and Pardon* (London: Routledge, 2003), p. 63.

70 Wirzba, *Food and Faith*, pp. 126, 168. Graham Ward quoted, p. 168.

71 Matthew 25.40. 'Integral' is a term that has featured in a range of twentieth-century theological contexts: integral mission, integral liberation, integral ecology all carry a shared emphasis on relations and parts within larger wholes. An important source for these integral theologies were early twentieth-century theologies which emphasized the integration of nature and grace, particularly in Roman Catholic theology. For 'integral liberation', see Gustavo Gutiérrez, *A Theology of Liberation*, trans. Sister Caridad Inda, John Eagleson (New York: Orbis, 1983), pp. 168–74. For integral ecology, see Pope Francis, *Laudato Si'*, in David J. O'Brien, Thomas A. Shannon, *Catholic Social Thought: Encyclicals and Documents from Pope Leo XIII to Pope Francis* (New York: Orbis, 2016), pp. 589–676. On integral mission, see Vinay Samuel and Albrecht Hauser, eds, *Proclaiming Christ in Christ's Way: Studies in Integral Mission* (Eugene: Wipf & Stock Publishers, 2007). On the relationship of nature and grace in early twentieth-century Roman Catholic theology, see Hans Boersma, 'Nature and Supernatural in *la nouvelle theologie*: The Recovery of a Sacramental Mindset', *New Blackfriars*, Vol. 93, No. 1043 (2011), pp. 34–46.

72 www.wnyc.org/story/wendell-berry/ (accessed 12 October 2019).

73 Berry, *Unsettling of America*, p. 22.

74 Ibid.

75 Is this an idealized account of Christianity? In the ancient near east, Israelite prophets and arable norms developed in contrast to Egyptian, imperial farming practices. In the Middle Ages, theologians like St Thomas Aquinas defended local cultures and customs against the centralizing and homogenizing tendencies of monarchical rule. Today, while the complicity of Christianity in destructive patterns of thought and action has been correctly noted, the task of unearthing what is legitimate in the tradition and deploying it to take a position in a long-standing conflict is urgent, necessary and appropriate. On the emergence of Israel and Egyptian farming, see Ellen F. Davis, *Scripture,*

*Culture and Agriculture: An Agrarian Reading of the Bible* (Cambridge: Cambridge University Press, 2008), pp. 66–79. On Thomas Aquinas and the defence of peasant cultures, see Alasdair MacIntyre, 'Natural Law as Subversive: The Case of Aquinas', in *Ethics and Politics: Selected Essays, Volume 2* (Cambridge: Cambridge University Press, 2006), pp. 41–63. On the multiple failings and ongoing utility of Christian theology in relation to ecology, see Leonardo Boff, *Cry of the Earth, Cry of the Poor*, trans. Philip Berryman (New York: Orbis Books, 1997), pp. 75–81.

76 Wirzba, *Food and Faith*, p. 173. In 'The Re-homing of the Human? A Theological Enquiry into whether Human Beings are at Home on Earth', the Anglican ecotheologian Professor Peter Scott says that the historical context of contemporary Christian theology is defeat: 'one in which theology has gradually given way in the task of providing persuasive explanations' of the world, its origin and its purpose. This defeat has been 'written on theology's body' and while it is possible that this defeat may help the church learn and theology progress, we also need to consider the possibility that theology's 'response to defeat led to the deepening of defeat through the narrowing of theology'. I take it that a part of what Scott is saying here is that the difficulty of the theological task moving forward is articulating plausible accounts of the Christian tradition without claiming a complete monopoly on the truth or possession of the only viable interpretation of the tradition. One instance in which theology has learnt from disciplines outside its immediate remit and its loss has simultaneously been its gain is in our changing understanding of hunger's cause. James Vernon writes in *Hunger: A Modern History* that 'between roughly the middle of the nineteenth and the middle of the twentieth centuries, the notion of hunger as either an unfortunate if unavoidable part of God's divine plan or the necessary sign of an individual's moral failure to learn the virtue of labour was gradually displaced, if never entirely superseded, by the discovery that hunger was a collective social problem.' See Peter Scott, 'The Re-homing of the Human? A Theological Enquiry into whether Human Beings are at Home on Earth', in Ernst M. Conradie, ed., *Christian Faith and the Earth: Current Paths and Emerging Horizons in Ecotheology* (London: T & T Clark, 2014), pp. 115–35, at pp. 119, 120. James Vernon, *Hunger: A Modern History* (Cambridge, MA: Belknap Press), p. 2.

77 Rachel Loopstra, Hannah Lambie-Mumford and Jasmine Fledderjohann, 'Food Bank Operational Characteristics and Rates of Food Bank Use across Britain', *BMC Public Health*, Vol. 19, No. 561 (2019), pp. 1–10. Riches, *Food Bank Nations*, p. 6.

78 A common definition of 'food insecurity', cited in *First World Hunger Revisited*, is 'limited or uncertain availability of nutritionally adequate and safe foods or limited or uncertain ability to acquire acceptable foods in socially acceptable ways'. Graham Riches, Tiina Silvasti, eds, *First World Hunger Revisited: Food Charity or the Right to Food* (New York: Palgrave Macmillan, 2014), p. 6.

79 Riches, *Food Bank Nations*, pp. 172, 173.

80 Karl Marx's observations about the need for unemployment in a capitalist system, to help suppress wages and give the employer a disciplinary tool ('work or I replace you') is still drawn on by academics who see economic utility – more profits – in current unemployment. See David McLellan, ed., *Karl Marx: Selected Writings* (Oxford: Oxford University Press, 2011), p. 518. David Graeber, *Bullshit Jobs: A Theory* (London: Allen Lane, 2018), p. 156. Lansley and Mack, *Breadline Britain*, pp. 101–3.

81 Riches and Silvasti, *First World Hunger Revisited*, p. 2.

82 Ibid.

83 Norman Wirzba, ed., *The Essential Agrarian Reader: The Future of Culture, Community, and the Land* (Berkeley: Counterpoint Press, 2003), p. 9.

84 George Monbiot, *Out of the Wreckage: A New Politics for an Age of Crisis* (London: Verso, 2018), p. 17.

85 Karl Polanyi, *The Great Transformation: The Political and Economic Origins of Our Time* (Boston: Beacon Press, 2001), p. 42.

86 Ibid., pp. 134, 135.

87 Ibid., p. 225.

88 Martijn Konings, *The Emotional Logic of Capitalism: What Progressives have Missed* (Stanford: Stanford University Press, 2015), p. 15.

89 Ibid., p. 2.

90 Konings, *The Emotional Logic of Capitalism*, p. 2.

91 Damien Cahill and Martijn Konings, *Neoliberalism* (Cambridge: Polity Press, 2017), pp. 110, 111.

92 Andrew Williams, Paul Cloke, Jon May and Mark Goodwin, 'Contested Space: The Contradictory Political Dynamics of Foodbanking in the UK', *Environment and Planning A*, Vol. 48, No. 11 (2016), pp. 2291–316. Chris Allen, 'Food Poverty and Christianity in Britain: A Theological Re-assessment', *Political Theology*, Vol. 17, No. 4 (2016), pp. 361–77.

93 International Panel of Experts on Sustainable Food System, *Too Big To Feed*, 2017, www.ipes-food.org/_img/upload/files/Concentration_FullReport.pdf (accessed 1 October 2019), p. 12.

94 The food sustainability agenda, Jennifer Clapp argues, has been deeply affected in recent years by the norms of 'agricultural trade liberalization'. In this book, the term sustainable is still used but as it is defined by Herman E. Daly when he writes that 'physical *throughput*, the entropic physical flow from nature's sources through the economy and back to nature's sinks, should be sustained and non-declining. More exactly, the capacity of the ecosystem to sustain energy/food flows over the long term is not to be run down.' Jennifer Clapp, 'The Trade-ification of the food sustainability agenda', *The Journal of Peasant Studies*, Vol. 44, No. 2 (2017), pp. 335–53. Herman E. Daly, 'Sustainable Economic Development', in Norman Wirzba, ed., *The Essential Agrarian Reader: The Future of Culture, Community, and the Land* (Berkeley: Counterpoint Press, 2003), pp. 62–79, at p. 62.

## Food Bank Lives

1 Rachel Loopstra and Doireann Lalor, *Financial Insecurity, Food Insecurity, and Disability: The Profile of People Receiving Emergency Food Assistance from The Trussell Trust Foodbank Network in Britain* (Salisbury: Trussell Trust, 2017), www.trusselltrust.org/wp-content/uploads/sites/2/2017/07/OU_Report_final_01_08_online2.pdf (accessed 19 July 2019). The Trussell Trust, to their credit, 'recognised the need to better understand who is receiving their emergency food parcels, and particularly, their short- and long-term financial circumstances, their experiences of food insecurity, and their health'. Ibid., p. 9.

2 Loopstra and Lalor, *Financial Insecurity, Food Insecurity, and Disability*, p. viii.

3 Ibid.

4 Ibid.

5 Ibid.

6 Ibid.

7 Ibid.

8 linkis.com/blacktrianglecampaign.org/d1Ume (accessed 16 July 2019).

9 Frances Ryan, 'How many benefits claimants have to kill themselves before something is done?' *The Guardian*, 10 February 2015, www.theguardian.com/commentisfree/2015/feb/10/benefits-sanctions-malcolm-burge-suicides (accessed 16 July 2019).

10 China Mills, 'Dead People Don't Claim: A Psychopolitical Autopsy of UK Austerity Suicides', *Critical Social Policy*, Vol. 38, No. 2 (2018), pp. 302–22, at p. 302. Also, see: Mandy Cheetham, Suzanne Moffatt and Michelle Addison, *It's Hitting People that Can Least Afford It the Hardest: The Impact of the Roll Out of Universal Credit in Two North East England Localities: A Qualitative Study*, 2018, www.gateshead.gov.uk/media/10665/The-impact-of-the-roll-out-of-Universal-Credit-in-two-North-East-England-localities-a-qualitative-study-November-2018/pdf/Universal_Credit_Report_2018pdf.pdf?m=63677883108163oooo (accessed 16 July 2019), p. 24.

11 Loopstra and Lalor, *Financial Insecurity, Food Insecurity, and Disability*, p. 22. Abigail Marks, Sue Cowan and Gavin Maclean, *Mental Health and Unemployment in Scotland: Understanding the Impact of Welfare Reforms in Scotland for Individuals with Mental Health Conditions* (2017), www.advocard.org.uk/wp-content/uploads/2017/02/2017-02-Heriot-Watt-Mental-Health-Report-on-WCA.pdf (accessed 16 July 2019), p. 17.

12 In addition, 11% of respondents provided no employment information, and 5% combined unemployment with economic inactivity. Loopstra and Lalor, *Financial Insecurity, Food Insecurity, and Disability*, p. 22.

13 Ibid., p. 25.

14 Ibid.

15 Ibid., p. 29.

16 Ibid.

17 Ibid., p. 32.

18 Ibid., p. 46.

19 Ibid., p. 34.

20 Ibid.

21 Ibid.

22 Ibid., p. 41.

23 Ibid.

24 Ibid., pp. 43, 46.

25 See A. Tinson, C. Ayrton, K. Barker, T. B. Born, H. Aldridge and P. Kenway, *Monitoring Poverty and Social Exclusion 2016* (New Policy Institute, 2016), www.jrf.org.uk/report/monitoring-poverty-and-social-exclusion-2016 (accessed 2 August 2018). Quoted in Loopstra and Lalor, *Financial Insecurity, Food Insecurity, and Disability*, p. 43.

26 See www.conservativehome.com/platform/2019/01/gareth-streeter-three-facts-which-suggest-a-rise-in-food-bank-use-is-not-just-down-to-universal-credit.html (accessed 16 July 2019) and www.dailymail.co.uk/news/article-3139159/I-welcome-food-banks-says-Iain-Duncan-Smith-claims-sign-decent-people-helping-difficulty.html (accessed 16 July 2019).

27 Loopstra and Lalor, *Financial Insecurity, Food Insecurity, and Disability*, p. 46.

28 Ibid.

29 Government policy relating to the level and causes of demand for food banks, and the broader provision of food assistance, is currently spread across eight departments: the Department for Work and Pensions (DWP) for social security benefits, Her Majesty's Revenue and Customs (HMRC) for tax credits, the Department for Business, Innovation and Skills (BIS) for labour market and wages policy, the Department for Environment,

Food and Rural Affairs (DEFRA) for food policy, the Department of Health for mal-nutrition, the Department of Energy and Climate Change (DECC) for energy costs, the Department for Education for school meals, and the Cabinet Office for voluntary provision. All-Party Parliamentary Inquiry into Hunger in the United Kingdom, *Feeding Britain: A Strategy for Zero Hunger in England, Wales, Scotland and Northern Ireland* (2014), https://feedingbritain.org/wp-content/uploads/2019/01/feeding_britain_report_2014-2.pdf (accessed 19 July 2019), p. 32.

30 Though limited by its unsustainable juxtaposition of the social and the economic, Karl Polanyi's account of the commodification of land and labour leading inevitably to the liquidification of the culture of any traditional community remains a seminal text in economic history and socialist theory. Karl Polanyi, *The Great Transformation: The Political and Economic Origins of our Time* (Boston: Beacon Press, 2001), pp. 158–70. For a recent criticism of Polanyi, see Adam Kotsko, *Neoliberalism's Demons: On the Political Theology of Late Capital* (Stanford: Stanford University Press, 2018), p. 134.

31 Norman Wirzba, ed., *The Essential Agrarian Reader: The Future of Culture, Community, and the Land* (Berkeley: Counterpoint Press, 2003), p. 9.

32 Ibid.

33 Ibid.

34 Ibid.

35 Guy Standing, *The Precariat: The New Dangerous Class* (London: Bloomsbury, 2016), p. 1.

36 Damien Cahill and Martijn Konings, *Neoliberalism* (Cambridge: Polity Press, 2017), p. 33.

37 Ibid.

38 Philip Goodchild writes in *Theology of Money* that 'economic globalization is the completion of this anti-political process throughout the world through millions of minor acts of alienation between people and people, people and land, and land its products or resources. It fragments the world of public representation through substitution and exchange.' Philip Goodchild, *Theology of Money* (London: SCM Press, 2007), p. 64. See also John Atherton, *Transfiguring Capitalism: An Enquiry into Religion and Global Change* (London: SCM Press, 2008), pp. 41–4, and David Harvey, *The New Imperialism* (Oxford: Oxford University Press, 2003), p. 62.

39 Standing, *Precariat*, p. 1. Growth of credit card debt is a very current manifestation of this tendency.

40 Standing, *Precariat*, pp. 32, 70, 32, 35, 34, 64.

41 Nick Srnicek and Alex Williams, *Inventing the Future: Postcapitalism and a World without Work* (London: Verso, 2016), p. 87.

42 Ibid., pp. 92, 93.

43 Standing, *Precariat*, p. 10. Srnicek and Williams, *Inventing the Future*, p. 93.

44 Lansley and Mack, *Breadline Britain*, p. 115.

45 See Chrystia Freeland, *Plutocrats: The Rise of the New Global Super-rich and the Fall of Everyone Else* (New York: Penguin, 2013).

46 Standing, *Precariat*, p. 8.

47 Standing, *Precariat*, p. 11.

48 Ibid., p. 12.

49 Ibid., pp. 13, 14.

50 Ibid., p. 28.

51 Ibid., p. 22.

52 Ibid., pp. 26–8.

53 Ibid., pp. 28, 29.

54 Ibid., p. 101.

55 Kotsko, *Neoliberalism's Demons*, pp. 72, 77–8.

56 Cahill, Konings, *Neoliberalism*, p. 75.

57 The Troubled Families programme was launched after the August Riots 2011 and targeted 120,000 families with the aim of turning them around by May 2015. David Cameron, in the aftermath of the riot, described the rioters' parents as 'often welfare reliant single mothers', 'without fathers', and the young people themselves as 'never wanting to work'. The programme was hailed as a success with a 73% turnaround rate, despite serious questions about the source of the 120,000 figure and lack of investigation into the families' socio-economic outcomes once they had been 'turned around'. Harriet Churchill, 'Turning Lives around? The Troubled Families Programme', in Liam Foster, Anne Brunton, Chris Deeming and Tina Haux, eds, *In Defence of Welfare* (York: Social Policy Association, 2015), www.social-policy.org.uk/what-we-do/publications/in-defence-of-welfare-2/ (accessed 12 October 2019), pp. 28–31.

58 https://parliamentlive.tv/event/index/4ed4b537-2726-41e0-b11c-e98e73c81ea2?in=14:35:50 (accessed 17 July 2019).

59 Standing, *Precariat*, p. 52.

60 See Jane Perry, *Paying Over the Odds? Real-life Experiences of the Poverty Premium* (Church Action on Poverty, 2010), www.church-poverty.org.uk/wp-content/uploads/2019/06/Paying-Over-the-Odds-report.pdf (accessed 11 October 2019).

61 Standing, *Precariat*, p. 52.

62 'Terminator' is also the name of a biological control mechanism, a technology which 'renders sterile the second generation of seed' forcing farmers to buy new seeds each year. The 'Big Six', some of whom have close links with 'genetic use restriction technologies (GURTs)', Syngenta, Bayer, DuPont, Monsanto, BASF, and Dow 'currently control both 60% of the global seed market and 75% of the global pesticide market'. See Ellen F. Davis, *Scripture, Culture and Agriculture: An Agrarian Reading of the Bible* (Cambridge: Cambridge University Press, 2008), p. 52. And International Panel of Experts on Sustainable Food System, *Too Big To Feed* (International Panel of Experts on Sustainable Food Systems, 2017), www.ipes-food.org/_img/upload/files/Concentration_FullReport.pdf (accessed 1 October 2019), p. 21. These agro-chemical giants control large proportions of the agriculture of the global South, keeping Southern farmers in a dependent relationship through seed, technology and farm supply monopolies while also manufacturing and transporting to the global North many of the products which will in the end be distributed through food banks.

63 See https://handcrafted.org.uk (accessed 11 October 2019).

64 David Graeber, *Bullshit Jobs: A Theory* (London: Allen Lane, 2018), p. 83.

65 Ibid.

66 Ibid., pp. 82, 209–11. The exception to the rule is doctors.

67 Ibid., p. xviii.

## International Growth of Food Banks

1 Rachel Loopstra and Doireann Lalor, *Financial Insecurity, Food Insecurity, and Disability: The Profile of People Receiving Emergency Food Assistance from The Trussell Trust Foodbank Network in Britain* (Salidbury: Trussell Trust, 2017), www.trusselltrust.org/wp-content/uploads/sites/2/2017/07/OU_Report_final_01_08_online2.pdf (accessed 19 July 2019), p. 47.

2 Ibid.

3 Rachel Loopstra, Hannah Lambie-Mumford and Jasmine Fledderjohann, 'Food Bank Operational Characteristics and Rates of Food Bank Use across Britain', *BMC Public Health*, Vol. 19, No. 561 (2019), pp. 1–10, at p. 2.

4 Ibid.

5 Ibid., p. 7. While Loopstra, through research on the Trussell Trust network, did find correlations between food bank accessibility and food bank use (which is worrying, as it suggests that limited accessibility in some areas will be inhibiting people's ability to engage with the service, particularly for disabled people), the relationships were not always obvious. Those in in-work poverty, for example, were not finding it harder to access food banks that were closed in the evening or at weekends. Ibid., pp. 8, 6.

6 Loopstra, Mumford and Fledderjohann, 'Food Bank Ooperational Characteristics', p. 8.

7 Janet Poppendieck, *Breadlines: Knee-Deep in Wheat, Food Assistance in the Great Depression* (Berkeley: University of California Press, 2014). Graham Riches, *Food Bank Nations: Poverty, Corporate Charity and the Right to Food* (London: Routledge, 2018), pp. 35, 36.

8 Riches, *Food Bank Nations*, p. 35.

9 Ibid., p. 36.

10 Ibid.

11 Douglas Martin, 'John van Hengel, 83, Dies; Set Up First Food Bank in U.S.', *New York Times*, 8 October 2005, www.nytimes.com/2005/10/08/us/john-van-hengel-83-dies-set-up-first-food-bank-in-us.html (accessed 29 July 2019).

12 Riches, *Food Bank Nations*, p. 36.

13 Ibid., p. 40.

14 www.eurofoodbank.org (accessed 4 April 2019).

15 Ibid.

16 Riches, *Food Bank Nations*, p. 41.

17 Ibid.

18 Ibid., p. 43.

19 Ibid., pp. 52, 53.

20 Ibid., pp. 54, 23.

21 Ibid., p. 45.

22 Ibid., p. 54.

23 Ibid., pp. 156–7.

24 Rebecca Wells and Martin Caraher, 'UK Print Media Coverage of the Food Bank Phenomenon: From Food Welfare to Food Charity?', *British Food Journal*, Vol. 116, No. 9, pp. 1426–45, at p. 1432.

25 Fareshare, *The Wasted Opportunity* (2018), fareshare.org.uk/wp-content/uploads/2018/10/J3503-Fareshare-Report_aw_no_crops.pdf (accessed 29 July 2019), p. 9.

26 fareshare.org.uk/what-we-do/our-impact/ (accessed 4 April 2019).

27 www.thegrocer.co.uk/home/topics/waste-not-want-not/asda-set-to-spend-20m-on-key-food-waste-charities/563157.article (accessed 4 April 2019).

28 https://fareshare.org.uk/what-we-do/hunger-food-waste/ (accessed 4 April 2019).

29 www.wrap.org.uk/content/surplus-food-redistribution-wrap-work (accessed 4 April 2019).

30 Fareshare, *The Wasted Opportunity* (2018), https://fareshare.org.uk/wp-content/uploads/2018/10/J3503-Fareshare-Report_aw_no_crops.pdf (accessed 29 July 2019), p. 5.

31 Riches, *Food Bank Nations*, pp. 166–7, https//feedingbritain.org/what-we-do/policy-issues/food-surplus-redistribution/ (accessed 4 April 2019). The British government confirms here that there are tax incentives for surplus redistribution of good quality food. Arguably, this is a tax which disincentivizes proportionate production and rewards the waste generated by an unsustainable food system.

32 Fareshare, *The Wasted Opportunity* (2018), https://fareshare.org.uk/wp-content/uploads/2018/10/J3503-Fareshare-Report_aw_no_crops.pdf (accessed 29 July 2019).

33 Fareshare state that 52,000 to 160,000 tonnes are lost during processing and manufacturing, 80,000–120,000 at wholesale and distribution and 47,000–110,000 at retail; there are also significant losses in waste from homes: fareshare.org.uk/what-we-do/hunger-food-waste/ (accessed 4 April 2019).

34 Wendell Berry, *The Art of Loading Brush: New Agrarian Writings* (Berkeley: Counterpoint, 2017), p. 40.

35 Food and Agriculture Organization of the United Nations, *Food Wastage Footprint: Impacts on Natural Resources* (2013), www.fao.org/3/i3347e/i3347e.pdf (accessed 4 April 2019).

36 Ibid., p. 6.

37 Ibid. Also see WRAP, *Surplus and Waste in the UK – Key Facts* (2019), www.wrap.org.uk/sites/files/wrap/Food%20Surplus%20and%20Waste%20in%20the%20UK%20Key%20Facts%20%2822%207%2019%29_0.pdf (accessed 12 October 2019), p. 13.

38 Food and Agriculture Organization, *Food Wastage Footprint*, p. 6.

39 www.youtube.com/watch?v=RcPaC8lsNhg (accessed 29 July 2019).

40 Riches, *Food Bank Nations*, p. 68.

41 Paul McMahon, *Feeding Frenzy: The New Politics of Food* (London: Profile Books, 2014), p. 94.

42 Ibid., pp. 94, 254–60, 45.

43 Ibid., p. 261. McMahon says that 'if there is one theme that runs throughout this book, it is that Government policy has a huge effect on food systems' and that taking this seriously in the present day means that 'commodity futures markets should be tightly regulated to ensure that they serve the interests of farmers, traders and consumers, rather than becoming a casino for financial speculators'. Ibid., pp. 268, 255.

44 www.reform-magazine.co.uk/2014/04/at-home-with-charity/ (accessed 3 July 2019).

45 Ibid.

46 Ibid.

47 Ibid.

48 Ibid.

49 Ibid.

50 Ibid.

51 Ibid.

52 www.trusselltrust.org/news-and-blog/latest-stats/ (accessed 29 July 2019).

53 www.trusselltrust.org/news-and-blog/latest-stats/end-year-stats/ (accessed 4 April 2019).

54 www.trusselltrust.org/what-we-do/more-than-food/ (accessed 4 April 2019).

55 www.trusselltrust.org/news-and-blog/latest-stats/end-year-stats/ (accessed 4 April 2019).

56 Ibid.

57 Wells and Caraher, 'Print Media Coverage of the Food Bank', *British Food*, p. 1427.

58 Ibid., p. 1434.

59 www.theguardian.com/politics/2013/dec/21/iain-duncan-smith-food-banks-charities (accessed 5 April 2019).

60 www.theguardian.com/global-development/2012/may/10/jacob-rees-mogg-overseas-aid (accessed 5 April 2019). Also www.independent.co.uk/news/uk/politics/jacob-rees-mogg-uk-food-bank-uplifting-conservative-mp-leader-a7946096.html (accessed 5 April 2019).

61 Kayleigh Garthwaite, *Hunger Pains: Life inside Foodbank Britain* (Bristol: Policy Press, 2016), p. 3.

62 Ibid., p. 7.

63 Ibid., p. 3.

64 Ibid., p. 11.

65 Ibid.

66 Ibid., p. 4.

67 Robert Colls and Bill Lancaster, eds, *Geordies* (Edinburgh: Edinburgh University Press, 1992), p. 39.

68 David Byrne, 'Industrial Culture in a Post-industrial World: The Case of the North East of England', *City*, Vol. 6, No. 3 (2002), pp. 279–89, at p. 282.

69 Ibid., p. 282.

70 Ibid.

71 Ibid., p. 281.

72 Ibid., p. 284.

73 Guy Standing, *Universal Basic Income: And How We Can Make it Happen* (London: Penguin, 2017), pp. 29, 30.

74 Colls and Lancaster, *Geordies*, p. 37.

75 Byrne, 'Industrial Culture', pp. 284, 281.

76 Colls and Lancaster, *Geordies*, p. 40.

77 Ibid., p. 39.

78 Ibid., p. 40.

79 Ibid., p. 42. A high value on the pound is problematic for exports, as goods produced in other countries with cheaper labour and currencies can sell at lower prices.

80 Cahill and Konings, *Neoliberalism*, p. 73.

81 Ibid., pp. 45, 46.

82 www.independent.co.uk/news/uk/home-news/north-south-divide-is-over-says-blair-744095.html (accessed 19 July 2019).

83 Tony Blair (Sedgefield), David Miliband (South Shields), Peter Mandelson (Hartlepool), Hilary Armstrong (North West Durham), Alan Milburn (Darlington), Mo Mowlam (Redcar) and Nick Brown (Newcastle East).

84 Louise Dalingwater, 'Regional Performance in the UK under New Labour', *Observatoire de la société britannique*, Vol. 10 (2011), pp. 115–36, journals.open edition.org/osb/1151#text (accessed 19 July 2019). Fred Robinson, Ian Zass-Ogilvie and Michael Jackson, *Never had it so good? The North East Under New Labour 1997–2007* (Durham: St Chad's College, Durham University, 2007).

85 Newcastle University Institute of Health and Society, *Visit by the UN Special Rapporteur on Extreme Poverty and Human Rights, Written Submission* (2018), www.ohchr.org/Documents/Issues/EPoverty/UnitedKingdom/2018/Academics/Newcastle_University_Institute_of_Health_and_Society.pdf (accessed 29 July 2019), p. 3.

86 Ibid., p. 2.

87 www.theguardian.com/business/2012/feb/05/financial-crisis-economics (accessed 19 July 2019).

88 Ibid.

89 Newcastle, *Visit by UN Special Rapporteur*, p. 4.

90 Ibid.

91 Ibid., p. 5.

92 Ibid., p. 6. For more, see: Lloyds Bank Foundation and New Policy Institute, *A Quiet Crisis: Local Government Spending on Disadvantage in England* (2018), www.lloydsbankfoundation.org.uk/A%20Quiet%20Crisis%20-%20Summary.pdf (accessed 29 July 2019).

93 www.theguardian.com/business/2012/feb/05/financial-crisis-economics (accessed 19 July 2019).

94 Data from the Office for National Statistics, www.tuc.org.uk/northern/news/400000-working-age-people-north-east-are-living-poverty (accessed 18 July 2019).

95 Andrew McCulloch, John Mohan and Peter Smith, 'Patterns of Social Capital, Voluntary Activity, and Area Deprivation in England', *Environment and Planning*, Vol. 44, No. 5 (2013), pp. 1130–47.

96 Newcastle, *Visit by UN Special Rapporteur*, p. 7.

97 Ibid.

98 www.bbc.co.uk/news/uk-england-tees-30483153 (accessed 29 September 2019).

99 http://apps.charitycommission.gov.uk/Accounts/Ends49/0001077549_AC_2017 1231_E_C.pdf (accessed 29 July 2019).

100 Riches, *Food Bank Nations*, p. 165.

101 Ibid., p. 167.

102 Robert Paarlberg, *Food Politics: What Everybody Needs to Know* (Oxford: Oxford University Press, 2010), pp. 22–5.

103 Vandana Shiva, *Making Peace with the Earth* (London: Pluto Press, 2013), p. 138.

104 Garthwaite, *Hunger Pains*, p. 10.

105 Ibid.

106 Wren-Lewis says that subjecting the British economy to austerity at such a vulnerable moment after the great recession 'was the equivalent of putting a sick patient on a starvation diet accompanied by cold showers'. The way austerity was targeted hit 'demand rich' areas like local authority budgets, welfare benefits and investment which spur output in the economy and solidify economic growth. Austerity went against economic orthodoxy, against the advice of the academic economic community, showed that Osborne had not learnt from the Japanese liquidity trap of the 1990s nor taken on board the limits of monetary policy when nominal interest rates hit their lower bound. Conversely, it showed Wren-Lewis how powerful media narratives ('mediamacro') can be in setting and reinforcing government economic policy. Wren-Lewis calls Osborne's austerity 'the most damaging UK macroeconomic policy mistake in my lifetime as an economist' and says that 'the real puzzle is why so many people think the Government is economically competent'. See Simon Wren-Lewis, *The Lies We Were Told* (Bristol: Bristol University Press, 2018), pp. 270, 33, 35, 44, 45, 53, 51, 124, 125, 51, 125.

107 Ibid., p. 52.

108 Phillip Mirowki recognizes that raising human welfare has been a part of neo-liberal discourse, but only in a highly contradictory way. He writes that neoliberals wish to have it both ways: 'To warn of the perils of expanding the purview of state activity *while simultaneously* imagining the strong state of their liking rendered harm-less through some instrumentality of "natural" regulation; to posit the free market as an ideal generator and a conveyor belt of information *while simultaneously* prosecuting a "war of ideas" on the ground strenuously and ruthlessly ... asserting that their pro-gram would lead to unfettered economic growth and enhanced human welfare *while simultaneously* suggesting that no human mind could ever really know any such thing, and therefore that it was illegitimate to justify their program by its consequences ... to portray the market as the *ne plus ultra* of all human institutions, *while simultaneously* suggesting that the market is in itself insufficient to attain and nourish the transeconomic values of a political, social, religious and cultural character.' Philip Mirowski and Dieter Plehwe, eds, *The Road from Mont Pèlerin, The Making of the Neoliberal Thought Collective* (London: Harvard University Press, 2009), pp. 442–3.

## Food, Faith, Food Banks

1 Rebecca de Souza, *Feeding the Other: Whiteness, Privilege and Neoliberal Stigma in Food Pantries* (London: MIT Press, 2019), p. 222.

2 Ibid., pp. 8, 11. De Souza traces a number of issues around food banks, particu-larly around stigma, back to Weber's account of the coincidence of a Christian mentality and an emerging economic practice. The difference between deserving and undeserving poor, economic success as a sign of God's blessing, the autonomy and importance of the individual, and how the value and importance of work and habits of working changed as people's view of the afterlife shifted are all elements of the present influenced by a Christian past, in de Souza's account. While she certainly does note alternative outlooks and inclinations in the Christian volunteers, her preponderant line of analysis is the con-flation of the economic, political and theological in her descriptions of the food banks she attended and what they promote. For her, they embody 'spiritual entrepreneurship' or 'pious neoliberalism'. The link between Christian Republicans and neoliberals in the twentieth- and twenty-first-century history of the United States makes these valid links to explore, given the failure of the USA to address its food insecurity problems, its ongoing issues around race and racism and its ecological footprint. What this analysis fails to account for are the differences between Protestant and proceeding Catholic engagements with money and the discontinuities between the parent Protestantism and its child capitalism, as noted by Weber himself and early interlocutors with his work like R. H. Tawney. See de Souza, *Feeding the Other*, pp. 141, 128, 134–56. For an excellent review of Roman Catholic approaches to money historically and what this implies for Weber, see Stefano Zamagni, 'Catholic Social Thought, Civil Economy, and the Spirit of Capitalism', in Daniel Finn, ed., *The True Wealth of Nations* (Oxford: Oxford Uni-versity Press, 2010), pp. 63–93. For Weber's differentiation of Protestant and capitalist societies, see Max Weber, *The Protestant Ethic and the Spirit of Capitalism*, trans. Talcott Parsons (London: Routledge, 2001), pp. 124–5. R. H. Tawney, *Religion and the Rise of Capitalism* (London: Butler & Tanner, 1969).

3 Todd LeVasseur, 'Introduction', in Todd LeVasseur, Pramod Parajuli and Norman Wirzba, eds, *Religion and Sustainable Agriculture: World Spiritual Traditions and Food Ethics* (Lexington: University of Kentucky Press, 2016), p. 2.

4 Gretel Van Wieren, *Food, Farming and Religion: Emerging Ethical Perspectives* (London: Routledge, 2018), p. 45.

5 Ibid., p. 139.

6 The term 'kenosis' refers to a Pauline text in Philippians 2 which states that Jesus 'did not regard equality with God as something to be exploited but emptied (*ekenōsen*) himself, taking the form of a slave, being born in human likeness, and being found in human form, he humbled himself and became obedient to the point of death – even death on a cross'. Kenosis, as Donald MacKinnon notes, has been a highly contested concept in Christology. MacKinnon asks whether it could be viably supposed 'that the Lord abandoned his cosmic functions for the period of the incarnation or even within the sphere of the incarnate life, withheld himself from their exercise'. Nevertheless, MacKinnon goes on, 'such paradoxes' are defensible not only because of their Pauline basis but because of 'the unfaltering stress of the Fourth Gospel on the Son's dependence on the Father, on an authority affirmed because of and in the context of a supreme humility, an "infinite self-abnegation". The concept of *kenosis* advertises the relevance of the costliness of the incarnate life to the absolute. If one cares, so to speak, it raises again the issue of divine impassibility by asking what light, if any, the manner of the ministry and passion of Jesus throws upon the being of the divine in itself, and on the nature of its relation to the created world.' In other words, kenosis is difficult to understand, and even harder to enact. John C. McDowell, Scott A. Kirkland and Ashley John Moyse, eds, *Kenotic Ecclesiology: Selected Writings of Donald M. MacKinnon* (Minneapolis: Fortress Press, 2016), p. 176. Cf. Philippians 2.6–8.

7 Corrie E. Norman, 'Food and Religion', in Jeffrey M. Pilcher, ed., *The Oxford Handbook of Food History* (Oxford: Oxford University Press, 2012), pp. 409–27, at p. 409.

8 LeVasseur, 'Introduction', *Religion and Sustainable Agriculture*, p. 1.

9 Vandana Shiva, 'Foreword', in Todd LeVasseur, Pramod Parajuli, Norman Wirzba, eds, *Religion and Sustainable Agriculture: World Spiritual Traditions and Food Ethics* (Lexington: University of Kentucky Press, 2016), pp. vii–x, at p. vii.

10 Ibid.

11 Ibid., pp. viii, vii.

12 David Grumett and Rachel Muers, *Theology on the Menu: Asceticism, Meat and Christian Diet* (London: Routledge, 2010), p. 1.

13 Ibid., p. 2.

14 Ibid., p. 5.

15 Ibid.

16 Ibid.

17 Ibid.

18 Ibid.

19 Ibid., p. 6.

20 Ibid., p. 32.

21 Ibid., p. 12.

22 Ibid., p. 13.

23 Ibid., p. 15.

24 Ibid., p. 16.

25 Ibid. When the donkey mysteriously disappears, the lion is suspected. He bears this stoically, before it is discovered that the donkey was stolen by camel drivers! Returned to the community by the lion, the donkey is saved and the lion's place in the community restored.

26 Ibid.

27 Ibid., p. 24.

28 Ibid.

29 Ibid. The contention that the modern, industrial food system is fundamentally defensible given that the medieval diet was bland and basic and sometimes insufficient is an important point and a legitimate warning against some forms of anachronism but ultimately unsustainable because the current food system is, ultimately, unsustainable. For a spirited defence of culinary modernism, see Rachel Laudan's article, 'A Plea for Culinary Modernism: Why We Should Love New, Fast, Processed Food', www.jacobin mag.com/2015/05/slow-food-artisanal-natural-preservatives (accessed 25 July 2019).

30 Grumett and Muers, pp. 25, 26.

31 Ibid., p. 35.

32 Ellen F. Davis, *Scripture, Culture and Agriculture: An Agrarian Reading of the Bible* (Cambridge: Cambridge University Press, 2008), p. 8.

33 Ibid., p. 2.

34 Deuteronomy 11.10–12.

35 Leviticus 25.23.

36 Davis, *Scripture, Culture and Agriculture*, p. 100.

37 Romans 8.18–23.

38 Davis, *Scripture, Culture and Agriculture*, p. 29.

39 Brian Swimme and Thomas Berry, *The Universe Story: From the Primordial Flaring Forth to the Ecozoic Era* (San Francisco: Harper, 1992), p. 243.

40 Norman Wirzba, quoted in Davis, *Scripture, Culture and Agriculture*, p. 32.

41 Davis, *Scripture, Culture and Agriculture*, p. 34. A similar point, noting the limits of the predominantly scientific framing of the climate change debate and welcoming perspectives from other social scientific and humanities disciplines, can be seen in Andrea Joslyn Nightingale and others, 'Beyond Technical Fixes: Climate Solutions and the Great Derangement', *Climate and Development*, published online 1 July 2019, www.tand fonline.com/doi/full/10.1080/17565529.2019.1624495 (accessed 17 November 2019).

42 Davis, *Scripture, Culture and Agriculture*, p. 36.

43 Grumett and Muers, *Theology on the Menu*, p. 86.

44 Ibid., p. 87.

45 The public theologian John Atherton says that 'the market plays a central part in the debate over well-being and has an indispensable part to play in the future, howbeit an evolving and reformulated one'. He goes on to write that 'with the price system matching supply and demand', modern complex societies have 'an indispensable information co-ordinating function and signalling system for the allocation of relatively scarce resources'. There is much truth to this and Atherton rightly notes that market exchanges have helped generate goods for many individuals and contributed to many being lifted from poverty. However, the utility of markets for processing information cannot fully replace the human attempt to discern the limits of the earth's resources or their best allocation. The great neoliberal economist F. A. Hayek's argument in *The Road to Serfdom* that market-led organization of goods was superior to any system of human (state) planning is not sustainable in its original form given the growing awareness that market prices do not factor in many important issues, like the external costs of pollution and even, according to Herman E. Daly, the value of natural resources. See John Atherton, *Transfiguring Capitalism: An Enquiry into Religion and Global Change* (London: SCM Press, 2008), pp. 139, 140; F. A. Hayek, *The Road to Serfdom* (London: The University of Chicago Press, 2007); Herman E. Daly, 'Sustainable Economic

Development', in Norman Wirzba, ed., *The Essential Agrarian Reader: The Future of Culture, Community, and the Land* (Berkeley: Counterpoint Press, 2003), pp. 62–79, at p. 70.

46 Barbara Kingsolver, quoted in Davis, *Scripture, Culture and Agriculture*, p. 37.

47 Ibid., p. 39.

48 Ibid.

49 Ibid., p. 110.

50 Wendell Berry, quoted in ibid., p. 16.

51 Davis, *Scripture, Culture and Agriculture*, p. 73.

52 Ibid., p. 94.

53 Ibid., p. 7. See John 4 and Revelation 21.

54 C. S. Lewis, *Miracles: A Preliminary Study* (London: Geoffrey Bles, 1947), p. 162.

55 Ibid., p. 163.

56 John 5.19; 6.5–13.

57 Jane S. Webster, *Ingesting Jesus: Eating and Drinking in the Gospel of John* (Atlanta: Society for Biblical Literature, 2003), p. 69.

58 Ibid., pp. 152–3; cf. John 6.35.

59 John 1.29.

60 Webster, p. 78.

61 See Exodus 3.14 and John 1.1–2.

62 Lewis, *Miracles*, p. 164.

63 Ibid., pp. 164, 165.

64 John 1.1–3.

65 Webster, p. 147.

66 Ibid., p. 149.

67 Ibid.

68 Ibid., p. 97.

69 John 13.8.

70 Webster, p. 114.

71 Ibid., p. 150.

72 John 4.35–38; 15.1–17; 21.15–17; 21.1–8.

73 Alexander Schmemann, *The Eucharist: Sacrament of the Kingdom*, trans. Paul Kachur (New York: St Vladimir's Seminary Press, 1988), p. 43.

74 Alexander Schmemann, *For the Life of the World* (New York: St Vladimir's Seminary Press, 1973), p. 16.

75 Ibid.

76 Ibid., p. 17.

77 Ibid., p. 43.

78 Ibid.

79 Alexander Schmemann, quoted in Angel F. Méndez-Montoya, *The Theology of Food: Eating and the Eucharist* (Chichester: Wiley-Blackwell, 2012), p. 86.

80 Schmemann, *For the Life*, p. 14.

81 Ibid., p. 15.

82 Ibid., p. 18.

83 Ibid., p. 8.

84 Wendell Berry, 'The Agrarian Standard', in Wirzba, ed., *The Essential Agrarian Reader*, p. 24.

85 Ibid., pp. 26–7.

86 Ibid., p. 27.

87 Ibid., p. 32.

88 Ibid., p. 27.

89 R. S. Thomas, *Collected Poems, 1945–1990* (London: Phoenix, 1993), p. 233.

90 Wendell Berry, *The Art of Loading Brush: New Agrarian Writings* (Berkeley: Counterpoint, 2017), p. 8. There is an ambiguity in the way Berry talks about 'nature's laws'. On the one hand his work, and the agrarian writers more generally, submit themselves to learning from and observing in practice the stable patterns of nature. On the other hand, Berry repeatedly affirms an incompleteness in our understanding of the natural world and that, consequently, the appropriate attitude to the natural world is awe, or a sense of mystery. Concluding an essay on representations of 'nature' in the Western literary canon, Berry says, 'I have heard Wes [Jackson] say many times that "the boundaries of causation always exceed the boundaries of consideration." The more I have thought about that statement, the more interesting it has become. The key word is "always". Mystery, the unknown, our ignorance, always will be with us, to be dealt with. The farther we extend the radius of our knowledge, the larger becomes the circumference of mystery. There is, in other words, a boundary that may move somewhat, but can never be removed, between what we know and what we don't, between our human minds and the mind of Nature or the mind of God.' Berry, *The Art of Loading Brush*, p. 171.

91 Ibid., p. 34.

92 Ibid., pp. 8, 9.

93 Ibid., p. 9.

94 Ibid., pp. 3, 11.

## Coincidences of the Neoliberal and the Food Banks

1 Wendell Berry, *The Unsettling of America: Culture and Agriculture* (New York: Avon, 1978), p. 46.

2 Wendell Berry, *The World-Ending Fire* (London: Penguin, 2018), p. 290.

3 'Industrial destructiveness, anyhow, is our disease. Most of our most popular worries – climate change, fossil fuel addiction, pollution, poverty, hunger, and the various forms of legitimated violence – are symptoms.' Ibid., p. 337.

4 Berry, *Unsettling of America*, p. 18.

5 Ibid., p. 19.

6 Ibid., p. 18.

7 Ibid.

8 Church House, the administrative headquarters for the Church of England, has been regularly rented out over the last few years to international arms dealers such as BAE Systems, Lockheed Martin and General Atomics for their conferences; see www.caat.org.uk/campaigns/arms-trade-out/church-of-england (accessed 22 October 2019).

9 See www.bbc.co.uk/news/business-28257351 (accessed 22 October 2019). The Church of England has now ended this small but embarrassing investment.

10 After Henry VIII's dissolution of the monasteries, land was transferred en masse to the Church of England. As Gill Barron writes in *The Land* magazine, in '1978 the Endowments and Glebe Measure 1976 came into effect. This Measure transferred the ownership and management of glebe land from incumbents to the Diocesan Boards of Finance (DBF). From 1978 onwards all income arising from glebe land has to be used towards the payment of stipends.' However, Barron also notes that there was a 'lack of

any apparent effort to quantify the remaining acres in the run-up to the Glebe Measure in 1976' and that without a complete Land Register, we still do not know how much land the Church of England has exactly. Using the example of St Albans diocese, which has 3,000 acres of farmland, Barron estimates that the Church of England's 43 dioceses make around £19 million a year from their land. Barron asks: 'What to do with all this real estate and colossal worldly wealth?' and suggests that 'it may be time to consider dissolving its assets and returning the proceeds – including all the land it hasn't so far managed to lose – to a common bank to be used for the common good.' See www. thelandmagazine.org.uk/articles/adios-landed-clergy (accessed 22 October 2019).

11 See Chapter 2.

12 Berry, *Unsettling of America*, p. 18.

13 Andrew Williams, Paul Cloke, Jon May and Mark Goodwin, 'Contested Space: The Contradictory Political Dynamics of Foodbanking in the UK', *Environment and Planning A*, Vol. 48, No. 11 (2016), pp. 2291–316.

14 Durham County Director of Public Health, *All the Lonely People: Social Isolation and Loneliness in County Durham* (2014), https://democracy.durham.gov.uk/documents/ s48104/Item%2016%20-%20Appendix%203%20-%20DPH%20Annual%20Report %20-%20All%20the%20Lonely%20People%20Social%20Isolation%20and%20 Loneliness%20in.pdf (accessed 5 August 2019).

15 Ibid., p. 13.

16 Ibid., p. 17. The report distinguishes between social isolation ('lack of frequency of social contacts') and loneliness ('a subjective experience related to the evaluation of the quality of social contacts an individual has').

17 Ibid., p. 10. Loneliness enhances the production of the stress hormone cortisol, which suppresses the immune system. Monbiot, *Out of the Wreckage*, p. 17.

18 Durham County, *All the Lonely People*, p. 11.

19 Trussell Trust, quoted in Garthwaite, *Hunger Pains*, p. 151.

20 James Vernon, *Hunger: A Modern History* (Cambridge, MA: Harvard University Press, 2007), p. 7.

21 Ibid., pp. 7, 8.

22 Méndez-Montoya, *The Theology of Food*, p. 36.

23 Ibid.

24 Ibid., pp. 40, 41.

25 Ibid., p. 41.

26 Ibid., p. 40.

27 Riches, *Food Bank Nations*, p. 10.

28 Williams and others, 'Contested Space', p. 2291.

29 Ibid., pp. 2292, 2309.

30 Ibid., pp. 2292, 2309, 2291.

31 Ibid., p. 2292.

32 Ibid., p. 2293.

33 Ibid.

34 Dowler quoted in ibid., p. 2293.

35 Ibid., p. 2295.

36 Van Wieren, *Food, Farming and Religion*, p. 15.

37 Vandana Shiva, *Making Peace with the Earth* (London: Pluto Press, 2013), pp. 17, 18.

38 Chris Allen, 'Food Poverty and Christianity in Britain: A Theological Re-assessment', *Political Theology*, Vol. 17, No. 4 (2016), pp. 361–77, at p. 365.

39 Ibid.
40 Ibid., p. 370.
41 Ibid.
42 Ibid., p. 364.
43 Ibid., p. 362.
44 In a longer review of Allen's article for the journal *Political Theology* I wrote:

The 'Food Banks and Food Poverty' briefing supplied to members of parliament in support of their duties and preparation for a parliamentary debate on the issue in 2014 for example notes that 'no government since the 1960s has undertaken any official empirical study of benefit adequacy, but independent estimates of "Minimum Income Standards" suggest that current out-of-work benefit rates for people of working age are significantly lower than the amounts necessary for a minimum acceptable standard of living.' In other words, not only does the British Government knowingly pay starvation level benefits to its subjects, it has also recently capped benefits at 1% (meaning a real term cut because of inflation and the linking of benefit payments to the Consumer Price Index (CPI) rather than the faster rising Retail Price Index (RPI)) and it has consistently underpaid a range of its benefits, to the tune of £10 billion in unpaid or unclaimed benefits in 2013/2014. The role of the law courts in enforcing the Government's public space protection orders and criminal behaviour orders also factors into contemporary British Governmental antipathy to the hungry, as a British Judge recently stated: 'I will be sending a man to prison for asking for food when he was hungry' when he sentenced a man to four months in prison for begging.

See Charles Pemberton, 'Between Ecclesiology and Ontology: A Response to Chris Allen on Food Banks', *Political Theology*, Vol. 20, No. 1 (2019), pp. 85–101; Emma Downing, Steven Kennedy and Mike Fell, *Food Banks and Food Poverty* (2014), http://research-briefings.parliament.uk/ResearchBriefing/Summary/SN06657 (accessed 28 May 2018), p. 25; Graham Riches and Tiina Silvasti, eds, *First World Hunger Revisited: Food Charity or the Right to Food* (New York: Palgrave Macmillan, 2014), p. 165; Garthwaite, *Hunger Pains*, p. 87; www.theguardian.com/society/2018/may/20/homeless-people-fined-imprisoned-pspo-england-wales?CMP=Share_iOSApp_Other, 2018 (accessed 28 May 2018); www.gloucestershirelive.co.uk/news/gloucester-news/man-breached-order-stop-him-242853 (accessed 28 May 2018).
45 Cahill and Konings, *Neoliberalism* (Cambridge: Polity Press, 2017), p. 56.
46 Ibid., p. 57.
47 Ibid.
48 Countries with newfound independence from colonial rule sought to emancipate themselves from import dependence during the 1960s and 1970s, but kick-starting this process included borrowing heavily from the West for industry, agriculture and infrastructure investment. As the global slowdown of the late 1970s hit, export costs fell for these countries and it became increasingly hard to keep up their debt repayments. Taking on new debts to serve the old ones, compounded by capital flight, led to the 'Third World Debt Crisis'. When these countries could no longer pay their loans, the IMF would step in and offer assistance, but such assistance was conditional 'on the receiving country committing itself to a wide range of market-orientated reforms, including cuts in government spending, deregulating and opening up markets, the privatization of public enterprises, and the removal of controls on foreign exchange and trade'. In this way, as Cahill and Konings say, neoliberalism began to take on a more organized global form. Ibid., pp. 60, 61.

49 Tim Ross, 'Ed Balls plans to keep Coalition spending cuts', *The Telegraph*, 3 June 2013, www.telegraph.co.uk/news/politics/labour/10096793/Ed-Balls-plans-to-keep-Coalition-spending-cuts.html (accessed 17 June 2019).

50 Cahill and Konings, *Neoliberalism*, p. 57.

51 Wren-Lewis, *The Lies We Were Told*, pp. 2, 17.

52 Allen, 'Food Poverty and Christianity', *Political Theology*, p. 369.

53 Ibid., p. 370. The use of 'consumers' is a little ungainly in this instance by Allen, as he goes on to critique 'consumerism' very extensively. In this instance, he uses consumerism to mean our participation in the world and in food systems as eaters. 'Consumerism' is, on the other hand, the egocentric mentality which sees the world as something *only* to be eaten and which '[circumscribes] our involvement in the relations of food production such that we ... have barely any direct involvement with the divine source of our lives' or 'membership of creation on which our lives depend'. Ibid., p. 371.

54 Allen, 'Food Poverty and Christianity', *Political Theology*, p. 371.

55 Williams, 'Contested Spaces', *Environment and Planning A*, p. 2309.

56 Ibid., p. 2293, 2294.

57 Frank Prochaska, *Christianity and Social Service in Modern Britain: The Disinherited Spirit* (Oxford: Oxford University Press, 2006), p. 149.

58 Ibid., p. 6.

59 For example, see Melinda Cooper, *Family Values: Between Neoliberalism and the New Social Conservatism* (New York: Zone, 2017).

60 Williams, 'Contested Spaces', *Environment and Planning A*, p. 2294.

61 The actual increased power of the state over the last 30 years shows that maximizing profits in reality requires a strong state and strong laws, the contradiction resides in neoliberalism's attack on the state and its simultaneous defence or extension of the state in other areas, as scholars like Mirowski have noted. See Philip Mirowski and Dieter Plehwe, eds, *The Road from Mont Pèlerin: The Making of the Neoliberal Thought Collective* (London: Harvard University Press, 2009).

62 Wren-Lewis, *The Lies We Were Told*, p. 42.

63 Marijn Konings, 'The Spirit of Austerity', *Journal of Cultural Economy*, Vol. 9, No. 1 (2016), pp. 86–100.

64 Kotsko, *Neoliberalism's Demons*, p.10.

65 These two aspects of neoliberalism are nicely contained by the North American geographer Jamie Peck when he defines neoliberalism as the ongoing process to 'abolish or weaken social transfer programs' like progressive taxation, rising welfare benefits, legal aid, drug and alcohol rehabilitation funding 'while actively fostering the "inclusion" of the poor and marginalised into the labour market, on the markets' terms'. Jamie Peck, 'Neoliberalizing States: thin policies/hard outcomes', *Progress in Human Geography*, Vol. 25, No. 3 (2001), pp. 445–55. Quoted in Geoffrey DeVerteuil, Robert Wilton, 'Spaces of Abeyance, Care and Survival: The addiction treatment system as a site of "regulatory richness"', *Political Geography*, Vol. 28, No. 8 (2009), pp. 463–72, at p. 464.

66 Kotsko, *Neoliberalism's Demons*, p. 3.

67 Ibid., p. 94.

68 Ibid., p. 95.

69 For an excellent article exploring this, the poor's disassociation of themselves from the term 'poverty' and possible reasons for it, see Tracy Shildrick, Robert MacDonald, 'Poverty talk: how people experiencing poverty deny their poverty and why they blame "the poor"', *The Sociological* Review, Vol. 61, No. 2 (2013), pp. 285–303.

70  Kotsko, *Neoliberalism's Demons*, p. 84, 90.

71  Two other issues that could be explored in this vein of investigation are: how is the nuclear family structured and supported under neoliberalism as a realm of both freedom and interdependence, and, second, political populism as a critique of market excesses – how populism includes its own critique of money and an implicit bias towards austerity. On family, see Kotsko, *Neoliberalism's Demons*, p. 88. On populism, see Konings, 'The Spirit of Austerity', *Journal of Cultural Economy*, pp. 86–100.

72  Williams, 'Contested Spaces', *Environment and Planning A*, p. 2294.

73  Ibid.

74  DeVerteuil, Wilton, p. 465. D. Conradson, 'Spaces of care in the city: the place of a community drop-in centre', *Social and Cultural Geography*, Vol. 4, No. 4 (2003), pp. 507–25.

75  Williams, 'Contested Spaces', *Environment and Planning A*, p. 2294. See H. Horst, S. Pascucci, W. Bol, 'The "dark side" of food banks? Exploring emotional responses of food bank receivers in the Netherlands', *British Food Journal*, Vol. 116, No. 9 (2014), pp. 1506–20. F. Douglas, J. Sapko, K. Kiezebrink, 'Resourcefulness, desperation, shame, gratitude and powerlessness: Common themes emerging from a study of food bank use in Northeast Scotland', *Public Health*, Vol. 2, No. 3 (2015), pp. 297–317.

76  Pat Caplan, 'Big Society or Broken Society?: Food Banks in the UK', *Anthropology Today*, Vol. 32, No. 1 (2016), pp. 5–9, at p. 7.

77  Williams, 'Contested Spaces', *Environment and Planning A*, p. 2294.

78  Caplan, 'Big Society or Broken Society?', *Anthropology Today*, p. 8.

79  Williams, 'Contested Spaces', *Environment and Planning A*, p. 2309.

80  Ibid., p. 2294.

81  Janet Poppendieck, *Breadlines: Knee-Deep in Wheat, Food Assistance in the Great Depression* (Berkley, University of California Press, 2014). Rebecca Anne Allahyari, *Visions of Charity: Volunteer Workers and Moral Community* (London: University of California Press, 2000).

82  De Souza, *Feeding the Other*, p. 133.

83  Ibid., p. 134.

84  Ibid.

85  Williams, 'Contested Spaces', *Environment and Planning A*, p. 2295. Though they do say that evidence for local authority funding has been contested.

86  Ibid., p. 2295. Evidence of 'the hold that neoliberal constructions of the deserving and undeserving welfare subject, and associated technologies, now enjoy'.

87  Williams, 'Contested Spaces', *Environment and Planning A*, p. 2296.

88  Ibid., p. 2296.

89  Williams, 'Contested Spaces', *Environment and Planning A*, p. 2304.

90  Ibid., p. 2304.

91  Ibid., p. 2311.

92  Williams, 'Contested Spaces', *Environment and Planning A*, p. 2304.

93  Sam Wells, quoted in Méndez-Montoya, *The Theology of Food*, p. 125.

94  Gustavo Gutiérrez, *We Drink from Our Own Wells*, trans. Matthew J. O'Connell (London: SCM Press, 1984), p. 28.

95  Ibid., p. 98.

96  Berry, *Unsettling of America*, p. 23.

97  Berry, *World Ending Fire*, p. 33.

98  Ibid., p. 33.

99  Ibid., p. 308.

100 Allen, 'Food Poverty and Christianity', *Political Theology*, p. 368, 372.

101 Ibid., p. 373. My criticism, in Charles Pemberton, 'Between Ecclesiology and Ontology: A Response to Chris Allen on Food Banks', *Political Theology*, Vol. 20, No. 1 (2019), pp. 85–101, was to ask why the church can't do both, if both state and the church body, as Allen contends, are under God's authority as parts of God's creation.

102 Allen, 'Food Poverty and Christianity', *Political Theology*, p. 373.

103 Ibid., p. 374.

## Political, Ecclesial and Personal Participation

1 Wirzba, *Food and Faith*, p. 210.

2 Aquinas, *Selected Political Writing*, trans. J. G. Dawson (Oxford: Basil Blackwell, 1954), pp. 109–11. Augustine, *City of God*, trans. Henry Bettenson (London: Penguin, 2003), pp. 872–4, 881.

3 Berry, *Art of Loading Brush*, p. 207; i.e. sustaining our current decline is unsuitable.

4 Field has been a protagonist in the last ten years of welfare reform and research into food insecurity, applying greater pressure to the sitting coalition government in 2014 by asking whether the government was suppressing a report by the Department for Environment, Food and Rural Affairs (DEFRA) which it was suspected laid much of the blame for food insecurity on government policies and why the government hadn't applied for a possible £200 million in funding for food banks, available from the European Union. See www.theguardian.com/society/patrick-butler-cuts-blog/2013/nov/28/poverty-mps-call-for-delayed-food-banks-report-to-be-published (accessed 14 July 2019) and www.frankfield.co.uk/upload/docs/Letter%20to%20David%20Cameron%20re%20food%20aid%20funidng%2028.01.14.pdf (accessed 14 July 2019).

5 www.frankfield.co.uk/campaigns/feeding-britain-appg-hunger.aspx (accessed 14 July 2019).

6 Ibid.

7 All-Party Parliamentary Inquiry into Hunger in the United Kingdom, *Feeding Britain: A Strategy for Zero Hunger in England, Wales, Scotland and Northern Ireland* (2014), https://feedingbritain.org/wp-content/uploads/2019/01/feeding_britain_report_2014-2.pdf (accessed 19 July 2019), p. 15.

8 Ibid.

9 Ibid.

10 Ibid., p. 19. End Hunger UK's *A Menu to End Hunger in the UK* made nine recommendations in 2018, including: a minister dedicated to dealing with hunger, yearly government measures of food insecurity, safeguarding child nutrition, reducing the poverty premium, welfare reform and employers paying the 'real' living wage. Later in the year, End Hunger UK published a further document on Universal Credit, which along with a series of suggestions for the short- and medium-term reform of Universal Credit asked for 'Universal Credit levels' to be 'brought in line with the actual cost of living'. Supported by Sustain, the Alliance for Better Food and Farming, the Independent Food Bank Network (IFAN), the Church of England, Nourish Scotland and the Child Poverty Action Group, End Hunger UK's priority is achieving the right to food for all people in the UK in socially acceptable ways; they prioritize participation by the public. See End Hunger UK, *A Menu to End Hunger in the UK* (2018), http://endhungeruk.org/menu/ (accessed 13 August 2019) and End Hunger UK, *Fix Universal Credit* (2018), http://endhungeruk.org/wp-content/uploads/2018/07/Fix-Universal-Credit-a-report-from-End-Hunger-UK.pdf (accessed 13 August 2019).

11 Malcolm Torry, *Citizen's Basic Income: A Christian Social Policy* (London: Darton, Longman and Todd, 2016), p. 4.

12 twitter.com/EmmaLewellBuck/status/1016649049326456837/photo/1 (accessed 16 August 2019). In the areas of welfare and pay there have been increases in the minimum wage which the APPG on Hunger has welcomed, to £7.83 in April 2018 for those over 25, and £7.38 for those under 25. They call, furthermore, for the expansion of those paying the living wage (as set by the Living Wage Foundation), which 6.2 million people are not yet paid (23% of all employee jobs). Along with these increases in the minimum wage, the APPG's report helped create the pressure that led the government to reduce the waiting time for the first Universal Credit payment from six weeks to five weeks, and made it easier for those applying for Universal Credit to get hardship payments and emergency loans. There has also been pressure from Feeding Britain for research, with money allocated by the government to investigate a 'yellow card' system for those being sanctioned (allowing them to appeal the sanctions brought against them, which they did successfully 6.5% of the time) and for holiday school food pilots to deal with British children that go hungry. However, further recommendations made to the sitting coalition government by Feeding Britain and later to the Conservative government have not been taken up. The government refused the APPG's request to continue to pay a minimum amount to those going through mandatory reconsideration periods (when a benefits claimant challenges an ESA decision) to stop a total loss of income. Feeding Britain's website reports that the government said that 'there are no legal grounds to make a payment of Employment and Support Allowance at this time', i.e. that the government is not obliged to make sure its citizens have enough food, so it would not. The government rejected the idea that there should be a clear two-way contract between claimant and Job Centre Plus and despite evidence that those being sanctioned have not been informed of the government's decision prior to its implementation, the government has decided to continue with its current sanctions practice. Feeding Britain invited the government to continue to support sanctioned people with Housing Benefit so that they were not made homeless during this period without income, another suggestion that government have not sought to enact. See https://feedingbritain.org/what-we-do/policy-issues/income-and-affordability-of-food/ (accessed 16 August 2019) and https://feedingbritain.org/what-we-do/policy-issues/welfare-reform/ (accessed 4 July 2019).

13 Guy Standing, *Universal Basic Income: And How We Can Make It Happen* (London: Penguin, 2017), p. 189.

14 Ibid., p. 190. Standing notes that only nine employers have been prosecuted for not paying the minimum wage since its launch in 1998 because it is so hard to monitor.

15 Ibid. Minimum wage increases can leave low-paid labourers worse off, Standing gives this example: 'suppose at a minimum wage of £10 an hour, a firm providing cleaning services hires 100 workers for thirty hours a week. If the minimum wage were raised to £12, the firm could cut the remunerated hours to twenty-five, leaving the payroll costs unchanged and the worker no better off. (Probably they would be worse off because they would have to do the same amount of cleaning in fewer hours, or work extra hours unpaid.)' After the introduction of the National Living Wage in 2015, this is what a firm that provided cleaning services to the government's tax office (HMRC) did to its employees. By cutting the cleaners' hours to 25, they further deprived them of working tax credits, cutting into their gross incomes, which are given to those working 30 hours a week.

16 Giupponi and Machin looked at the effect of introducing the living wage in the care sector and found that, combined with the limited ability care providers had to control

prices because they are local authority funded, the biggest concern was reductions in the quality of the service. See www.weforum.org/agenda/2018/08/impacts-of-changing-the-structure-of-minimum-wages (accessed 19 November 2019). Giulia Giupponi, Stephen Machin, *Changing the Structure of Minimum Wages: Firm Adjustment and Wage Spill-overs* (2018), http://cep.lse.ac.uk/pubs/download/dp1533.pdf (accessed 19 November 2019). Jonathan Wadsworth, *Did the National Minimum Wage Affect UK Prices?* (2009), http://ftp.iza.org/dp4433.pdf (accessed 19 November 2019).

17 Increased minimum standards still leave the benefits system highly bureaucratized and expensive: administration cost the Department for Work and Pensions £8 billion of its £172 budget in 2013–14. Standing, *Universal Basic Income*, p. 131.

18 Fisher, *Capitalist Realism*, p. 20.

19 Ibid.

20 Torry, *Citizen's Basic Income*, p. 113. Standing says that Jobseeker's Allowance is now claimed successfully by only half of those entitled to it, approximately £2.4 billion in 2014–15. Standing, *Universal Basic Income*, p. 195.

21 Ibid., pp. 193, 194.

22 Monbiot, *Out of the Wreckage*, pp. 108–12. Graeber, *Bullshit Jobs*, pp. 271–85. Kotsko, *Neoliberalism's Demons*, pp. 140, 141. Lansley and Mack, *Breadline Britain*, p. 237. Standing, *Universal Basic Income*, pp. ix–xiii. Srnicek and Williams, *Inventing the Future*, pp. 118–24.

23 Kotsko, *Neoliberalism's Demons*, pp. 140, 141, 136.

24 Srnicek and Williams, *Inventing the Future*, p. 119.

25 Ibid., p. 120.

26 Ibid., pp. 120–2. For Standing, the difference between work and labour – one paid and the other not – is often arbitrary and perverse. Standing is fond of economist Pigou's observation that 'if he hired a housekeeper, national income went up, economic growth increased, employment rose and unemployment fell. If he subsequently married her, and she continued to do precisely the same activities, national income and growth went down, employment fell and unemployment rose. This is absurd (and sexist).' It is sexist because the majority of domestic work is done by women, who now often have to bear the triple burden of caring for the young and the old and earning a wage. According to the Office for National Statistics, the value of formal volunteering alone (not includ-ing other forms of care) is around £22 billion a year. UBI presents us with a means for beginning to undermine the fallacies of the (un/paid) current distinction between work and labour. Unlike means-tested assistance, volunteers and clients at the food bank *both* stand to mutually gain from a UBI. It is a policy that makes common cause. Standing, *Universal Basic Income*, p.157. Torry, *Citizen's Basic Income*, p. 81. Standing, *The Precariat*, pp. 146–8. Office for National Statistics, *Changes in the Value and Division of Unpaid Volunteering in the UK: 2000 to 2015* (2017), www.ons.gov.uk/economy/nationalaccounts/satelliteaccounts/articles/changesinthevalueanddivisionofunpaidcare workintheuk/2000to2015 (accessed 16 August 2019), p. 21. Standing, *Universal Basic Income*, p. 157.

27 www.cato-unbound.org/print-issue/1805, (accessed 6 November 2019). Graeber, *Bullshit Jobs*, p. 271.

28 Standing, *Universal Basic Income*, p. 3.

29 Ibid.

30 Ibid., p. 4. Coote and Yaziki (2019) critique UBI on the grounds that 'models of UBI that are universal and sufficient are not affordable, and models that are affordable are not universal', i.e, if all non-health benefits were collected and distributed through

a UBI with the same tax rates, would UBI not be too low for the poorest individuals? Conversely, if a UBI at a sustainable level were paid to all, would taxes not have to be excessively high, leading to capital flight and the withdrawal of international businesses from the UK? Standing addresses these concerns and the 'back of an envelope' calculations (which the *Economist* blog has, for example, undertaken, allocating the Finnish $10,500 a year, the UK $5,800 and the Mexican citizen $900 per year) on which they are based by raising a number of concerns with their methods and presuppositions. For Standing, these calculations fail to consider simple means for taking a UBI back from the top earners through simple tax adjustments; second, they fail to account for the administrative savings on current means-tested benefits. Standing continues: what about possible spending change priorities (such as the £200 billion that will be spent on renewing the British nuclear submarine programme, Trident) or the current £93 billion that the UK tax payer gives to businesses in corporate welfare incentives. Neither the mountain of escalating taxes nor the valley of indefinite poverty are inevitable repercussions of introducing a UBI, both the RSA and Compass have costed UBI schemes in the UK which *retain* current benefit payments *along with* generous universal payments and 'strict revenue neutrality' by abolishing income tax personal allowances (which cost the British tax payer £100 billion a year and give greater savings to the rich rather than the poor) and raising taxes by 3 points per band. These hybrid or transitional schemes, at the cost of £700 million a year (Compass) to £9.8 billion a year (RSA), would give the UK citizen a payment of £61 per week (Compass) to £143, £71 and £82.5 for pensioners, adults and children respectively (RSA). These figures represent £3,172 to £7,436 a year on top of existing support to the most deprived people in our society. See Anna Coote and Edanur Yaziki, *Universal Basic Income: A Union Perspective* (Ferney-Voltaire, France: Public Services International, 2019), www.world-psi.org/sites/default/files/documents/research/en_ubi_full_report_2019.pdf (accessed 7 November 2019), p. 4. Standing, *Universal Basic Income*, pp. 135, 132, 139, 133, 135. Compass, *Universal Basic Income*, 2016, www.compassonline.org.uk/wp-content/uploads/2016/05/UniversalBasicIncomeByCompass-Spreads.pdf (accessed 6 November 2019). Aditya Chakrabortty, 'The £93bn Handshake: Businesses Pocket Huge Subsidies and Tax Breaks', *The Guardian*, 7 July 2015, www.theguardian.com/politics/2015/jul/07/corporate-welfare-a-93bn-handshake (accessed 24 June 2019). Anthony Painter and Chris Thoung, *Creative Citizen, Creative State: The Principled and Pragmatic Case for a Universal Basic Income* (London: RSA, 2015), www.thersa.org/discover/publications-and-articles/reports/basic-income (accessed 6 November 2019).

31 Standing, *Universal Basic Income*, p. 5. For Torry, migrants would have to be legally resident for a required period of time before becoming eligible to receive UBI. Torry, *Citizen's Basic Income*, p. 8.

32 Standing, *Universal Basic Income*, p. 5.

33 Ibid., p. 6.

34 Ibid., p. 7.

35 Ibid., p. 108.

36 https://basicincome.org/news/2016/11/new-academic-research-shows-basic-income-improves-health/ (accessed 24 June 2019). Lynn McIntyre, Daniel Dutton, Cynthia Kwok and J. Herbert Emery, 'Reduction of Food Insecurity among Low-Income Canadian Seniors as a Likely Impact of a Guaranteed Annual Income', *Canadian Public Policy*, Vol. 42, No. 3 (2016), pp. 274–86.

37 www.foodbankscanada.ca/getmedia/01e662ba-f1d7-419d-b40c-bcc71a9f943c/HungerCount2015_singles.pdf.aspx (accessed 24 June 2019).

38 John Hoddinott and others, *Enhancing WFP's Capacity and Experience to Design, Implement, Monitor, and Evaluate Vouchers and Cash Transfer Programmes: Study Summary* (2013), http://ebrary.ifpri.org/utils/getfile/collection/p15738coll2/id/127961/filename/128172.pdf (accessed 24 June 2019).

39 Thomas Paine, *Agrarian Justice* (1797), online edition, 1999, http://piketty.pse.ens.fr/files/Paine1795.pdf (accessed 16 August 2019), p. iii.

40 Ibid., p. 8.

41 Ibid., pp. 8, 9. Likewise, there is a theological element to Paine's account of the rights of man, as he says 'every history of the creation, and every traditional account ... all agree in establishing one point, *the unity of man*; by which I mean, that men are all of *one degree,* and consequently that all men are born equal, and with equal natural right ... every child born into the world must be considered as deriving its existence from God.' Thomas Paine, *Rights of Man* (1791; London: Penguin Books, 1984), p. 66.

42 Ibid., p. 10.

43 Standing writes that UBI is ecologically friendly in another sense: 'a basic income would encourage people to shift some of their time from resource-depleting labour activities to resource-preserving "reproductive" activities such as caring or voluntary work', or, as he says later in the book, 'shorter working hours in jobs are correlated with smaller ecological footprints'. Standing, *Universal Basic Income*, pp. 39, 180.

44 Ibid., p. 9. For more on the question of ownership and the production of profits, see notes 54 and 150 below.

45 Ibid., p. 18.

46 Along with the sale of state assets and commodity monopolies to individuals (Russian steel after the fall of the Soviet Union, or Carlos Slim's Mexican telecommunications monopoly, for example) there are a series of state technological innovations which came from state funding. As Srnicek and Williams write, 'Developments like railways, the internet, computing, supersonic flight, space travel, satellites, pharmaceuticals, voice-recognition software, nanotechnology, touch-screens and clean energy have all been nurtured and guided by states, not corporations.' Finally, the bank bailout following the great recession is just one example of the close relationships between financers and government regulators which has helped generate large profits in the financial industries. Freeland, in her book on the emergence of a new global super-rich, says: 'as with the sale of state assets in developing economies, the role of deregulation in creating a plutocracy turns classic thinking about rent-seeking upside down. Deregulation was part of a global liberalization drive whose goal was to pull the state out of the economy and let market forces rule. But one of its consequences was to give the state a direct role in choosing winner and losers – in this case, giving financial engineers a leg up.' Srnicek and Williams, *Inventing the Future*, p. 178; Freeland, *Plutocrats*, p. 222.

47 Paine, *Agrarian Justice*, p. 11.

48 Ibid., p. 16.

49 Ibid., p. 15.

50 Ibid.

51 Ibid.

52 Monbiot, *Out of the Wreckage*, p. 110.

53 Ibid., pp. 104, 111. Until recently, the possibility of a groundrent has been impossible given the reluctance of the UK Land Registry to keep a public record of private land ownership in the UK. Guy Shrubsole's very valuable piece of work *Who Owns England* reports that the 2017 Housing White Paper 'announced that the Land Register would aim to fully complete its register by 2030' and that the Labour Party would 'for the first

time consider a land value tax' in its manifesto. Guy Shrubsole, *Who Owns England?* (London: William Collins, 2019), pp. 42, 43.

54 Monbiot, *Out of the Wreckage*, p. 105. Those who own land can extract value from it through rents; this income is enhanced by anything that raises the land's value. Monbiot writes that 'we enhance the proprietors' unearned income by providing, through our taxes, the infrastructure and services that raise the value of the land.' He reinforces this argument with reference to an excellent passage, written in 1909 by Winston Churchill, which states: 'Roads are made, streets are made, services are improved, electric light turns night into day, water is brought from reservoirs a hundred miles off in the mountains – and all the while the landlord sits still. Every one of those improvements is effected by the labour and cost of other people and the taxpayer. To not one of those improvements does the land monopolist, as a land monopolist, contribute, and yet by every one of them the value of his land is enhanced. He renders no service to the community, he contributes nothing to the general welfare, he contributes nothing to the process from which his own enrichment is derived.' Ibid., p. 103.

55 Monbiot, *Out of the Wreckage*, pp. 105, 111. A sovereign wealth fund, similar to that proposed by Monbiot, is also desirable to Standing. See Standing, *Universal Basic Income*, pp. 150–3.

56 Monbiot, *Out of the Wreckage*, p. 102.

57 Ibid., pp. 102, 139–45, 109, 110.

58 There are potential benefits for families when UBI is compared to the current benefits regime: 'perhaps counterintuitively, treating everyone as an individual would be good for families,' Torry says. The current benefits system allocates its payments to households, not individuals, and this produces a number of problematic anomalies. One of the partners getting a job, for example, can lead to little or no rise in disposable income for the whole family (a facet of the increasing polarization of British families into work-rich – two jobs – and work-poor – no-work households). Living apart can be more financially beneficial for parents than living together, as two individuals would normally receive higher benefit payments than if they cohabited, disincentivizing family formation. Conversely, a recent report highlighted by the Trussell Trust called *Benefits or barriers? Making Social Security Work for Survivors of Violence and Abuse across the UK's Four Nations* found that the current benefits regime can reinforce patterns of domestic abuse. A number of characteristics of the current system, such as payments into single bank accounts, domestic abuse survivors having to wait five weeks before receiving a new benefits payment, along with a general depreciation of the worth of benefit associated with the benefit cap, social security cuts and two-child limit, can leave women trapped in abusive households or unable to leave for new accommodation. A UBI will not abolish all poverty overnight, Standing says, but it could be a significant factor in helping free partners from abusive spouses and make it possible for those who want to share space to do so on a stable financial keel. Torry, *Citizen's Basic Income*, p. 34; Standing, *Universal Basic Income*, p. 197; Marilyn Howard, *Benefits or Barriers? Making Social Security Work for Survivors of Violence and Abuse across the UK's Four Nations* (London: Women's Budget Group, 2019), https://wbg.org.uk/media/press-releases/governments-commitments-in-domestic-abuse-bill-undermined-by-the-social-security-system/ (accessed 24 June 2019); Standing, *Universal Basic Income*, p. 79.

59 On the question of work incentives and the human enjoyment of being a 'cause', see the conclusion of Chapter 1. In regard to the trial runs of UBI and its effects on work, Standing summarizes the United States and Canadian trials by saying that Gary Burtles found that a Basic Income led to 'modest reduction in work', while Karl Widerquist,

surveying the extensive literature that has been generated by these projects, concluded that the 'impact on labour supply was mostly statistically insignificant or so small as to be of no serious concern to policy makers'. Where there were drops in work, these were mothers spending longer with their children or teenagers whose graduation rates rose because they did not have to work part-time while doing their studies. In pilots in Namibia and India, productivity in areas which have tried UBIs has risen as people have the security, confidence and means to start small businesses, retrain or further their education. Standing, *Universal Basic Income*, pp. 163, 166, 122.

60 Torry, *Citizen's Basic Income*, p. 81.

61 Ibid., p. 4.

62 https://feedingbritain.org/what-we-do/policy-issues/childhood-hunger/ (accessed 14 July 2019).

63 Torry, *Citizen's Basic Income*, p. 105. Lansley and Mack write that 'until the mid 1980s, the UK tax system was mildly progressive, taking a higher proportion of high than of low incomes. Since then it has become regressive. In 1979, the top fifth paid 37.6% of their incomes in tax and the poorest fifth only 30.5%. By 2011, this pattern had reversed with the bottom paying, at 36.6%, more than all other groups including the top fifth, at 35.5%.' Lansley and Mack, *Breadline Britain*, p. 237.

64 Monbiot, *Out of the Wreckage*, p. 58.

65 Jane Wills, *Locating Localism: Statecraft, Citizenship and Democracy* (Bristol: Polity Press, 2016), p. 87.

66 Ibid., p. 88.

67 Ibid., p. 93. There are some facts that buck this trend; membership of arts and cultural organizations are up along with human rights groups, and the numbers of those undertaking 'market-orientated activism' such as boycotting products for ethical or environmental reasons is up from 4% in 1984 to 26% in 2002. Ibid., pp. 88–93.

68 Torry, *Citizen's Basic Income*, p. 20.

69 Ibid., pp. 56, 96, 36, 31, 52–5, 42–8, 78.

70 See note 30 above.

71 Standing, *Universal Basic Income*, p. 122.

72 Torry, *Citizen's Basic Income*, p. 135. With the long-term economic trend towards returns on capital exceeding growth in the economy (as analysed by Piketty), there is scope to even use 'Government money creation to fill the gap between the total productive capacity of the economy and the proportion paid out in wages'. Piketty shows that the rich are getting richer from their riches, while those who work receive less renumeration as a proportion of total productivity through wages. With the exception of the period following on from the Second World War the trajectory of twentieth-century capitalism was towards increasingly concentrated wealth. Thomas Piketty, *Capital in the Twenty-first Century* (Cambridge, MA: Belknap Press, 2014), p. 353. Torry, *Citizen's Basic Income*, p. 135.

73 Standing, *Universal Basic Income*, p. 146. The Tax Justice Network estimates between $21 and $32 trillion of private financial wealth is in lightly or untaxed secrecy jurisdictions around the world: www.financialsecrecyindex.com. The Tax Justice Network publishes a 'Secrecy Ranking' which identifies the countries most prone to sustaining institutions which design and market offshore structures for their clients. In the summer of 2019, the Tax Justice Network reported that the UK bore 'the lion's share of responsibility through its controlled network of satellite jurisdictions' internationally for helping corporations dodge £500 billion in tax a year, enough to pay

for the UN's humanitarian budget 20 times every year: www.taxjustice.net/2019/05/28/
new-ranking-reveals-corporate-tax-havens-behind-breakdown-of-global-corporate-
tax-system-toll-of-uks-tax-war-exposed/ (accessed 24 June 2019). By delaying the
implementation of a bill requiring all its overseas territories to keep a register of
share ownership, the UK government has given the tax avoiders until 2023 to continue their practices or move their operations into other territories. Patrick Wintour,
'Delay to tax havens' public registers "risks national security"', *The Guardian*, 21
February 2019, www.theguardian.com/world/2019/feb/21/delay-to-tax-havens-public
registers-risks-national-security (accessed 24 June 2019).

74 Standing, *Universal Basic Income*, pp.166, 167, 235, 236.

75 Graeber, *Bullshit Jobs*, p. 285.

76 Ibid. For a broad definition of the 'value' of work, which Graeber concludes is
'care', see ibid., pp. 201, 207–21, 231, 237.

77 Torry, *Citizen's Basic Income*, p. 25.

78 Jason Beattie, '27 bishops slam David Cameron's welfare reforms as creating a
national crisis in unprecedented attack', *The Mirror*, 19 February 2014, www.mirror.
co.uk/news/uk-news/27-bishops-slam-david-camerons-3164033 (accessed 7 November
2019).

79 Ibid.

80 Nico Koopman, 'The Reception of the Barmen Declaration in South Africa', *The
Ecumenical Review*, Vol. 61, No. 1. (2009), pp. 60–71. Koopman draws attention to
the impact of Karl Barth's 'Barmen Declaration' on the work of the Church in South
Africa during the time of apartheid. The Barmen Declaration provided the former Dutch
Reformed Mission Church with a model (the Confession of Belhar, 1986) for argu-
ing that racial segregation was against the nature of the gospel and incompatible with
Christian belief.

81 Ibid., p. 65.

82 Karl Barth, quoted in Koopman, 'The Reception of the Barmen Declaration',
p. 64.

83 Gustavo Gutiérrez, *We Drink from Our Own Wells*, trans. Matthew J. O'Connell
(London: SCM Press, 1984), p. 123.

84 David Fergusson, *Church, State and Civil Society* (Cambridge: Cambridge University Press, 2004), p. 168.

85 Ibid.

86 Ibid.

87 As defenders of Church of England establishment such as Richard Hooker and
John Milbank have argued. See Richard Hooker, *Of the Laws of Ecclesiastical Polity*
(1593– ; Oxford: Oxford University Press, 2013), pp. 188–264. John Milbank and
Adrian Pabst, *The Politics of Virtue: Post-Liberalism and the Human Future* (London:
Rowman & Littlefield, 2016), p. 208.

88 Fergusson, *Church, State*, p. 177. Mark Chapman, Judith Maltby and William
Whyte, eds, *The Established Church: Past, Present and Future* (London: T & T Clark
International, 2011), p. 80.

89 Nigel Biggar, *Between Kin and Cosmopolis: An Ethic of the Nation* (Cambridge:
James Clarke, 2014), p. 9.

90 Ibid.

91 Nigel Biggar, *Good Life* (London: SPCK, 1997), p. 110.

92 Italics in original. Ibid., p. 123.

93 Ibid., pp. 113, 124, 125.

94 See Samantha Walker, Jill Annison and Sharon Beckett, 'Transforming Rehabilitation: The Impact of Austerity and Privatisation on Day-to-day Cultures and Working Practices in "Probation"', *Probation Journal*, Vol. 66, No. 1 (2019), pp. 113–30. The BMJ, *Bigger Cuts to Sure Start Children's Centres in More Disadvantaged Areas* (2017), www.bmj.com/content/359/bmj.j5332/rr (accessed 10 November 2019).

95 Nigel Biggar, 'Why the Establishment of the Church of England is a Good for a Liberal Society', in Chapman, Maltby and Whyte, eds, *Established Church*, pp. 1–25, at p. 2.

96 Ibid.

97 Ibid., p. 3. In 'Establishment and Liberalism: A Response to Nigel Biggar', the theologian Theo Hobson says that Biggar's 'brisk treatment of the religious case for disestablishment is hugely inadequate'. I agree, while also recognizing that the theological investigation of disestablishment is minor in this essay compared to Biggar's obvious concern with modern liberal thought. Theo Hobson, 'Establishment and Liberalism: A Response to Nigel Biggar', *Theology*, Vol. 115, No. 3 (2012), pp. 163–74, at p. 165.

98 Biggar, 'Establishment of the Church of England', *Established Church*, p. 2. According to William Whyte, writing in the same volume, 'the Bishops are very rarely present in the House of Lords and never have a decisive effect on votes there.' William Whyte, 'What Future for Establishment?', in Chapman, Maltby and Whyte, eds, *Established Church*, pp. 180–95, at p. 184. While this is overstating the case, it certainly is a check on the 'vast opportunities' that establishment brought and General Synod bishops threw back at Bishop Colin Buchanan when he proposed the removal of state controls over episcopal appointments in July 1994. For an empirical review of the works of the Lords Spiritual, see Anna Harlow, Frank Cranmer and Norman Doe, 'Bishops in the House of Lords: a Critical Analysis', *Public Law*, Autumn (2008), pp. 490–509.

99 Biggar, 'Establishment of the Church of England', *Established Church*, p. 3. Given the current arrangement in which the British government has a decisive role in choosing the church's leadership, Biggar's indictment of the vertiginous refusal of the responsibility to make a decision sounds equally apt when applied to the Church of England's own structures and processes for choosing a leader. Donald MacKinnon's statement on this issue is worth quoting: 'No one has yet suggested in so many words that the Patronage Secretary has replaced the Holy Ghost in the Church of England's understanding of the proper method for choosing its chief pastors, but its practice encourages the belief that such a substitution has taken place, or that we shall soon hear that the passages in the Fourth Gospel relating to the "Other Advocate" are to be demythologized in terms of the gift of such a functionary.' McDowell, Kirklan and Moyse, *Kenotic Ecclesiology*, p. 187.

100 Biggar, 'Establishment of the Church of England', *Established Church*, p. 3.

101 Whyte, 'Future for Establishment', *Established Church*, p. 194.

102 Italics in original. Biggar, 'Establishment of the Church of England', *Established Church*, p. 1.

103 Whyte, 'Future for Establishment', *Established Church*, p. 185.

104 Biggar, 'Establishment of the Church of England', *Established Church*, pp. 3, 7, 14.

105 Biggar, 'Establishment of the Church of England', *Established Church*, p. 21.

106 Tariq Modood, quoted in ibid., p. 16.

107 J. Watkins, W. Wulaningsih, C. Da Zhou et al., 'Effects of Health and Social Care Spending Constraints on Mortality in England: A Time Trend Analysis', *BMJ Open*, Vol. 7 (2017), pp. 1–9.

108 Fergusson, *Church, State*, p. 179.

109 Donald MacKinnon, quoted in ibid., p. 179.

110 Fergusson, *Church, State*, p. 43.

111 British society has reduced its carbon footprint over the last 20 years. The government has committed itself to zero net carbon by 2050, but this is not ambitious enough, includes international offsets, and does not include imports. Considering that British society was not on course to meet its previous greenhouse gas emission targets, an easy set of promises have been made but proportionate action has not been taken on this or the other ecological catastrophes (soil erosion, biodiversity decline) that we are currently going through. Caroline Lucas MP, a member of the Green Party, draws attention to support for fracking, blocking onshore wind, and the support for new roads and runways that marked Theresa May's record on carbon emissions. Leaving the European Union may give British society the chance to reform significant sectors like agriculture, but, as Isabella Tree warns, the EU has driven British green agendas in numerous ways. Tree writes: 'As the UK begins to divorce itself from European regulations and reconsider the costs of farming subsidies, there are big choices to be made. One of them will be how far to encourage environmental protection. Historically, UK policy does not have a good track record. It took EU legislation to clean up the rivers, beaches and bathing water of the "the Dirty Man of Europe". The EU changed our approaches to sewage treatment and releases of nitrates. It was the EU's air-quality framework directive that reduced our emissions of sulphur dioxide and nitrous oxide, and that, in 2015, fined the UK Government for continuing to fail air-pollution standards in London and other major cities. In 2017 the environmental law organization ClientEarth took legal action against the UK Government for the third time after it still failed to deliver improvements to air pollution. It was Natura 2000 and European habitats directives that obliged the UK Government to provide protected wildlife zones and encouraged the reintroduction of the beaver. With the notable exception of climate-change legislation, the UK has consistently failed to lead environmental policies in Europe.' Tree, *Wilding*, pp. 299, 300. See www.sciencemediacentre.org/expert-reaction-to-the-net-zero-report/ (accessed 10 November 2019). Caroline Lucas, 'Theresa May's net-zero emissions target is a lot less impressive than it looks', *The Guardian*, 12 June 2019, www.theguardian.com/commentisfree/2019/jun/12/theresa-may-net-zero-emissions-target-climate-change (accessed 15 November 2019).

112 Iain Mclean and Scot Peterson, 'Uniform Establishment', in Chapman, Maltby and Whyte, eds, *Established Church*, pp. 141–57, at p. 154.

113 McDowell, Kirklan and Moyse, *Kenotic Ecclesiology*, p. 210.

114 Ibid., p. 193.

115 Ibid., pp. 194, 195.

116 www.monbiot.com/2018/01/17/eating-the-earth/ (accessed 30 May 2018). 'The global footprint (land use) associated with UK's food and feed supply increased by 2022 kilohectares (kha) from 1986 to 2009, a rise of 28% ... the UK is currently importing over 50% of its food and feed, whereas 70% and 64% of the associated cropland and greenhouse gas emission impacts were located abroad. Feeding the UK, in other words, is increasingly using more of other people's land.' Tim Lang, Erik Millstone and Terry Marsden, *A Food Brexit: Time to Get Real* (Sussex: Science Policy Research Unit, 2017), www.sussex.ac.uk/webteam/gateway/file.php?name=foodbrexitreport-langmillstonemarsden-july2017pdf.pdf&site=25 (accessed 17 January 2019), p. 21.

117 Accord to George Monbiot, drawing on work from the UN, at the current rate of soil deterioration, the earth has 60 years of viable harvests remaining. George

Monbiot, 'We're treating soil like dirt. It's a fatal mistake, as our lives depend on it', *The Guardian*, 25 March 2015, www.theguardian.com/commentisfree/2015/mar/25/treating-soil-like-dirt-fatal-mistake-human-life (accessed 30 May 2018). A large number of people have transitioned to plant-based diets in the last few years, following the recognition that addressing climate change requires confronting how we produce food and what we eat. Between 2018 and 2019 there was a 3% increase in consumers who are reducing or considering reducing the amounts of meat in their diets: www.igd.com/articles/article-viewer/t/the-rise-of-plant-based-living/i/22613 (accessed 15 November 2019). The number of vegans in the UK quadrupled between 2014 and 2019, from 150,000 to 600,000 people: www.vegansociety.com/news/media/statistics (accessed 15 November 2019).

118 Berry, *World-Ending Fire*, p. 338.

119 Ibid., p. 310.

120 Ibid.

121 Ibid., p. 311.

122 'The main conclusion to be drawn from this exercise is that organic livestock-based agriculture, practised by orthodox methods and without supplementary measures, has the most difficulty sustaining the full UK population on the land available.' Simon Fairlie, 'Can Britain Feed Itself?', *The Land*, 4, 2007–08, www.thelandmagazine.org.uk/articles/can-britain-feed-itself (accessed 30 May 2018), pp. 18–26, at p. 25.

123 Fairlie, 'Can Britain Feed Itself?', p. 25. Fairlie, and Wirzba addresses this too, is not suggesting that everyone becomes a farmer. Not everyone is suited to it. Norman Wirzba, *From Nature to Creation: A Christian Vision for Understanding and Loving our World* (Grand Rapids: Baker Academic, 2015), p. 98. Berry's suggestion, in the closing pages on *Unsettling of America* is rather that 'low-interest loans ought to be made available to people wishing to buy family-size farms'. Berry, *Unsettling of America*, p. 22.

124 Fairlie, 'Can Britain Feed Itself?', p. 22.

125 What about organic: Fairlie compares permaculture and organic by saying 'the Livestock Permaculture land economy outlined [in this text] produces all its food, a substantial proportion of its textiles, and the energy for cultivating its fields, on 13.4 million hectares, a little over half the entire country. The more orthodox organic system in [this text] requires nearly 16 million hectares, it doesn't produce any fuel, it is low on fat, and it produces less meat: only 187 calories in the daily ration, compared with 272 in the permaculture model. The improvement comes through using animals for what they are best at, recycling nutrients and waste – and avoiding feeding them grains.' Fairlie, 'Can Britain Feed Itself?', p. 24.

126 Shiva writes that 'data shows that, everywhere in the world, biodiverse small farms produce more agricultural output per unit area than large farms' and 'industrial agriculture contributes to climate change through the direct use of fossil fuels and the emission of $CO_2$, as well as through the use of fossil fuel-based nitrogen fertilisers which emit nitrogen oxide, which is 300 times more damaging to the climate than $CO_2$. Organic farming and organic soils contribute to mitigation of climate change by (a) getting rid of agri-chemicals like synthetic fertilisers; (b) sequestering carbon in the soil.' Shiva, *Making Peace with the Earth*, pp. 230, 151.

127 Ibid., p. 147.

128 Dee Butterly and Ian Fitzpatrick, *People's Food Policy* (2017), www.peoplesfoodpolicy.org (accessed 10 November 2019), p. 32.

129 Ibid.

130 Ibid.

131 The document continues: 'There is an irony here, as spending in local food outlets generates 10 times the local economic wealth and three times the number of people in employment for each £1 of turnover compared with spending in supermarkets.' On production, manufacturing and retail, *A People's Food Policy* laments significant consolidation and homogenization in the industry. 'Over the past few decades there has been a major consolidation of production, manufacturing and retail enterprises across the food supply chain. A rich diversity of independent shops, small farms and craft producers have faded out of existence. Today, the UK grocery market is worth £180 billion, and is highly concentrated, with eight supermarkets holding a 93% market share of food retailing. 58% of food is bought from supermarkets or hypermarkets, 21% from convenience stores, 16% from discounters or online, and 6% from other retailers. In food manufacturing, 6% of enterprises are responsible for 76% of turnover. In the past 60 years 100,000 specialist food stores have closed across the UK.' Butterly and Fitzpatrick, *People's Food Policy*, pp. 32, 78.

132 Berry, *Unsettling of America*, pp. 23, 24.

133 Van Wieren, *Food, Farming and Religion*, p. 65.

134 Ibid., p. 98. Methane and nitrous oxide are even more problematic than $CO_2$; livestock production is worse for global warming than the global transport sector.

135 Ibid.

136 www.vegansociety.com/whats-new/blog/should-christians-be-vegan (accessed 11 November 2019).

137 Ibid. Two-thirds of the world's arable land and a quarter of the total ice-free land surface is used for raising livestock. On top of soil compaction, run-off and clearing of natural habitats for grazing or intensive farming, this huge concentration of single species leads to the loss of biodiversity and proliferation of arable monocultures, which then in turn are liable to rely on synthetic fertilizers which require fossil fuel; 8% of global water use is related directly to livestock. See Van Wieren, *Food, Farming and Religion*, pp. 98, 66. Eleonora Gullone, 'Why Eating Animals Is Not Good for Us', *Journal of Animal Ethics*, Vol. 7, No. 1 (2007), pp. 31–62, at p. 53.

138 Lang, *Food Brexit*, p. 21.

139 Including heart disease, cancer, type 2 diabetes and strokes. See www.vegan society.com/whats-new/blog/should-christians-be-vegan (accessed 11 November 2019). Eleonora Gullone argues, I think correctly, that our awareness of animal suffering in the industrial food industry, whether consciously or intuitively, inhibits our capacity for empathy more broadly and means that our 'system requires management of incongruences' in order to stabilize and perpetuate itself. She asks whether we sustain, collectively, coping strategies for dealing with the schism between what we know and what we do by having different animal welfare laws for domestic or 'economic' animals, calling the animal one name and the meat another – pigs/pork etc. – exaggerating the animal–human difference, perpetuate stereotypes like the association of masculinity with carnivorousness and bolstering half-truths like the need for meat in a healthy diet: the 'a plant based diet is really inhibiting that rhino's ability to put on muscle mass' argument. Gullone even notes, suggestively, that the 'irony is that it is in those countries where there are more companion animals [pets] that the diet comprises of more animal-based foods (i.e. the Western diet). So, it is in those very nations where animals are welcomed into our lives, families, and homes and treated as nonhuman "people" where the largest numbers of nonhuman animals are forced to live short miserable lives in intensive factory farms, where their sentience and their capacity to suffer are largely

denied in the interest of profits.' Gullone, 'Why Eating Animals is Not Good', *Journal of Animal Ethics*, pp. 35, 36, 45–6, 54.

140 Grumett and Muers, *Theology of the Menu*, p. 70, 105.

141 Genesis 1; Psalm 145; Luke 12.6.

142 Wirzba, *Faith and Food*, p. 201.

143 Ibid. For individuals and churches who are interested in learning more about the food brands they eat, Oxfam's 'Behind the Brands' paper and accompanying document can give information on the 'Big Ten' food companies: Associated British Foods, Coca-Cola, Danone, General Mills, Kellogg, Mars, Mondelez International, Nestlé, PepsiCo and Unilever. This work by Oxfam can help people learn where their food was sourced, how these companies treated their labourers and whether it was produced sustainably. See Oxfam, *Behind the Brands: Food Justice and the 'Big 10' Food and Beverage Companies* (2013), www-cdn.oxfam.org/s3fs-public/file_attachments/bp166-behind-the-brands-260213-en_2.pdf (accessed 15 November 2019). An up-to-date associated website which tracks the progress or decline of these companies can be found here: www.behindthebrands.org.

144 Lang, *Food Brexit*, p. 68.

145 Ibid., p. 6.

146 Ibid., p. 11.

147 Ibid., pp. 49, 74. There are around 200,000 people on zero hours contracts in these sectors, according to Lang.

148 Ibid., p. 74.

149 Ibid., pp. 72–4.

150 In *How Good We Can Be*, Hutton says that 'put at its rawest, our private institutions provide insufficient widespread social or public good to justify their continuing unreformed autonomy'. The dereliction of duty is once again partly political as 'wealth generation is not some magic left to business, enterprise and individuals in their low-taxed private garden: it reflects how companies are owned, financed and incentivised within a framework of public law'; we need deep changes 'in the way wealth generation is approached: substantive reforms in the ways companies are owned and financed – the heart of the matter financially – along with suggestions as to how public action can capitalise on those reforms to enlarge the scope for innovation and investment'. Filling out this ambition, Hutton goes on to suggest more robust protections for British businesses from foreign takeovers and a 'new approach to ownership' through a 'Companies Act for the twenty-first century' in which 'companies will be required to declare their business purpose on incorporation: they should incorporate to deliver particular goods and services that serve a societal or economic need and will need particular capabilities and skills. It is through delivering of their purpose that they should seek to make profits.' All Hutton's further suggestions – the publication of pay scales, worker representation on operational management boards, protections from short-term share inflation or asset stripping by attaching shareholder voting to the duration a share is owned, and employee share ownership schemes – are orientated to creating the legal horizon which nurtures companies that are orientated to realizing social goods and have long-term stability. Will Hutton, *How Good We Can Be* (London: Abacus, 2015), pp. 128, 130, 137.

151 Norman Wirzba, ed., *The Essential Agrarian Reader: The Future of Culture, Community, and the Land* (Berkeley: Counterpoint Press, 2003), p. 9.

152 Berry, *Unsettling of America*, p. 13.

153 Ibid., p. 14.

## Conclusion

1 John 10.10.

2 Herman E. Daly, 'Sustainable Economic Development: Definitions, Principles, Policies', in Norman Wirzba, ed., *The Essential Agrarian Reader: The Future of Culture, Community, and the Land* (Berkeley, Counterpoint Press, 2003), pp. 62–79, at pp. 70, 71.

3 Norman Wirzba, quoted in Chris Allen, 'Food Poverty and Christianity in Britain: A Theological Re-assessment', *Political Theology*, Vol. 17, No. 4 (2016), pp. 361–77, at p. 368.

4 Wirzba, *Essential Agrarian Reader*, p. 8.

5 David B. Burrell, Carlo Cogliati, Janet M. Soskice and William R. Stoeger, eds, *Creation and the God of Abraham* (Cambridge: Cambridge University Press, 2010), p. 3.

6 The language used here is key. To suggest that God wills something other than God to be, and that when this happened creation happened, is not to suggest that God is in any way lacking or deficient in a way that creation completes. Creation depends on God, God does not depend on creation, the relationship is a 'non-reciprocal relation of dependence' in honour of the complete uniqueness of the Creator–creation relation. See Peter Scott, 'Creation', in Peter M. Scott and William T. Cavanaugh, eds, *Political Theology* (Oxford: Blackwell Publishing, 2007) and Burrell et al., *Creation and the God of Abraham*, p. 45.

7 Burrell et al., *Creation and the God of Abraham*, p. 43.

8 The passage continues: And being found in human form, he humbled himself and became obedient to the point of death – even death on a cross.' Philippians 2.6–8.

9 John 10.11.

10 John 13.1.

11 De Souza quotes a retired teacher in her book who said: 'that's a risk of providing any charity; it becomes institutionalized, if you will. I have been here twenty years, and you know, our goal always was to be redundant and I have not seen much progress in that direction.' See de Souza, *Feeding the Other*, p. 107.

12 Riches, *Food Bank Nations*, p. 165.

13 Monbiot, *Out of the Wreckage*, p. 29.

14 Wells and Caraher, 'UK Print Media Coverage of the Food Bank', p. 1428.

15 McKendrick, quoted in ibid.

16 Berry, *Unsettling of America*, p. 13.

17 Along with some of the examples given in Grumett and Muers' history of Christian engagements with food, there are the works of the contemporary Catholic Workers' Movement and their farms, Tradecraft, A Rocha UK and their resources for doing 'eco-church', and a very significant and welcome proliferation of local markets and direct buying from farms, or local purchasing co-operatives.

18 Wirzba, *Essential Agrarian Reader*, p. 4.

19 Ibid.

20 Ibid., p. 140.

21 Along with Shiva, who draws upon Hindu ideas to develop her defence of agrarianism, Masanobu Fukuoka's text *The One-Straw Revolution* is an excellent example of the integration of Buddhist and agrarian ideas. Masanobu Fukuoka, *The One-Straw Revolution* (New York: New York Review of Books, 2009).

22 Wirzba, *Essential Agrarian Reader*, p. 94.

23 Ibid., p. 84.

24 Ibid., p. 95.

# Bibliography

## Books

Augustine, *City of God*, trans. Henry Bettenson (London: Penguin, 2003).

Allahyari, Rebecca Anne, *Visions of Charity: Volunteer Workers and Moral Community* (London: University of California Press, 2000).

Anderson, Gary A., *Charity* (London: Yale University Press, 2013).

Aquinas, *Selected Political Writing*, trans. J. G. Dawson (Oxford: Basil Blackwell, 1954).

Atherton, John, *Transfiguring Capitalism: An Enquiry into Religion and Global Change* (London: SCM Press, 2008).

Beaumont, Justin and Paul Cloke, eds, *Faith-Based Organisations and Exclusion in European Cities* (Bristol: Policy Press, 2012).

Berry, Wendell, *The Unsettling of America: Culture and Agriculture* (New York: Avon, 1978).

Berry, Wendell, *The World-Ending Fire* (London: Penguin, 2018).

Berry, Wendell, *The Art of Loading Brush: New Agrarian Writings* (Berkeley: Counterpoint, 2017).

Biggar, Nigel, *Good Life* (London: SPCK, 1997).

Biggar, Nigel, *Between Kin and Cosmopolis: An Ethic of the Nation* (Cambridge: James Clarke, 2014).

Boff, Leonardo, *Cry of the Earth, Cry of the Poor*, trans. Philip Berryman (New York: Orbis Books, 1997).

Burrell, David B., Cogliati, Carlo, Soskice, Janet M. and Stoeger, William R., eds, *Creation and the God of Abraham* (Cambridge: Cambridge University Press, 2010).

Cahill, Damien and Konings, Martijn, *Neoliberalism* (Cambridge: Polity Press, 2017).

Cahill, Lisa Sowle, *Global Justice, Christology and Christian Ethics* (Cambridge: Cambridge University Press, 2013).

Chapman, Mark, Maltby, Judith and Whyte, William, eds, *The Established Church: Past, Present and Future* (London: T & T Clark International, 2011).

Colls, Robert and Lancaster, Bill, eds, *Geordies* (Edinburgh: Edinburgh University Press, 1992).

Conradie, Ernst M., ed., *Christian Faith and the Earth: Current Paths and Emerging Horizons in Ecotheology* (London: T & T Clark, 2014).

Cooper, Melinda, *Family Values: Between Neoliberalism and the New Social Conservatism* (New York: Zone, 2017).

De Bolla, Peter, *The Architecture of Concepts: The Historical Formation of Human Rights* (New York: Fordham University Press, 2013).

De Souza, Rebecca, *Feeding the Other: Whiteness, Privilege and Neoliberal Stigma in Food Pantries* (London: MIT Press, 2019).

Davis, Ellen F., *Scripture, Culture and Agriculture: An Agrarian Reading of the Bible* (Cambridge: Cambridge University Press, 2008).

Durkheim, Emile, *The Division of Labour in Society*, trans. George Simpson (New York: The Macmillan Company, 1960).

Fergusson, David, *Church, State and Civil Society* (Cambridge: Cambridge University Press, 2004).

Finn, Daniel, ed., *The True Wealth of Nations* (Oxford: Oxford University Press, 2010).

Fisher, Mark, *Capitalist Realism* (Winchester: Zero Books, 2009).

Freeland, Chrystia, *Plutocrats: The Rise of the New Global Super-Rich and the Fall of Everyone Else* (New York: Penguin, 2013).

Fukuoka, Masanobu, *The One-Straw Revolution* (New York: New York Review of Books, 2009).

Garthwaite, Kayleigh, *Hunger Pains: Life inside Foodbank Britain* (Bristol: Policy Press, 2016).

Goodchild, Phillip, *Theology of Money* (London: SCM Press, 2007).

Graeber, David, *Bullshit Jobs: A Theory* (London: Allen Lane, 2018).

Graham, Elaine, *Between a Rock and a Hard Place: Public Theology in a Post-Secular Age* (London: SCM Press, 2013).

Grumett, David and Muers, Rachel, *Theology on the Menu: Asceticism, Meat and Christian Diet* (London: Routledge, 2010).

Gutiérrez, Gustavo, *A Theology of Liberation*, trans. Sister Caridad Inda and John Eagleson (New York: Orbis, 1983).

Gutiérrez, Gustavo, *We Drink from Our Own Wells*, trans. Matthew J. O'Connell (London: SCM Press, 1984).

Harvey, David, *The New Imperialism* (Oxford: Oxford University Press, 2003).

Hayek, F. A., *The Road to Serfdom* (London: The University of Chicago Press, 2007).

Hooker, Richard, *Of the Laws of Ecclesiastical Polity* (1563– ; Oxford: Oxford University Press, 2013).

Hutton, Will, *How Good We Can Be* (London: Abacus, 2015).

Konings, Martijn, *The Emotional Logic of Capitalism: What Progressives Have Missed* (Stanford: Stanford University Press, 2015).

Kotsko, Adam, *Neoliberalism's Demons: On the Political Theology of Late Capital* (Stanford: Stanford University Press, 2018).

Lansley, Stewart and Mack, Joanna, *Breadline Britain: The Rise of Mass Poverty* (London: Oneworld, 2015).

LeVasseur, Todd, Parajuli, Pramod and Wirzba, Norman, eds, *Religion and Sustainable Agriculture: World Spiritual Traditions and Food Ethics* (Lexington: University of Kentucky Press, 2016).

Lewis, C. S., *Miracles: A Preliminary Study* (London: Geoffrey Bles, 1947).

Lindbeck, George A., *The Nature of Doctrine* (Louisville: Westminster John Knox Press, 1984).

Lorey, Isabell, *State of Insecurity: Government of the Precarious* (London: Verso, 2015).

MacIntyre, Alasdair, *Ethics and Politics: Selected Essays, Volume 2* (Cambridge: Cambridge University Press, 2006).

MacIntyre, Alasdair, *After Virtue* (London: Duckworth, 2007).

McDowell, John C., Kirkland, Scott A. and Moyse, Ashley John, eds, *Kenotic Ecclesiology: Selected Writings of Donald M. MacKinnon* (Minneapolis: Fortress Press, 2016).

McLellan, David, ed., *Karl Marx: Selected Writings* (Oxford: Oxford University Press, 2011).

McMahon, Paul, *Feeding Frenzy: The New Politics of Food* (London: Profile Books, 2014).

Méndez-Montoya, Angel F., *The Theology of Food: Eating and the Eucharist* (Chichester: Wiley-Blackwell, 2012).

Milbank, John, *Being Reconciled: Ontology and Pardon* (London: Routledge, 2003).

Milbank, John, *Theology and Social Theory: Beyond Secular Reason* (Oxford: Blackwell Publishing, 2006).

Milbank, John, Pabst, Adria, *The Politics of Virtue: Post-Liberalism and the Human Future* (London: Rowman & Littlefield, 2016).

Mirowski, Philip and Plehwe, Dieter, eds, *The Road from Mont Pèlerin: The Making of the Neoliberal Thought Collective* (London: Harvard University Press, 2009).

Monbiot, George, *Out of the Wreckage: A New Politics for an Age of Crisis* (London: Verso, 2018).

O'Brien, David J. and Shannon, Thomas A., *Catholic Social Thought: Encyclicals and Documents from Pope Leo XIII to Pope Francis* (New York: Orbis, 2016).

Paarlberg, Robert, *Food Politics: What Everybody Needs to Know* (Oxford: Oxford University Press, 2010).

Paine, Thomas, *Rights of Man* (London: Penguin Books, 1984).

Piketty, Thomas, *Capital in the Twenty-first Century* (Cambridge, MA: Belknap Press, 2014).

Pilcher, Jeffrey M., ed., *The Oxford Handbook of Food History* (Oxford: Oxford University Press, 2012).

Polanyi, Karl, *The Great Transformation: The Political and Economic Origins of Our Time* (Boston: Beacon Press, 2001).

Poppendieck, Janet, *Breadlines: Knee-Deep in Wheat, Food Assistance in the Great Depression* (Berkley: University of California Press, 2014).

Prochaska, Frank, *Christianity and Social Service in Modern Britain: The Disinherited Spirit* (Oxford: Oxford University Press, 2006).

Riches, Graham, *Food Bank Nations: Poverty, Corporate Charity and the Right to Food* (London: Routledge, 2018).

Riches, Graham and Silvasti, Tiina, eds, *First World Hunger Revisited: Food Charity or the Right to Food* (New York: Palgrave Macmillan, 2014).

Robinson, Fred, Zass-Ogilvie, Ian and Jackson, Michael, *Never Had It so Good? The North East Under New Labour 1997–2007* (Durham: St Chad's College, Durham University, 2007).

Samuel, Vinay and Hauser, Albrecht, eds, *Proclaiming Christ in Christ's Way: Studies in Integral Mission* (Eugene: Wipf & Stock Publishers, 2007).

Schmemann, Alexander, *For the Life of the World* (New York: St Vladimir's Seminary Press, 1973).

Schmemann, Alexander, *The Eucharist: Sacrament of the Kingdom*, trans. Paul Kachur (New York: St Vladimir's Seminary Press, 1988).

Scott, Peter M., and Cavanaugh, William T., eds, *Political Theology* (Oxford: Blackwell Publishing, 2007).

Shiva, Vandana, *Making Peace with the Earth* (London: Pluto Press, 2013).

Shrubsole, Guy, *Who Owns England?* (London: William Collins, 2019).

Srnicek, Nick, Williams, Alex, *Inventing the Future: Postcapitalism and a World without Work* (London: Verso, 2016).

Standing, Guy, *The Precariat: The New Dangerous Class* (London: Bloomsbury, 2016).

Standing, Guy, *Universal Basic Income: And How We Can Make It Happen* (London: Penguin, 2017).

Swimme, Brian and Berry, Thomas, *The Universe Story: From the Primordial Flaring Forth to the Ecozoic Era* (San Francisco: Harper, 1992).

Tawney, R. H., *Religion and the Rise of Capitalism* (London: Butler & Tanner, 1969).

Taylor, Charles, *Sources of the Self: The Making of Modern Identity* (Cambridge: Cambridge University Press, 1992).

Taylor, Charles, *A Secular Age* (Cambridge, MA: Harvard University Press, 2007).

Thomas, R. S., *Collected Poems, 1945–1990* (London: Phoenix, 1993).

Torry, Malcolm, *Citizen's Basic Income: A Christian Social Policy* (London: Darton, Longman and Todd, 2016).

Tree, Isabella, *Wilding: The Return of Nature to a British Farm* (London: Picador, 2018).

Van Wieren, Gretel, *Food, Farming and Religion: Emerging Ethical Perspectives* (London: Routledge, 2018).

Vernon, James, *Hunger: A Modern History* (Cambridge, MA: Belknap, 2007).

Weber, Max, *The Protestant Ethic and the Spirit of Capitalism*, trans. Talcott Parsons (London: Routledge, 2001).

Webster, Jane S., *Ingesting Jesus: Eating and Drinking in the Gospel of John* (Atlanta: Society for Biblical Literature, 2003).

Wills, Jane, *Locating Localism: Statecraft, Citizenship and Democracy* (Bristol: Policy Press, 2016).

Wirzba, Norman, ed., *The Essential Agrarian Reader: The Future of Culture, Community, and the Land* (Berkeley: Counterpoint Press, 2003).

Wirzba, Norman, *Food and Faith: A Theology of Eating* (Cambridge: Cambridge University Press, 2011).

Wirzba, Norman, *From Nature to Creation: A Christian Vision for Understanding and Loving our World* (Grand Rapids: Baker Academic, 2015).

Wood, Ben, ed., *Renewing the Self: Contemporary Religious Perspectives* (Newcastle-upon-Tyne: Cambridge Scholars Publishing, 2017).

Wren-Lewis, Simon, *The Lies We Were Told* (Bristol: Bristol University Press, 2018).

Wright, Christopher J. H., *God's People in God's Land: Family, Land and Property in the Old Testament* (Grand Rapids: William B. Eerdmans Publishing Company, 1990).

## Journals

Adams, Nicholas and Elliott, Charles, 'Ethnography is Dogmatics: Making Description Central to Systematic Theology', *Scottish Journal of Theology*, Vol. 53, No. 3 (2000), pp. 339–64.

Allen, Chris, 'Food Poverty and Christianity in Britain: A Theological Re-assessment', *Political Theology*, Vol. 17, No. 4 (2016), pp. 361–77.

Boersma, Hans, 'Nature and Supernatural in *la nouvelle theologie*: The Recovery of a Sacramental Mindset', *New Blackfriars*, Vol. 93, No. 1043 (2011), pp. 34–46.

Byrne, David, 'Industrial Culture in a Post-industrial World: The Case of the North East of England', *City*, Vol. 6, No. 3 (2002), pp. 279–89.

Caplan, Pat, 'Big Society or Broken Society? Food Banks in the UK', *Anthropology Today*, Vol. 32, No. 1 (2016), pp. 5–9.

Castel, Robert, 'The Rise of Uncertainties', *Critical Horizons*, Vol. 17, No. 2 (2016), pp. 160–7.

Clapp, Jennifer, 'The Trade-ification of the Food Sustainability Agenda', *The Journal of Peasant Studies*, Vol. 44, No. 2 (2017), pp. 335–53.

Conradson, D., 'Spaces of Care in the City: The Place of a Community Drop-in Centre', *Social and Cultural Geography*, Vol. 4, No. 4 (2003), pp. 507–25.

Dalingwater, Louise, 'Regional Performance in the UK under New Labour', *Observatoire de la société britannique*, Vol. 10 (2011), pp. 115–36. Available at journals. openedition.org/osb/1151#text. Accessed 19 July 2019.

Davis, Owen and Geiger, Ben Baumberg, 'Did Food Insecurity Rise across Europe after the 2008 Crisis? An Analysis Across Welfare Regimes', *Social Policy and Society*, Vol. 16, No. 3 (2017), pp. 343–60.

DeVerteuil, Geoffrey and Wilton, Robert, 'Spaces of Abeyance, Care and Survival: The Addiction Treatment System as a Site of "Regulatory Richness"', *Political Geography*, Vol. 28, No. 8 (2009), pp. 463–72.

Douglas, F., Sapko, J. and Kiezebrink, K., 'Resourcefulness, Desperation, Shame, Gratitude and Powerlessness: Common Themes Emerging from a Study of Food Bank Use in Northeast Scotland', *Public Health*, Vol. 2, No. 3 (2015), pp. 297–317.

Gullone, Eleonora, 'Why Eating Animals Is Not Good for Us', *Journal of Animal Ethics*, Vol. 7, No. 1 (2007), pp. 31–62.

Harlow, Anna, Cranmer, Frank and Doe, Norman, 'Bishops in the House of Lords: a Critical Analysis', *Public Law*, Autumn (2008), pp. 490–509.

Hobson, Theo, 'Establishment and Liberalism: A Response to Nigel Biggar', *Theology*, Vol. 115, No. 3 (2012), pp. 163–74.

Jenkins, Willis, 'After Lynn White: Religious Ethics and Environmental Problems', *Journal of Religious Ethics*, Vol. 37, No. 2 (2009), pp. 283–309.

Koopman, Nico, 'The Reception of the Barmen Declaration in South Africa', *The Ecumenical Review*, Vol. 61, No. 1 (2009), pp. 60–71.

Konings, Marijn, 'The Spirit of Austerity', *Journal of Cultural Economy*, Vol. 9, No. 1 (2016), pp. 86–100.

Loopstra, Rachel, Lambie-Mumford, Hannah and Fledderjohann, Jasmine, 'Food Bank Operational Characteristics and Rates of Food Bank Use across Britain', *BMC Public Health*, Vol. 19, No. 561 (2019), pp. 1–10.

Horst, H., Pascucci, S. and Bol, W., 'The "Dark Side" of Food Banks? Exploring Emotional Responses of Food Bank Receivers in the Netherlands', *British Food Journal*, Vol. 116, No. 9 (2014), pp. 1506–20.

McCulloch, Andrew, Mohan, John and Smith, Peter, 'Patterns of Social Capital, Voluntary Activity, and Area Deprivation in England', *Environment and Planning*, Vol. 44, No. 5 (2012), pp. 1130–47.

McIntyre, Lynn, Dutton, Daniel, Kwok J., Cynthia and Emery, Herbert, 'Reduction of Food Insecurity among Low-Income Canadian Seniors as a Likely Impact of a Guaranteed Annual Income', *Canadian Public Policy*, Vol. 42, No. 3 (2016), pp. 274–86.

Mills, China, 'Dead People Don't Claim: A Psychopolitical Autopsy of UK Austerity Suicides', *Critical Social Policy*, Vol. 38, No. 2 (2018), pp. 302–22.

Nightingale, Andrea Joslyn, Eriksen, Siri, Taylor, Marcus, Forsyth, Timothy, Pelling, Mark, Newsham, Andrew, Boyd, Emily, Brown, Katrina, Harvey, Blane, Jones, Lindsey, Kerr, Rachel Bezner, Mehta, Lyla, Naess, Lars Otto, Ockwell, David, Scoones, Ian, Tanner, Thomas and Whitfield, Stephen, 'Beyond Technical Fixes: Climate Solutions and the Great Derangement', *Climate and Development*, www.tandfonline. com/doi/full/10.1080/17565529.2019.1624495, published online 1 July 2019.

Peck, Jamie, 'Neoliberalizing States: Thin Policies/Hard Outcomes', *Progress in Human Geography*, Vol. 25, No. 3 (2001), pp. 445–55.

Pemberton, Charles, 'Between Ecclesiology and Ontology: A Response to Chris Allen on Food Banks', *Political Theology*, Vol. 20, No. 1 (2019), pp. 85–101.

Shildrick, Tracy and MacDonald, Robert, 'Poverty Talk: How People Experiencing Poverty Deny their Poverty and Why they Blame "The Poor"', *The Sociological Review*, Vol. 61, No. 2 (2013), pp. 285–303.

Walker, Samantha, Annison, Jill and Beckett, Sharon, 'Transforming Rehabilitation: The Impact of Austerity and Privatisation on Day-to-day Cultures and Working Practices in "Probation"', *Probation Journal*, Vol. 66, No. 1 (2019), pp. 113–30.

Watkins, J,. Wulaningsih, W., Da Zhou, C., et al., 'Effects of Health and Social Care Spending Constraints on Mortality in England: A Time Trend Analysis', *BMJ Open*, Vol. 7 (2017), pp. 1–9.

Wells, Rebecca and Caraher, Martin, 'UK Print Media Coverage of the Food Bank Phenomenon: From Food Welfare to Food Charity?', *British Food Journal*, Vol. 116, No. 9, pp. 1426–45.

Williams, Andrew, Cloke, Paul, May, Jon and Goodwin, Mark, 'Contested Space: The Contradictory Political Dynamics of Foodbanking in the UK', *Environment and Planning A*, Vol. 48, No. 11 (2016), pp. 2291—316.

## Reports

All-Party Parliamentary Inquiry into Hunger in the United Kingdom, *Feeding Britain: A Strategy for Zero Hunger in England, Wales, Scotland and Northern Ireland*, 2014. https://feedingbritain.org/wp-content/uploads/2019/01/feeding_britain_report_2014-2.pdf. Accessed 19 July 2019.

BMJ, *Bigger Cuts to Sure Start Children's Centres in More Disadvantaged Areas*, 2017. www.bmj.com/content/359/bmj.j5332/rr. Accessed 10 November 2019.

Butterly, Dee and Fitzpatrick, Ian, *People's Food Policy*, 2017. www.peoplesfood policy.org. Accessed 10 November 2019.

Centre for Social Justice, *Signed On, Written Off*, 2013. www.centreforsocialjustice. org.uk/library/signed-written-off-inquiry-welfare-dependency-britain. Accessed 14 November 2019.

Cheetham, Mandy, Moffatt, Suzanne and Addison, Michelle, *It's Hitting People that Can Least Afford it the Hardest: The Impact of the Roll Out of Universal Credit in Two North East England Localities: a Qualitative Study*, 2018. www.gateshead. gov.uk/media/10665/The-impact-of-the-roll-out-of-Universal-Credit-in-two-North-East-England-localities-a-qualitative-study-November-2018/pdf/Universal_Credit_Report_2018pdf.pdf?m=636778831081630000. Accessed 16 July 2019.

Church Urban Fund, *Hungry for More*, 2013. www2.cuf.org.uk/research/hungry-more. Accessed 30 September 2019.

Compass, *Universal Basic Income*, 2016. www.compassonline.org.uk/wp-content/uploads/2016/05/UniversalBasicIncomeByCompass-Spreads.pdf. Accessed 6 November 2019.

Cooper, Niall and Dumpleton, Sarah, *Walking the Breadline: The Scandal of Food Poverty in 21st Century Britain*, 2013. https://policy-practice.oxfam.org.uk/publications/walking-the-breadline-the-scandal-of-food-poverty-in-21st-century-britain-292978. Accessed 1 June 2018.

Coote, Anna and Yaziki, Edanur, *Universal Basic Income: A Union Perspective* (Ferney-Voltaire, France: Public Services International, 2019). www.world-psi. org/sites/default/files/documents/research/en_ubi_full_report_2019.pdf. Accessed 7 November 2019.

DeStress Project, *Poverty, Pathology and Pills*, 2019. http://destressproject.org.uk/ wp-content/uploads/2019/05/Final-report-8-May-2019-FT.pdf. Accessed 17 November 2019.

Downing, Emma, Kennedy, Steven and Fell, Mike, *Food Banks and Food Poverty*, 2014. http://researchbriefings.parliament.uk/ResearchBriefing/Summary/SN06657. Accessed 28 May 2018.

Durham County Director of Public Health, *All the Lonely People: Social Isolation and Loneliness in County Durham*, 2014. https://democracy.durham.gov.uk/documents/ s48104/Item%2016%20-%20Appendix%203%20-%20DPH%20Annual%20 Report%20-%20All%20the%20Lonely%20People%20Social%20Isolation%20 and%20Loneliness%20in.pdf. Accessed 5 August 2019.

End Hunger UK, *Fix Universal Credit*, 2018. http://endhungeruk.org/wp-content/ uploads/2018/07/Fix-Universal-Credit-a-report-from-End-Hunger-UK.pdf. Accessed 13 August 2019.

End Hunger UK, *A Menu to End Hunger in the UK*, 2018. http://endhungeruk.org/ menu/. Accessed 13 August 2019.

End Hunger UK, *Why End Hunger?*, 2019. www.endhungeruk.org/2019/11/06/ whyendukhunger/. Accessed 14 November 2019.

Fairlie, Simon, 'Can Britain Feed Itself?', 2009. www.thelandmagazine.org.uk/articles/ can-britain-feed-itself. Accessed 30 May 2018.

*Faith in Foodbanks?* (London: Joint Public Issues Team, 2014), www.jointpublicissues. org.uk/wp-content/uploads/Faith-in-Foodbanks-Report.pdf. Accessed 4 January 2020.

Fareshare, *The Wasted Opportunity*, 2018. https://fareshare.org.uk/wp-content/ uploads/2018/10/J3503-Fareshare-Report_aw_no_crops.pdf. Accessed 29 July 2019.

Food and Agriculture Organization of the United Nations, *Food Wastage Footprint: Impacts on Natural Resources*, 2013. www.fao.org/3/i3347e/i3347e.pdf. Accessed 4 April 2019.

Food and Agriculture Organization of the United Nations, *The State of Food Security and Nutrition in the World*, 2018. www.fao.org/3/I9553EN/i9553en.pdf. Accessed 15 November 2019.

Foster, Liam, Brunton, Anne, Deeming, Chris and Haux, Tina, *In Defence of Welfare*, 2015. www.social-policy.org.uk/what-we-do/publications/in-defence-of-welfare-2/. Accessed 12 October 2019.

Giupponi, Giulia and Machin, Stephen, *Changing the Structure of Minimum Wages: Firm Adjustment and Wage Spillovers*, 2018. http://cep.lse.ac.uk/pubs/download/ dp1533.pdf. Accessed 19 November 2019.

Gladek, Eva, Fraser, Matthew, Roemers, Gerard, Munoz, Oscar Sabag, Kennedy, Erin and Hirsch, Peter, *The Global Food System: An Analysis*, 2016. www.metabolic.nl/ publications/global-food-system-an-analysis/. Accessed 28 September 2019.

Haddad, Moussa, Perry, Jane and Madfield-Spoor, Mia, *Emergency Use Only: Update 2017, Change is Possible*, 2017. www.trusselltrust.org/wp-content/uploads/ sites/2/2017/12/EUOII.pdf. Accessed 29 September 2019.

Hoddinott, John, Gilligan, Daniel, Hidrobo, Melissa, Margolies, Amy, Roy, Shalini, Sandstöm, Susanna, Schwab, Benjamin and Upton, Joanna, *Enhancing WFP's*

*Capacity and Experience to Design, Implement, Monitor, and Evaluate Vouchers and Cash Transfer Programmes: Study Summary*, 2013. http://ebrary.ifpri.org/utils/getfile/collection/p15738coll2/id/127961/filename/128172.pdf. Accessed 24 June 2019.

Howard, Marilyn, *Benefits or Barriers? Making Social Security Work for Survivors of Violence and Abuse across the UK's Four Nations*, 2019. https://wbg.org.uk/media/press-releases/governments-commitments-in-domestic-abuse-bill-undermined-by-the-social-security-system/. Accessed 24 June 2019.

International Panel of Experts on Sustainable Food System, *Too Big To Feed*, 2017. www.ipes-food.org/_img/upload/files/Concentration_FullReport.pdf. Accessed 1 October 2019.

Lambie-Mumford, Hannah, Crossley, Daniel, Verbeke, Monae and Dowler, Elizabeth, *Household Food Security in the UK: A Review of the Food Aid*, 2014. https://assets.publishing.service.gov.uk/government/uploads/system/uploads/attachment_data/file/283071/household-food-security-uk-140219.pdf. Accessed 29 September 2019 .

Lang, Tim, Millstone, Erik and Marsden, Terry, *A Food Brexit: Time to Get Real*, 2017. www.sussex.ac.uk/webteam/gateway/file.php?name=foodbrexitreport-langmillstonemarsden-july2017pdf.pdf&site=25. Accessed 30 May 2018.

Loopstra, Rachel and Lalor, Doireann, *Financial Insecurity, Food Insecurity, and Disability: The Profile of People Receiving Emergency Food Assistance from The Trussell Trust Foodbank Network in Britain* (Salisbury: Trussell Trust, 2017). www.trusselltrust.org/wp-content/uploads/sites/2/2017/07/OU_Report_final_01_08_online2.pdf. Accessed 19 July 2019.

Lloyds Bank Foundation and New Policy Institute, *A Quiet Crisis: Local Government Spending on Disadvantage in England*, 2018. www.lloydsbankfoundation.org.uk/A%20Quiet%20Crisis%20-%20Summary.pdf. Accessed 29 July 2019.

Marks, Abigail, Cowan, Sue and Maclean, Gavin, *Mental Health and Unemployment in Scotland: Understanding the Impact of Welfare Reforms in Scotland for Individuals with Mental Health Conditions*, 2017. www.advocard.org.uk/wp-content/uploads/2017/02/2017-02-Heriot-Watt-Mental-Health-Report-on-WCA.pdf. Accessed 16 July 2019.

Newcastle University Institute of Health and Society, *Visit by the UN Special Rapporteur on Extreme Poverty and Human Rights, Written Submission*, 2018. www.ohchr.org/Documents/Issues/EPoverty/UnitedKingdom/2018/Academics/Newcastle_University_Institute_of_Health_and_Society.pdf. Accessed 29 July 2019.

Office for National Statistics, *Changes in the Value and Division of Unpaid Volunteering in the UK: 2000 to 2015*, 2017. www.ons.gov.uk/economy/nationalaccounts/satelliteaccounts/articles/changesinthevalueanddivisionofunpaidcareworkintheuk/2000to2015. Accessed 16 August 2019.

Oxfam, *Behind the Brands: Food Justice and the 'Big 10' Food and Beverage Companies*, 2013. www-cdn.oxfam.org/s3fs-public/file_attachments/bp166-behind-the-brands-260213-en_2.pdf. Accessed 15 November 2019.

Paine, Thomas, *Agrarian Justice*, 1999. http://piketty.pse.ens.fr/files/Paine1795.pdf. Accessed 16 August 2019.

Perry, Jane, *Paying Over the Odds? Real-life Experiences of the Poverty Premium*, 2010. www.church-poverty.org.uk/wp-content/uploads/2019/06/Paying-Over-the-Odds-report.pdf. Accessed 11 October 2019.

Perry, Jane, Williams, Martin, Sefton, Tom and Haddad, Moussa, *Emergency Use Only: Understanding and Reducing the Use of Food Banks in the UK*, 2014. www.

trusselltrust.org/wp-content/uploads/sites/2/2016/01/foodbank-report.pdf. Accessed 29 September 2019.

Policy Exchange, *Smarter Sanctions*, 2014. https://policyexchange.org.uk/wp-content/uploads/2016/09/smarter-sanctions-1.pdf. Accessed 14 November 2019.

Richards, Anne, *Liberation and Entrapment Project, Mission and Food Banks*, 2017. www.churchofengland.org/sites/default/files/2017-11/MTAG%20Mission%20and%20Food%20Banks.pdf. Accessed 29 September 2019.

Painter, Anthony and Thoung, Chris, *Creative Citizen, Creative State: The Principled and Pragmatic Case for a Universal Basic Income* (London: RSA, 2015). www.thersa.org/discover/publications-and-articles/reports/basic-income. Accessed 6 November 2019.

Taylor, Matthew, Marsh, Greg, Nicol, Diane and Broadbent, Paul, *Good Work: The Taylor Review of Modern Working Practices*, 2017. www.gov.uk/government/publications/good-work-the-taylor-review-of-modern-working-practices. Accessed 29 September 2019.

Tinson, A., Ayrton, C., Barker, K., Born, T. B., Aldridge, H. and Kenway, P., *Monitoring Poverty and Social Exclusion*, 2016. www.jrf.org.uk/report/monitoring-poverty-and-social-exclusion-2016. Accessed 2 August 2018.

United Nations Educational, Scientific and Cultural Organization, *Human Rights: Comments and Interpretations*, 1948. https://unesdoc.unesco.org/ark:/48223/pf0000155042. Accessed 29 September 2019.

Wadsworth, Jonathan, *Did the National Minimum Wage Affect UK Prices?*, 2009. http://ftp.iza.org/dp4433.pdf. Accessed 19 November 2019.

## Websites

http://apps.charitycommission.gov.uk/Accounts/Ends49/0001077549_AC_20171231_E_C.pdf. Accessed 29 July 2019.

https://basicincome.org/news/2016/11/new-academic-research-shows-basic-income-improves-health/. Accessed 24 June 2019.

www.bbc.co.uk/news/business-28257351. Accessed 22 October 2019.

www.bbc.co.uk/news/uk-england-tees-30483153. Accessed 29 September 2019.

www.brin.ac.uk/figures/attitudes-towards-the-disestablishment-of-the-church-of-england/. Accessed 9 November 2019.

www.caat.org.uk/campaigns/arms-trade-out/church-of-england. Accessed 22 October 2019.

www.cato-unbound.org/print-issue/1805. Accessed 06 November 2019.

www.conservativehome.com/platform/2019/01/gareth-streeter-three-facts-which-suggest-a-rise-in-food-bank-use-is-not-just-down-to-universal-credit.html. Accessed 16 July 2019.

www.dailymail.co.uk/news/article-2606573/Food-bank-charity-misleading-public-Claim-1m-need-food-parcels-just-self-promotion.html. Accessed 29 September 2019.

www.dailymail.co.uk/news/article-3139159/I-welcome-food-banks-says-Iain-Duncan-Smith-claims-sign-decent-people-helping-difficulty.html. Accessed 16 July 2019.

www.eurofoodbank.org. Accessed 4 April 2019.

https://fareshare.org.uk/what-we-do/our-impact/. Accessed 4 April 2019.

https://feedingbritain.org/what-we-do/policy-issues/food-surplus-redistribution/. Accessed 4 April 2019.

https://feedingbritain.org/what-we-do/policy-issues/income-and-affordability-of-food/. Accessed 16 August 2019.

https://feedingbritain.org/what-we-do/policy-issues/welfare-reform/. Accessed 4 July 2019.

www.foodbankscanada.ca/getmedia/01e662ba-f1d7-419d-b40c-bcc71a9f943c/Hunger Count2015_singles.pdf.aspx. Accessed 24 June 2019.

www.frankfield.co.uk/upload/docs/Letter%20to%20David%20Cameron%20re%20 food%20aid%20funidng%2028.01.14.pdf. Accessed 14 July 2019.

www.frankfield.co.uk/campaigns/feeding-britain-appg-hunger.aspx. Accessed 14 July 2019.

www.gloucestershirelive.co.uk/news/gloucester-news/man-breached-order-stop-him-242853. Accessed 28 May 2018.

www.igd.com/articles/article-viewer/t/the-rise-of-plant-based-living/i/22613. Accessed 15 November 2019.

www.independent.co.uk/news/uk/politics/jacob-rees-mogg-uk-food-bank-uplifting-conservative-mp-leader-a7946096.html. Accessed 5 April 2019.

www.independent.co.uk/news/uk/home-news/north-south-divide-is-over-says-blair-744095.html. Accessed 19 July 2019.

www.jacobinmag.com/2015/05/slow-food-artisanal-natural-preservatives. Accessed 25 July 2019.

linkis.com/blacktrianglecampaign.org/d1Ume. Accessed 16 July 2019.

www.metamute.org/editorial/articles/precarious-precarisation-precariat. Accessed 29 September 2019.

www.mirror.co.uk/news/uk-news/foodbank-charity-threatened-closure-government-3682914. Accessed 29 September 2019.

www.mirror.co.uk/news/uk-news/27-bishops-slam-david-camerons-3164033. Accessed 7 November 2019.

www.monbiot.com/2018/01/17/eating-the-earth/. Accessed 30 May 2018.

www.nytimes.com/2005/10/08/us/john-van-hengel-83-dies-set-up-first-food-bank-in-us.html. Accessed 29 July 2019.

https://parliamentlive.tv/event/index/4ed4b537-2726-41e0-b11c-e98e73c81ea2?in= 14:35:50. Accessed 17 July 2019.

www.reform-magazine.co.uk/2014/04/at-home-with-charity/. Accessed 3 July 2019.

www.sciencemediacentre.org/expert-reaction-to-the-net-zero-report/. Accessed 10 November 2019.

www.taxjustice.net/2019/05/28/new-ranking-reveals-corporate-tax-havens-behind-breakdown-of-global-corporate-tax-system-toll-of-uks-tax-war-exposed/. Accessed 24 June 2019.

www.telegraph.co.uk/news/politics/labour/10096793/Ed-Balls-plans-to-keep-Coalition-spending-cuts.html. Accessed 17 June 2019.

www.thegrocer.co.uk/home/topics/waste-not-want-not/asda-set-to-spend-20m-on-key-food-waste-charities/563157.article. Accessed 4 April 2019.

www.theguardian.com/business/2019/jan/07/average-uk-household-debt-now-stands-at-record-15400. Accessed 15 November 2019.

www.theguardian.com/commentisfree/2015/mar/25/treating-soil-like-dirt-fatal-mistake-human-life. Accessed 30 May 2018.

www.theguardian.com/commentisfree/2019/jun/12/theresa-may-net-zero-emissions-target-climate-change. Accessed 15 November 2019.

www.theguardian.com/society/2018/may/20/homeless-people-fined-imprisoned-pspo-england-wales?CMP=Share_iOSApp_Other. Accessed 28 May 2018.

www.theguardian.com/politics/2013/dec/21/iain-duncan-smith-food-banks-charities. Accessed 5 April 2019.

www.theguardian.com/politics/2015/jul/07/corporate-welfare-a-93bn-handshake. Accessed 24 June 2019.

www.theguardian.com/global-development/2012/may/10/jacob-rees-mogg-overseas-aid. Accessed 5 April 2019.

www.theguardian.com/business/2012/feb/05/financial-crisis-economics. Accessed 19 July 2019.

www.theguardian.com/society/patrick-butler-cuts-blog/2013/nov/28/poverty-mps-call-for-delayed-food-banks-report-to-be-published. Accessed 14 July 2019.

www.theguardian.com/world/2019/feb/21/delay-to-tax-havens-public-registers-risks-national-security. Accessed 24 June 2019.

www.thelandmagazine.org.uk/articles/adios-landed-clergy. Accessed 22 October 2019.

www.thetimes.co.uk/article/ministers-hide-surge-in-use-of-food-banks-w590ndckf6d. Accessed 29 September 2019.

www.trusselltrust.org/news-and-blog/latest-stats/. Accessed 29 July 2019.

www.trusselltrust.org/news-and-blog/latest-stats/end-year-stats/. Accessed 4 April 2019.

www.trusselltrust.org/what-we-do/more-than-food/. Accessed 4 April 2019.

www.tuc.org.uk/northern/news/400000-working-age-people-north-east-are-living-poverty. Accessed 18 July 2019.

twitter.com/EmmaLewellBuck/status/1016649049326456837/photo/1. Accessed 16 August 2019.

www.vegansociety.com/news/media/statistics. Accessed 15 November 2019.

www.vegansociety.com/whats-new/blog/should-christians-be-vegan. Accessed 11 November 2019.

www.weforum.org/agenda/2018/08/impacts-of-changing-the-structure-of-minimum-wages. Accessed 19 November 2019.

www.wnyc.org/story/wendell-berry/. Accessed 12 October 2019.

www.wrap.org.uk/content/surplus-food-redistribution-wrap-work. Accessed 4 April 2019.

www.youtube.com/watch?v=RcPaC8lsNhg. Accessed 29 July 2019.

# Index of Names and Subjects